Circus as Multimodal Discourse

Also available from Bloomsbury

A Buddhist Theory of Semiotics, *Fabio Rambelli*
Introduction to Peircean Visual Semiotics, *Tony Jappy*
Semiotics of Drink and Drinking, *Paul Manning*
Semiotics of Happiness, *Ashley Frawley*
Semiotics of Religion, *Robert Yelle*
The Language of War Monuments, *Gill Abousnnouga and David Machin*
The Semiotics of Che Guevara, *Maria-Carolina Cambre*
The Semiotics of Clowns and Clowning, *Paul Bouissac*
The Visual Language of Comics, *Neil Cohn*

Circus as Multimodal Discourse

Performance, Meaning, and Ritual

Paul Bouissac

BLOOMSBURY
LONDON • NEW DELHI • NEW YORK • SYDNEY

Bloomsbury Academic
An imprint of Bloomsbury Publishing Plc

50 Bedford Square
London
WC1B 3DP
UK

1385 Broadway
New York
NY 10018
USA

www.bloomsbury.com

Bloomsbury is a registered trade mark of Bloomsbury Publishing Plc

First published by Continuum International Publishing Group 2012

Paperback edition first published by Bloomsbury Academic 2014

© Paul Bouissac, 2012, 2014

Paul Bouissac has asserted his right under the Copyright, Designs and Patents Act, 1988, to be identified as the Author of this work.

All rights reserved. No part of this publication may be reproduced or transmitted in any form or by any means, electronic or mechanical, including photocopying, recording, or any information storage or retrieval system, without prior permission in writing from the publishers.

No responsibility for loss caused to any individual or organization acting on or refraining from action as a result of the material in this publication can be accepted by Bloomsbury or the author.

British Library Cataloguing-in-Publication Data
A catalogue record for this book is available from the British Library.

ISBN: HB: 978-1-4411-2563-7
      PB: 978-1-4725-6947-9
      ePDF: 978-1-4411-0261-4
      ePub: 978-1-4411-3575-9

Library of Congress Cataloging-in-Publication Data
A catalog record for this book is available at the Library of Congress.

Typeset by Newgen Knowledge Works (P) Ltd., Chennai, India
Printed and bound in Great Britain

To Alexander Lacey, mansuetarius princeps[1]

---

[1] In ancient Rome, the *mansuetarii* were wild-animal trainers who used nonviolent methods to tame their animals and were performing tricks in close contact with them. These lions, tigers, and bears could be safely touched (*mansuetus* means accustomed to the hand).

Contents

Introduction: Playing with Fire		1
1	Circus Performances as Rituals: Participative Ethnography	10
2	The "Textility" of Circus Acts: Disentangling Cognition and Pleasure	28
3	Magic in the Ring	48
4	Horses which Speak, Count, and Laugh	58
5	Steeds and Symbols: Multimodal Metaphors	74
6	The Staging of Actions: Heroes, Antiheroes, and Animal Actors	92
7	Circus Animals as Symbols, Actors, and Persons	104
8	Dancing with Tigers, Lying with Lions: Translating Biology into Art	115
9	Clowns at Work: A Sociocritical Discourse	144
10	The Imaginary Circus	159
11	Ideology and Politics in the Circus Ring	170
12	The Postanimal Circus	188
Conclusion: Pleasures of the Circus: Attraction, Emotion, and Addiction		199
Bibliography		209
Index		215

Introduction

Playing with Fire

This book is about circus, a generic form of popular entertainment whose roots are lost in the deep time of immemorial traditions. The iconography of the most ancient cultures provides evidence that the body techniques and the tricks we admire in the ring were practiced millennia ago in temples, royal courts, and public spaces. The circus's modern avatar is a secular institution which developed during the past three centuries. It has maintained a resilient presence until today, constantly adapting to the evolution of its cultural, technological, and socioeconomic contexts. Through the 12 chapters which compose this volume, I endeavor to describe and document some typical circus acts and to reflect upon the meanings they create for their audience. My examples come from the direct observations of performances in the Americas, Europe, and India. The latter is evoked by the illustration on this book's cover. From time to time, I will interrupt the flow of the ethnographic and analytical discourse to offer, in italics, anecdotal glimpses of the circumstances which brought me during the past four decades in direct contact with the fascinating world of the circus.

My plane to Bombay—which had not yet reversed to the precolonial name Mumbai—had landed well before daybreak. I was now in a taxi rushing toward my hotel in Kolaba. It seemed the city never slept. The driver was an educated Muslim who proudly pointed to the mosques we were passing on the way. Suddenly, as he slowed down at a crossroad before running a red light, I noticed an emaciated, longhaired, half-naked, ageless man who was standing still in front of a tall fire which was brightly burning between two venerable trees. It was quite warm outside. I turned to the driver with an inquisitive look. "Oh! That? Hindu religion! They worship fire. They call it Agni. The Parsis do something like that too. They keep an ancient fire in their temple but you cannot see it. They don't let anybody inside." As the taxi speeded up along Cuffe Parade, memories were now flocking to my mind from the time when I was studying Greek and Roman mythologies. Fire was ever present in narratives and rituals. During my childhood, the most daring boys and girls were jumping over the fires we were lighting each year at the summer solstice. As St. John's fires, they had become a part of the Catholic yearly public celebrations but kept for us their mysterious pagan attractiveness. Later, I learned that making cattle and other animals cross over burning fences or clear a gap through a circle of flames were common rituals in India's villages. So were people who walked on red hot charcoal. I discovered that the fire-eaters I often saw perform on Paris's and New York's sidewalks were perpetuating a long tradition of priests and magicians whose secrets had been divulged and downgraded to street entertainment tricks.

"Playing with fire" is both a metaphor which applies to the circus in general and a literal reference to some actual acts: jumping through fiery hoops of various diameters is indeed performed by acrobats, horses, and, more commonly, by lions and tigers; the clearing of burning barriers by various animals can also be observed in the ring; the climax of jugglers' displays often consists of manipulating torches alight; hula-hoop dancers at times undulate within a swirling metallic circle to which burning pieces of rope soaked in fuel are attached, a prop which replicates the wheel of flames of Shiva, the Hindu dancing god of destruction and death. The most glaring example, though, is the fire-eaters who use immemorial techniques to shock and awe their audience. Magicians are keen on producing flames from thin air or making live doves rise, like the Phoenix, from the ashes of a pyre. Trigger, a horse we will meet later in this book, was trained to extinguish a small fire in the ring with his hooves. Fireworks often conclude circus programs.

Fire plays a part also in some clown acts. In a classic slapstick comedy, for instance, the "firemen" soak in water another clown whose hat has caught fire "because he was thinking too hard." Candles, explosions, and smoke are often used in gags. But few acts are more telling than the traditional act called "The match" which was recorded in Tristan Remy's repertory of standard circus comedies. There are three characters: the culturally sophisticated whiteface clown, the scruffy tramplike, uneducated *auguste*, as he is called in the continental tradition, and the master of ceremonies (MC) who oversees the formal unfolding of the program. As the MC introduces the whiteface, the latter boasts that he is a prize-winning sharpshooter. To prove his skill, he pulls a revolver from his pocket and explains that if the MC agrees to hold a burning match between his fingers, he will extinguish the flame in no time with a single shot. The trusting MC is willing to cooperate in the experiment. The whiteface strikes a match and hands it over to the MC who holds it straight up between his fingers while, at a distance, the sharpshooter takes aim at the target, steps back, moves a little to the right, then to the left, until suddenly the MC utters a cry of pain because during all this process of aiming the match has been completely consumed and the fire has reached his hand. That was a practical joke which exploited the trust and naivety of his friend! To placate the MC, the whiteface suggests that he should play the trick on the *auguste* who at this precise moment enters the ring just as the whiteface leaves. So, the joke claims another victim. The MC, in turn, consoles the *auguste* by remarking that the whiteface has not seen what happened and could be tricked into holding the match. As the whiteface returns to the ring, the *auguste* boasts about his own shooting skill and hands over to him a burning match. Surprise! The match keeps burning endlessly in the whiteface's hand without burning his fingers while the puzzled *auguste* takes all the time he can to calculate the distance and adjust his aim. The reason for this mystery is revealed when the whiteface shows with a laugh that he had substituted the match with a coiled waxed taper, which he moved up between his fingers as time passed.

There is more in this act than meets the eyes. Three different modalities of fire are indeed involved: explosion (which remains virtual since the gun is not fired), fast burning, and slow combustion. The whiteface, who is the embodiment of the highest forms of culture, demonstrates both his absolute mastery of fire and his ability to trick lesser people into getting burnt. This is the history of humanity in a nutshell. The production of fire was an instant achievement but what was a priceless progress was undoubtedly its conservation over long periods of time and the advantages it conferred to those who had managed to control combustion both instant (explosion) and slow (preservation). It is impossible to know how far in the past such ritualistic games were created and which forms they took as they traveled through time, cultures, and languages. Because of their exclusively oral and gestural transmission, the circus arts point to unbroken chains of ageless techniques and meanings whose transformations can hardly be retraced. But some constants are obvious as soon as we reflect upon the nature of the acts themselves as I have undertaken to do through a long familiarity with circus performances.

This volume is indeed about circus performances, the ways they unfold in the ring, and the meanings they create in the minds of their audiences. Acrobats, animal trainers, and clowns display extreme situations. They achieve feats that nobody among their public could survive. They do so with solemnity, following like a ritual the conventions of their trade; they confront dangers and take risks which are carefully staged: the freestanding ladders on which they balance sway at times beyond belief; they trust their head to the sharp teeth of lions which were angrily roaring a moment earlier; they slap and trip each other while keeping true violence at bay. We could say that they play with fire, albeit not in a literal sense. This common metaphor indeed designates behaviors on the edge of catastrophes. When a fire is started, it can easily get out of hand. Cities—and many tenting circuses—have been destroyed in this manner. Challenging the limits of gravity, bluffing large predators, and testing the tolerance of one's neighbors in tussling and tumbling games, can be rightly perceived as courting death. The spectators experience strong emotions which are commensurate with the apparent uncertainty of the outcome. Periodically, the circus reenacts these dramas which always gratify its audience with the same intensity.

The brief example of a clown's practical joke, which was sketched above, offers a preview of the general approach which the following chapters illustrate: first, a precise description of the multimodal unfolding of the acts; second, an understanding of the contexts of their performance with respect to other acts of the same kind belonging to the circus tradition; and finally, an interpretation of their significance in the broader perspective of their sociocultural environment. The three characters of "the match" embody a dramatic structure which defines a fundamental circus paradigm: the triangle formed by the straight man (or woman in some cases) who connects a hypercultured actor and an undercultured one who represents a state of nature, a kind of precivilized, childish, naïve, unsophisticated partner. A reflection on their antics shows that the contents of their gags are far from being trivial once we relate the objects and behaviors they display to the cultural categories they signify. In that case, the issue is the control of fire which is coterminous with the triumph of civilization, for the better and for the worse.

Figure 0.1 In the 1981 program of Swiss National Circus Knie, a Zebra liberty act included jumping through a hoop of fire. (Rendering of an illustration from the printed program by David Blostein.)

Figure 0.2 A classic of cage act consists of training lions and tigers to leap through a flaming circle. (Rendering by David Blostein of a blog of Munroe County, Illinois, advertising the Ainad Shrine Circus in June 2010.)

Chapter 1 argues that circus spectacles are secular rituals in the sense that they have become purely humanistic with hardly any hint of supernatural input for their public. They preserve, though, some remarkable properties which evoke religious behavior through their structure and the emotional experience they procure for their audiences. This raises the question of their origins and the nature of their function in contemporary societies.

Chapter 2 addresses methodological issues. How to provide a textual equivalent of the fast and tumultuous multimodal unfolding of a circus performance? How to avoid the pitfalls of naïve ethnography? We will encounter on our way the extraordinary attempts by two graphic artists, the Vesque sisters, to immortalize through drawings and writings the circus acts they admired during their lifetime which coincided with a Golden Age of the European circus (ca 1890–1940). The advantages and limits of the method of our approach will be discussed in this chapter.

Figure 0.3 Christianity in Europe assimilated some ancient rituals which were too resilient to be eradicated. They were reinterpreted in view of the new religious symbolism. This drawing shows Catholic priests blessing fire on Easter Vigil. (Drawing by David Blostein.)

Chapter 3 will move to the circus performances themselves, starting with magic. Originally, the tricks which became the substance of today's circus acts were experienced as magic before they were admired as skills. But magic acts remain an important part of the circus's offerings. They still, at times, puzzle their audience and give rise to anxiety and fear in children. Circus magicians play with dangerous props: swords, water, fire, chains, saws, guillotines, and wild animals. They make things and people disappear. They threaten the stability of common existences by transforming one category into another by a sleight of hand. What sort of perverse pleasure do we derive from watching such unnatural production and destruction processes?

Chapters 4 and 5 will focus our attention on the part played by the horses in circus performances: first, as individual, personalized actors whose performances have long been interpreted as magic; second, as groups which can be semiotically manipulated to the extent that horses can be used as a secondary modeling system to express social relations and transformations.

Chapter 6 deals with other domestic animals, more particularly dogs. We will see that this most trainable pet allows the circus to produce the equivalent of a metalanguage of training by featuring animals which "mock" their trainers by engaging in antiperformances. They are trained to do nothing, literally, and appear to cause their masters to toil in their place. This will be an opportunity to review the general system of factitive actions in relation to the various species which are trained to perform in circus rings.

Chapter 7 will address the issue of the changing attitude toward animals in contemporary societies. This reflexive pause is indeed in order at a time when one of the cornerstones of the circus tradition has come under fire. It will be shown that ethical objections regarding circus animals result from a much wider cultural transformation of the moral and legal status of animals, and involve both ideology and politics which converge toward prohibition and abolitionism.

Chapter 8 will document the kind of acts which will probably disappear from the cultural landscape in the years to come: lion and tiger acts. These performances have played a crucial role in the history of the circus during the past 200 years or so. The transformation of biology into art, which they achieved at a cost that has now become objectionable, remains a cultural phenomenon deserving ethnographic attention. The taming of the wild and the triumph over predators seem irrelevant and obsolete in a world in which wilderness is constantly receding and former lethal predators now need human protection if they are to survive.

Chapter 9 will bring in the clowns. As hinted through the example above, circus clowning is not the mindless chaos it usually appears to be. In any given circus program, clowns have to keep their audience interested, motivated, and laughing for a sizeable portion of the time. They interpret short comedies from a rich traditional repertory which they constantly update and creatively adjust to the sociocultural evolution of their context. We will analyze in detail several such comedies and demonstrate the relevance of their multimodal discourse to deep social issues.

Chapter 10 addresses the semiotic gap that exists between the contents of the acts performed by actual circus acrobats and clowns, and their images in literature and art. This chapter explores the distance that separates the real circus as an institution and its productions from the imaginary circus which has been fostered by poets and visual artists in the wake of Romanticism and Symbolism. It shows that this parallel multimodal discourse not only influences the ways in which audiences perceive circus spectacles but also interferes with the very production of some acts which tend to meet the expectations of their public. The chapter concludes with evidence of such cross-modal intertextuality with reference to high-wire walkers or funambulists.

Chapter 11 discusses the ability of the circus as a visual language to articulate political content. Examples are presented to support the claim that circus acts are relevant to sexual politics and other issues pertaining to the body politic in general. Feminism, gay liberation, community relations, social issues, and the like, are often expressed through the nature and staging of circus acts.

Chapter 12 briefly retraces the evolution of the circus during the past 50 years with the arrival of newcomers in the trade and the emergence of the ethos of conservation which clashed with ancestral traditions. The latter had assimilated the ideology of colonialism and thrived on featuring captive exotic animals. A new aesthetic and a new morality blended with various forms of activism as all the traditional skills became at the same time democratized through the numerous circus schools which blossomed in the world. In the meantime, the traditional circus has shown impressive resilience but probably will not be able to maintain for long the exhibition of trained animals. This is why this chapter is titled "The postanimal circus." It outlines possible new directions for an art which remains attractive to a vast global audience.

The conclusion to this volume asks: what is the source of the pleasure we derive from circus performances? Why audiences are repeatedly attracted to these spectacles which offer relatively little variation? What is the nature of the emotions the public experiences? Why so many people seem to be addicted to this unique form of entertainment? As hinted in some of the forthcoming chapters, the game structure of circus acts may explain their attractiveness. These multimodal performances are essentially open narratives which keep us on edge until they are provisionally resolved, only to start again afresh through endless ritual cycles.

The chapters in this book are based on over four decades of fieldwork which was supported by a number of research grants for which grateful acknowledgment is expressed here: the Netherlands Institute for Advanced Research (1972–3); the John Simon Guggenheim Foundation (1973–4); the Social Science and Humanities Research Council of Canada (1977–8); the Wenner-Gren Foundation for Anthropological Research (1976 and 1984–5); the Connaught Fellowship (1989); the Killam Fellowship (1990–2); and, last but not least, Victoria University in the University of Toronto for numerous smaller grants which allowed me to pursue my inquiry into the circus of the twenty-first century. Finally, the original illustrations which document the circus acts I discuss in this volume were made possible by a generous grant from the Senate of Victoria University in Toronto.

Special thanks are due to Gurdeep Mattu, Senior Commissioning Editor at Bloomsbury Academic, for his encouragements and enlightened advice during the writing of this book; my colleague David Blostein for his deft rendering of acrobatic moments which are not easy to catch with clarity on film; my friend Zbigniew Roguszka for his daring close-up pictures of the lions and tigers of Alexander Lacey as well as other illustrations; Alexander Lacey, of course, to whom this book is dedicated, and Sascha Grodotzki from Zirkus Charles Knie for his kind cooperation during the most recent research on which this volume is based; and last but not least my partner Stephen H. Riggins for his patient and careful copy editing of the text.

1

Circus Performances as Rituals: Participative Ethnography

Circus online

As I surf the internet in search of circus itineraries, I come across the website of Zirkus Charles Knie which advertises its traditional program and indicates the German cities where it will perform in the weeks ahead. The dates for Heidelberg are ideal. I can make a stopover in this venerable university town on my way to Munich, the city from which I am due to fly back home a few days later.

The traveler in search of a circus can easily follow its tracks on the World Wide Web. Most circus companies maintain websites that list their current programs and display some visual documents, even in some cases, brief videos of the acts they want to highlight. For Germany, Austria, Switzerland, and the Netherlands, www.circus-gastspiele.de/Gastspiele/TourneeKarten/ provides such information in great detail with, in addition, links to the city maps on which the ephemeral locations of the circuses are indicated. Similar information can be found for France in the daily updated website www.aucirque.com. In early 2011, I had reviewed 31 such websites for Germany alone when Zirkus Charles Knie caught my attention. Not only was it going to be coincidentally on my path but also its traditional program, as far as I could judge from the brief video clips it had put online, was extremely attractive for my research purpose. The whole array of circus specialties was represented in this program: ground acrobatics, flying trapeze, lions and tigers, clowns, exotic animal displays, and three different kinds of equestrian acts. It was obvious from the glimpses offered by the clip that the show was staged with artistic flair, a treat for an ethnographer of the circus in the twenty-first century.

Research on contemporary circus indeed starts online. The websites put up by individual artists, troupes, agencies, and companies provide a wealth of information not only on the organization of the trade but also on the contents of the spectacles they advertise. Virtual data, both visual and verbal, and the musical background that comes with the video clips are relevant to the inquiry of the ethnographer who endeavors to explore the interface between the circus and its audience. Such websites are modern versions of the posters and placards which were once displayed in cities and villages in advance to announce the forthcoming visits of circuses as the only means available to reach potential audiences. The modern websites are also extensions of the traditional façades which decorate the front of circus tents with their banners, painted panels, loudspeakers that blast alluring music, and other devices, which call the attention of passersby and entice them to purchase admission tickets. Many circuses also provide the means of buying seats online ahead of time rather than queuing in front of the wickets after the traveling circus has set up its tent on the lot. Contemporary information technologies, though, have not cancelled the traditional publicizing strategies. They reflect and expand them beyond the printed media and the direct displays which require larger budgets than the fees of a single webmaster. In fact, most circuses now use all these promotional tools in combinations which maximize their public exposure toward enticing and securing audiences.

This book endeavors to document and analyze the circus as a multimodal discourse which plays an important part in the contemporary landscape of mass entertainments and feeds people's imaginations with rich icons and narratives. To do so, it will exploit all sources of information available, both through perusing circus websites and providing detailed descriptions of actual performances in all their multisensorial dimensions. Indeed both virtual and live experiences belong to the modern enjoyment of the circus.

But speaking about the circus in general terms, as is often done in essays and journalistic reports, misses a crucial point: each circus is an organization with its own social identity and symbolic character. Although all traditional circuses present the same kinds of acts, each company has a unique profile that is rooted in its history and the past experience of several generations of spectators. Some circuses have been family-owned for more than a century; others have kept the name alive over several transfers of ownership when the company identity tags were purchased with the animals and equipment. There are some brand names in the circus world which are important assets because in some populations they evoke rich associations with exotic and daring displays. These names mean "circus" and they radiate such an aura of magic that retired owners of such names often lease out the right to use them as a marketing device for lesser-known companies. It is interesting to note that the value of these prestigious names is grounded in their history and the memory of the spectators who attended the performances which were delivered under their labels over several generations. The symbolic value of these names is purely historical and circumstantial. In most cases, there is nothing fancy in their phonetics and semantics with respect to the languages of the countries in which they operate.

There was indeed nothing extraordinary in the name of a circus which periodically illuminated my childhood in southwestern France. Cirque Bureau could hardly have borne a more pedestrian name, the equivalent in English of "Circus Office" or "Circus Desk," given the double meaning of this common French word which can also occur as a family name, hence the name of this company which had been founded by Jean Bureau in 1851 and was still owned by one of his descendants in the 1940s. In my preteen years, "Bureau" was for me endowed with all the glamour of another, marvelous, world. My grandfather was speaking with awe of the shows he had seen in this circus when he was younger. Circus Bureau's slogan was *Le cirque sans bluff* [the circus that does not bluff]. It cultivated an ethos of respectability and, at the time when I saw it, presented only horses and, occasionally, dogs, in addition to the expectable assortment of acrobats and clowns. Its posters were considered reliable reflections of the actual program that would be seen under the big top. "The musical horses," for example, were depicting six horses engaged in producing sounds from some adapted instruments: an oversized keyboard; a drum connected to a pedal that a stomping hoof could activate; bells that could be shaken on command; two honking horns that could be squeezed by a horse's mouth; and a podium for the conductor which was briefly holding a baton between its teeth or, otherwise, agitated its head furiously as if it were giving the beat that was actually produced by the circus musicians.

This circus had twelve mares, four white, four brown, and four black, whose names we knew because they were inscribed on wooden plates hanging in front of their individual stalls under the tent which served as a temporary stable. There was also a special one, Roxane, the gray mare who every year danced to different tunes and rhythms. For naïve spectators, the behavior of the horses in the ring was nothing short of miraculous. One year, they would enter the ring in haphazard order, each wearing a number fixed on its harness. While they were cantering around with all the numbers mixed up, the trainer would order them to take their right place and, in no time, number one would be first in line and so on until they all had taken the slot indicated on their backs. Another year, they would wear the names of the twelve months and similarly they would rearrange themselves from chaos to cosmic order. They were told to trot two by two, three by three, or four by four. They would all be mixed up and asked to sort themselves out by colors. Some years the horses would wear extravagant yellow and orange plumes and elegant harnesses decorated with shiny copper nails. Some other years, they would perform bare as if they were wild horses, running faster and jumping to a fast, exotic music rather than cantering and pirouetting in perfect order to some Viennese waltz melodies. This was what Cirque Bureau meant for me and for all the families who would not have missed, if they could afford it, the annual visit to the circus which pitched its blue and yellow tent on the central market square of the city, surrounded by its trucks and trailers painted in the same colors as the tent.

The identity kit of a circus, its public profile, is a visual set of qualities that distinguishes it from its competitors and from other kinds of commercial enterprises. Since the late eighteenth century, when circuses became a legitimate business in Europe and America, the printed media extended to a wide audience the interface of circuses with the population at large through images and texts. But the direct impact of the actual presence of a circus in a city depends on its capacity to stand out against a duller background as was the case when traveling troupes were performing in seasonal fairs and were vying to catch the public's attention. Still, nowadays, traditional companies display distinctive colors and decorative patterns that characterize their trucks and trailers, their tents, and the souvenirs they peddle to their audience. Vivid, even gaudy colors mean "circus" and their particular chromatic combinations which evoke ancient coats of arms indicate the brand, so to speak, as much as their large painted names, which cannot be missed from a distance.

This distinctiveness has been transferred to the electronic media. Clicking on Zirkus Charles Knie in Google brings up pages that introduce present and past programs with abundant pictures and video clips. Other links take us to views of the big top with its elegant white and red stripes, its electric giant sign in the form of an arch which reads "Super Circus" above "Zirkus Charles Knie"; the illuminated glittering front and entrance; its welcoming smaller tent in which visitors will wait and socialize around the booths selling programs, drinks, and circus food before the beginning of the show and during the intermission. At the same time joyful circus music seeps from the computer's speakers. The current program is announced on a star-studded intense pink background through five blue circles which frame highlights from the show: a young lady facing the muzzle of her seal; a pickpocket who has jokingly robbed an unsuspecting spectator of his watch, wallet, and tie; a five-member flying trapeze troupe with a glimpse of their act in the background; an equestrian whose face is intimately close to the head of his white steed; the charismatic portrait of a trainer with two tigers standing on each side. These are the icons of the spectacle. The blue medallions of three different sizes are artistically circled by a thin yellow line, which makes them appear to be windows revealing the inside of the circus. Parts of the images are protruding out of their frames, thus creating a three-dimensional effect as if the horse's head was halfway out the window or the smiling pickpocket who is represented with four arms handing back his catch to his victims. This multitude of limbs, evocative of the supernatural power of a Hindu god, suggests that his hands can reach into the pockets of many unsuspecting spectators. He is shown on the poster holding a watch, a wallet, car keys, and a tie as if he were returning these objects to their owners after having skillfully stolen them. The stars display friendly, inviting faces. These images are reproduced on the posters and the printed programs which will later form the permanent anchors of the spectators' memories.

Clicking on another link provided by the *circus-gastspiele* hub, I come across the website of Circus William which has titled its current program "World of Circus." The visitor is immediately introduced to the four brothers who run the company and, obviously, provide the main items on the program. Four medallions decorated by a lion-and-tiger motif feature in succession: Manuel Wille holding a white tiger on a leash; Roberto Wille next to a bridled antelope; Markus Wille close to the head of a black horse; and Manolito with a microphone in his hand, indicating that he is the presenter of the show. They all wear traditional Brandenburg uniforms with gold or silver braids embroidered on the chest symbolizing traditional military formality and heroism. The homepage features buttons which lead to their Christmas festival and to their current summer season programs.

Self-presentations vary as we keep exploring other websites. Circus Constanze Busch, for example, offers a sumptuous red, deep blue, and golden yellow baroque design. Its main page emphasizes the circus team around the larger medallion showing the smiling but bossy director. Ten frames of lesser dimensions portray on the top row the younger men who are in charge of the exotic animal act, the horse displays, and the tiger number respectively, and the woman who is the artistic director of the show. The lower row features the superintendent, the accountant, the public relations person, the office manager, and the transportation supervisor. A successful circus performance does indeed depend on a robust organizational infrastructure, a fact that is forcefully conveyed by the visual structure of this page. As we have seen above, some other circuses foreground the stars of the program, thus emphasizing the magic of the spectacle rather than the work of those who toil behind the scene.

Another significant variation concerns the social characteristics which are implied by the choice of the images selected for the website. Circus William, for instance, underlines the family unit since four brothers provide both the leadership and the program. Zirkus Charles Knie points to international artists. Circus Constanze Busch displays a social organization sustained by the common will or complementary needs of unrelated individuals since each one has a different family name, which is provided with the specification of his or her function. The emphasis is on team work under the leadership of a father figure.

The second page of the Circus Constanze Busch is an aerial view of the circus set up in a field in the outskirts of a city. The white trucks and the long white stable tent are lined up to form a perfect square with an opening at the front for the admission gate and the covered access to the big top which stands at the center of the square with its triangular blue and white stripes radiating from the top toward the blue and yellow side which encloses the circus space. Order and hierarchy are the dominant notes but the smiling eyes and relaxed expressions of the team's faces as well as the vivid colors of the canvas bring a playful flavor of benevolent paternalism to this invitation to come to the circus. These three examples show that the various online manifestations of the circus are a rich source of information concerning a range of aspects which will be scrutinized and discussed in this book.

First, a website is a deliberate semiotic gesture toward the population at large. It combines images, texts, and music designed to introduce the provider of a service and to offer virtual samples of the goods. As a move of self-introduction, it selects and organizes a seductive multimodal discourse which endeavors to establish its truthful representation in an entertainment paradigm that was traditionally associated with unethical promotional strategies. The hit and run mode of operation, which could rely on the short-term effects of deceptive posters, is not any longer an option. In the age of Twitter, Facebook, and other social networks, information instantly runs fast and far. No circus could outrun a spontaneous negative wave. But, in the competitive context of live entertainments, companies still need to deploy rhetorical resources aimed at persuading potential audiences. Indeed, a performance is an act of communication not only at the level of each number in a program but also, prominently, as a service provided by a company, a family, or even often a single individual. It is with this personalized agency that audiences strike an implicit contract when they purchase an admission ticket. The program itself is embedded within this fundamental fiduciary structure. Therefore, it is crucial that the provider establish and maintain its virtual credentials within a wider interactive framework. Contemporary media such as television talk shows, newspaper interviews, and, most importantly, the internet offer means through which circus agencies construct themselves as icons larger than nature: the donators of the wonder that is circus. Many city councils in Europe periodically take over this role. During the past few decades, elected officials have launched circus festivals which are sponsored by the city's councils. Once a year, for a limited number of days, they hire a tent, organize a program in collaboration with artistic agencies, and give trophies to the best acts selected by a jury. They reproduce on a smaller scale the International Circus Festival which started in 1970 as an initiative of Prince Rainier of Monaco and has been ever since a major annual event now sponsored by his heirs. All these festivals also run their own websites.

Perusing the sites of all these circuses and festivals on the internet reveals a great variety of statuses and styles. Whether a small circus has used an open source template and posted some amateurish pictures or a wealthier company has been able to afford a professional web designer with the latest IT range of possibilities, the information which can thus be collected is greatly relevant to the ethnographer's inquiry. The selection of highlights or simply representative pictures by the circus companies is an explicit semiotic gesture that is meant to communicate contents and create a virtual experience but it also discloses, as was noted above, the implicit subtext which can be inferred from the websites' organization and architecture.

Another kind of precious information provided by the internet concerns the spectacles themselves. Program composition is the rhetorical form in which the multimodal discourse of the circus is delivered. As we will see in Chapter 2, individual acts can be abstractly considered as self-contained units but they never appear in isolation. They are always parts of the complex set of a program. Most of them are context-dependent in the sense that their interpretation by the audience is somewhat constrained by their order of appearance and the contrasts or complementarities they implement with respect to each other. Some acts involving parody or intertextual references are even determined in their form and meaning by the act(s) which preceded them in the program. Even, at times, as we will see in later chapters, a retroactive semiotic effect is obtained when an act is performed in the nostalgic mode. The structure of circus programs is indeed an important source of data for the ethnographer of the circus. In the past century, there was no other way than traveling to circuses or examining printed programs when such documents were available for sale or in public or private archives. But, in the internet age, most of the programs of circuses in a given season can be collected and compared.

Circus in the field

The iconography which circus websites display is a rich source of information concerning two crucial aspects of the acts. First, it allows for the precise recording of the styles and colors of the costumes, the props, and the animals' decorations. Of course, these may change from performance to performance and from program to program in successive years because acrobats usually carry several sets of costumes and may change their musical accompaniments to fit the garbs or the reverse. From this point of view there is no internet shortcut to a troupe's complete wardrobe and range of styles of performance but websites provide a robust perceptual anchor. Secondly, these images and occasional brief video clips have been chosen by the circus itself as representative of particular acts. It is a reliable guide to what performers and producers consider as the typical visual expressions of their specialties, what they want to foreground in the public representation of their artistic identities without disclosing the full contents of their acts. There are, however, some cases in which fairly long performance samples can be found online. These are posted by independent artists who want to advertise their acts in a very competitive market without using the costly channel of artistic agencies. Or they have been made by amateurs in spite of the reluctance of circuses to let anybody freely film their shows. These snippets of performance are often of low visual quality but they are nevertheless a precious source of ethnographic information and also bear witness to the special interests of members of circus audiences by revealing what is the focus of their individual attention, that is, what is worth being recorded and memorialized. But for all its interest and informative value, the virtual reality of the circus institution and its works cannot compare with the actual experience of going to the circus and being part of an audience.

> The first taxi I approached in front of the Heidelberg train station was reluctant to drive me to the Messplatz, in the outskirts of the city, where Zirkus Charles Knie had pitched its tent. He summoned another driver, a friendly middle-aged woman who did not waste any time to tell me that she loved the circus. She does not mind waiting until I have purchased my ticket for the evening performance to drive me back to my hotel. It is raining. The circus is located beyond an industrial zone in a sort of no-man's land between sport fields, construction sites, and the countryside. I am the only person walking to the wicket under the pouring rain. A friendly word with the cashier who speaks English warms me up to this circus but nobody else seems to be around. A circus at standstill in a muddy field in mid-morning under a summer's windy rain is a rather unattractive sight. I recognize, though, the elegant big top with red and white stripes, and the banners and posters which had arrested my attention as I was surfing the internet a few days earlier. On the way back to the city I learn that my driver, Marga, works part-time for the owner of a one-car taxi company. She does the morning shifts when he happens to be busy with other business. But, if I want, Edmund will pick me up later at the hotel in time for the show. He too is fond of circuses. We agree that for the next five days I can call their cell phone any time I need to be driven to or from the circus lot.
>
> Shortly before show time, I proceed toward the gate and the two cheerful uniformed young men who casually check the admission vouchers let me in. The glitter in their eyes tells something about the relaxed atmosphere which prevails in this circus. Pop music comes from the tent's belly. On the right side, in front of the imposing trailer with a flashing Kassa sign, two long lines of visitors wait to purchase their tickets. The rain has stopped. The big top is illuminated with a profusion of garlands of electric bulbs which offset the gray clouds of the dusk. The canvas undulates under the wind. It is already teeming with life inside. I get the seat I had chosen, on the eighth row from the ring, slightly on the side of the entrance. The inner space is of human proportions, all in curves, warm and cozy. It smells of fresh sawdust and horses. The circus is half full. People continuously ooze in. I am drowned in a rich hum like I imagine the noise of a beehive must be. Some excited children run or scream for candy floss. Young women sell the colorful program which features the portrait of the trainer who is dwarfed next to the face of a serene lion sporting an abundant mane. The beginning of the show is obviously delayed because the public keeps coming in. Soon, the circus is packed. The orchestra wakes up; the audience stops humming; the spotlights are dimmed and it can all start as music fills the tent.
>
> The introductory tableau emerges from darkness and reveals a Gypsy camp which has been hastily set in the ring in the intimacy of a dreamy penumbra, a poetic reminder of the roots of the circus among nomadic troupes which crisscrossed

the Eurasian continent from immemorial times. The spotlights briefly bring to life emblematic snapshots: somersaults, pyramids, rope walking, and juggling. The music is sentimental and nostalgic, evocative of street violinists and Gypsy bands playing for weddings in Mittel-Europa. The artists who portray the men in typical casual clothes and the women with their long dark hair and full-length undulating, colorful dresses take carefully choreographed poses and engage in brief stereotyped interactions, dancing, whispering at times, and giggling. There is a campfire on one side, with children weaving reed baskets and a small group of women on the other side with one of them reading the future in another's palm. The audience is eased into another world when suddenly a fire-eater appears, juggling with torches alight and finally produces from his mouth a huge geyser of flames which illuminates the whole tent and spreads an acrid smell like wild incense. As the dancers vanish in the background, clearing the ring of their props, the first act starts: two black horses surge from the red curtain with a couple balancing on their backs while the music, slow and intense, with the deep accents of a religious chant, espouses the rhythm of their pace.

From the seat I chose when I bought my ticket, I can see the whole area of the ring from an elevated position that is not encumbered by a supporting pole. The first time is always for the pleasure. When I return, the next day, I will bring my notebook which I will have prepared in advance in view of the acts I plan to document. The *pas de deux* [steps of two], a French technical expression borrowed from the ballet, refers to the exercises which the man and the woman, Dany and Denisa, execute as they keep their balance on the two horses trotting side by side around the ring. The man has one foot on each horse and the woman rests on the right one between the acrobatic poses she takes on the shoulders of her partner. The act unfolds with precision and solemnity, ending with a daring, breathtaking feat: Denisa keeps her balance while standing straight up with her feet on the head of Dany for the full length of a spin around the ring. I join the thundering hand clapping which salutes the couple as they leave the ring, the man supporting his partner high on his muscular right arm.

In a fleeting moment, the music switches to a cheerful tune as Mexican clown Versace enters with three tiny toy elephants one of whose actual identity will be revealed at the end when a smartly trained dog emerges from this disguise. But this will be performed as a resurrection after the elephant "dies," causing the brief, touching distress of its master.

Lavishly costumed dancers periodically invade the ring, providing inklings of the theme of the act which follows. Now comes a cohort of girls which introduces a scantily dressed oriental princess who will display graceful hula-hoop expertise. Her supple hips and torso undulate in suggestive waves while the hoops gyrate up and down along her attractive body. She concludes her act by catching a dozen hoops which are thrown toward her in fast succession by the dancers.

The tent is suddenly flushed with pungent odors as camels, lamas, zebras, and exotic cattle from Asia and Africa fill the ring under the direction of a spectacularly dressed trainer. It is a classic of circus programs but it is here orchestrated very effectively with haunting musical accompaniments which match the gait of the successive animal species moving around the ring under stunning artistic lighting.

The smell of gasoline now permeates the atmosphere as the Mairen Brothers drive their roaring red motorcycle to the center. Rock music takes over as the two athletic and handsome boys ascend the platform which is fixed to the vehicle and display their feats of strength and balance. Applause is enthusiastic and sustained. Their youth and charismatic smiles have obviously triggered a deep empathy in the public.

The orchestra is now going classical with Ravel's Bolero as Flamenco dancers set a fast Spanish pace. Six Friesian horses go through the traditional routines of liberty horse acts. Then, Dany and Denisa succeed them on their mounts of the same breed and deploy a classy high-school repertory of equine allures and paces while the band strives to make the music match the movements of the animals. After this black, red, and gold display, a chromatic relief comes in the form of three bay and three white horses decorated with orange-red trappings under the direction of their trainer semicasually dressed in a suit of the same color. The music is cheerful and modern.

First Versace, then the dancers capture the attention of the public while a large safety net is set up all across the ring. South American rhythms follow the entrance of the three men and two women who form the flying trapeze group. The Flying Mendoca climb the rope ladders which take them to their suspended platform and trapezes. A different tempo takes hold of the circus: the time it takes for a full swing from the point of departure to the point of arrival when the flyer grasps the hands of the catcher after having propelled himself or herself through space. The audience is all the more elated by their daring skill because the presence of the safety net allows them to focus on the beauty of the acrobats and their gracious movements without fearing a deadly fall. There is some perceptible tension, though, when the triple somersault is announced by the presenter. This is the grail of flying trapeze acts. Only a few can perform this demanding trick. Tonight, it is a flawless demonstration. Spontaneously the public stands up while vigorously clapping their hands. This is not perfunctory applause. Like everybody else, I had jumped on my feet, filled with a warm feeling of enthusiasm, an irrational sense of solidarity, with tears coming to my eyes. It takes some time for the thundering noise to die out and people to sit down. The acrobats' faces radiate joy and gratitude and send back kisses with their hands toward the public. I remember how hard and rough is the skin of these graceful palms used to grab in midair the bar of their trapeze with a firm grip.

The lights are dimmed and a 20-minute intermission is announced. The crowd has suddenly become more communicative. Strangers exchange a few appreciative words about the performance. As I leave my seat, I share a glance with my neighbor and make the gesture of clapping my hands in silence. He nods his head approvingly. I try my broken German with another one. "Are you French?" she asks in English and she adds in broken French that she too loved that performance. The hospitality tent, just outside, is quickly packed. Everybody drinks beer or pop. Hot *bratwursts*, steaming between slices of fresh bread, are very popular. Emotions make people hungry. A perceptible unanimity and human warmth pervade this cramped space, as is sometimes the case in religious gatherings or national celebrations.

I soon regain my seat as I want to observe the setting up of the steel arena and the preparations for the cage act. I count the number of stools as they are arranged in a semicircle. There will be 11 animals in this act. The trainer, in a gown that hides his stage costume, checks the stability of the pedestals. The public is back. The performance starts. I am familiar with this trainer as I have seen earlier versions of his act in other circuses for almost a decade. Alexander Lacey, to whom this book is dedicated, is the very best of a generation of modern circus trainers. He is now in full action under the glare of the spotlights surrounded by lions and tigers with which he constantly establishes hand or face contacts, using the rod he holds in his hand as a conductor's baton rather than a stick. His outstanding act will be described in detail in Chapter 8. At the end, when he dances with two tigers, the audience is transfixed and he receives the third triumphal homage of this evening.

The clown sustains the public's interest while the steel arena is taken apart and rushed to the backstage. The equestrians, Dany and Denisa, now present an aerial act hanging from two ribbons which they use as substitutes for a trapeze, forming knots and loops, climbing up and sliding down.

Then two playful seals follow Mona, the charming young woman who earlier did the hula-hoop routine under the name of Monika. Her costume is now an unlikely, albeit attractive mixture of swimming outfit and sailor uniform which evokes "the kingdom of Neptune" as the caption of her photo in the program claims. Indeed effluvia of the sea seep into the atmosphere as she carries a pail full of fresh herrings which are destined to reward Manta and Stefanie, the seals, after they have performed each trick. The interactions between these marine animals, which spend most of their time in a large artificial pool of water erected on the circus lot, and Mona, are intense and cheerful. Whether they are eager to do their tricks or get their reward is, of course, a matter of appreciation. But the illusion is perfect and nobody, including the seals, seems to object.

The clown returns with an act full of surprises which builds on the cheerful mood of the seal display. His wit elicits smiles rather than laughter. I will take some notes tomorrow.

During a brief blackout, something has been brought to the center of the ring. When the blue light softly comes back, sacred music by Johann Sebastian Bach gives the tent the serenity and plenitude of a cathedral. On a low, white platform, a young man lightly dressed in white slowly balances from one hand to the other. He appears to be weightless, moving as in a dream, combining strength and contortions. It is an adagio of athletic virtuosity, a kind of offering which invents its own spiritual choreography. I experience again a moment of intense emotion. I check the program. His name is Iurie Basiul. He comes from Moldova. The audience offers him a triumphal exit.

Still two acts to go before the finale. A hilarious ventriloquist reminds me that the circus inherited all the magical techniques, which from the depth of human history filled people with awe and fear. As I anticipate the writing of this book, I decide to devote a chapter to these techniques and their meanings as they remain at the core of the circus discourse, sometimes under the guise of another specialty.

The Nistorovs will conclude the program with a dazzling roller-skating act. The man keeps gyrating at high speed on a small elevated stand, holding his partner by her teeth, or her foot and other daring acrobatic configurations.

The time for the finale has come. All the artists return to the ring and acknowledge the intense standing ovation they receive from the public. However, the staging of the ritual is not over. The audience will emotionally be eased out, thus avoiding the shock of finding themselves too brutally confronted to the night of their quiet city, under the rain. A warm moment of lightness and poetry is now in the making. A Montgolfier is being inflated and starts ascending toward the top of the tent. Versace, the gentle clown is there, holding a little boy. As they rise, they gesture good-bye to the crowd and shower them with confetti. They will be back next year with more wonders to feed their dreams.

It takes me time to settle down as Marga drives me back to the hotel. Edmund will pick me up tomorrow afternoon for the matinee and she will come back to drive me to the evening show. How many times do you see the same show? She asks. The first time is for pleasure. Then, I try to record all the details, all the things which no film could ever register, because there is an infinity of moments in such works of art which no single act of attention could possibly encompass and understand. It is this infinity of gestures, facial expressions, smells, colors, lights, sounds, feelings, and ideas which overwhelm the minds and hearts of the audience. Look at their faces when they leave the circus: they have been transformed by the experience. They are able to dream again.

The spectator as ethnographer

The predicaments of traditional ethnography have been thoroughly exposed during the past three decades. Its political and epistemological roots have been scrutinized and its works have been radically criticized. The positivist enterprise of describing the social and cultural behavior of an exotic other by an observer who is assumed to be objective and scientific has been denounced as a fallacy. The ethnographer, usually under the protection of a colonial power, was supposed to record what he or she witnessed as if they were themselves invisible. Even in participatory observation any kind of personal involvement would have been considered a bias that could invalidate the data. But the cultural biases of the investigators themselves tended to be ignored and the impact of their own presence was deemed negligible. They relied on uncritically trusted informants to learn what the observed behaviors meant to particular ethnic groups. They were keen on identifying differences that set the culture of these groups apart and would make their reports interesting for their home disciplinary establishments. Brief stays in exotic countries at times of peace and not too harsh seasonal weather or in agreeable year-round climates empowered those ethnographers to produce riveting generalizations on how "others" lived their lives and made sense of themselves and their environments within drastically different cultural modes and social organizations. The overarching notion of "primitive" populations—that is, populations which were not using modern technologies—tended to construe these groups as prehistoric in the sense that their illiteracy had prevented them from evolving a cumulative culture. A great deal of idealization played an important part in the twentieth-century glamour of ethnography.

Then, progressively emerged the acute awareness that ethnography was grounded in written texts, which relied on all the same stylistic and rhetorical devices as those used in literary works (e.g. Clifford and Marcus 1986). Were these tropes of objectivity and scientific metaphors mere stylistic devices which established ethnography as a creative genre among others? The critical literature has indeed soon distinguished subgenres which owed their characteristics to style rather that method: realist, confessional, and impressionistic tales characterize the various ways in which the data obtained through observation and interaction are translated into a discourse that may privilege the dialogic nature of the investigation or the dispassionate reporting of witnessed events (e.g. Van Maanen 1988). Was the recognition of ethnography as a form of writing enough to invalidate the epistemological relevance of its works? Even if it could be shown that ethnographic accounts yielded as much information about the ethnographers as about the populations which were probed, there was some knowledge to be gained in both cases even if this knowledge had to be contextualized. Martyn Hammersley's *What's Wrong with Ethnography?* (1992) is a deliberately ambiguous title. Ethnography has emerged from two decades of questioning as a stronger and epistemologically mature enterprise.

Why do circus ethnography? What kind of ethnography does this book propose to engage in? It is well established that, at least from the end of the eighteenth century, complex spectacles involving horsemanship, acrobatics, and clowning have become a part of popular entertainment in Europe and the Americas. These performances were taking place both in urban stable, albeit often temporary structures, and under traveling tents. There are countless mentions of, and allusions to these events and the attraction they exercised on the population at large. The emerging printed media and the legal records, as well as the literary works of the time, provide abundant data concerning the institutions and the characters which embodied the circus as a prominent presence in popular culture. However, precious little information has been preserved concerning the actual contents of the performances themselves. Only a few highlights have been described in some detail but always partially. It is noticeable that excellent works by historians who have retraced the history of the circus in England (e.g. Assael 2005) and in Germany (e.g. Otte 2006) during the nineteenth and early twentieth centuries provide only sporadic details about the countless spectacles which were produced during this long period of time. While these historical accounts possess an ethnographic dimension in as much as they illustrate the lives and conditions of the owners and performers of circuses in their social and cultural contexts, they could not rely on any kind of archives which would have made it possible to describe the spectacles themselves. They produce a sort of derivative ethnography based on information provided by, or inferred from archives whose initial purposes were not to document what was displayed in circus rings for the whole duration of the performances.

There are, though, a few remarkable exceptions. For instance, we will discuss in Chapter 4 the case of a traveling horse act that was presented on market squares and fairgrounds in the late sixteenth century throughout Europe. A French essayist, Michel de Lestoile, described this performance in exquisite detail because the master of the horse had been accused of witchcraft and had, for his defense, explained how the animal had been trained. But by and large the performances which took place and thrilled audiences for over two centuries since the beginning of the nineteenth century in the institutional setting of the modern circus constitute a "black box." We have only glimpses and shadows of its contents because nobody ever undertook the ethnography of these spectacles, that is, exhaustive descriptions of the performances and their reception in real time by actual audiences.

The goal of this book is to make up for this lack of documentation, at least as far as the contemporary circus is concerned, and to contribute to the ethnography of circus performances in the two decades at the cusp of the present century, a period of time which is witnessing an extraordinary renaissance of the circus both in its traditional forms and in newly emerged modes of staging and marketing. Of course, this book cannot offer detailed descriptions of circus acts which were presented in the past—live performances are ephemeral phenomena which leave only fragile echoes in the memory of their audience and in the writings of their contemporaries—but it is possible to make use of the visual recordings which were made once television started broadcasting whole circus programs to bring some shows to people's homes. There also exist some rare, mostly unpublished ethnographic documents which were constituted by passionate amateurs of the circus art such as, the rich legacy of Juliette and Marthe Vesque, two French visual artists who devoted their whole lives to the graphic recording of the circus performances they attended between the late nineteenth and mid-twentieth centuries. We will briefly examine their precious contribution to the ethnography of the circus in the next chapter when we address the critical issue of "writing the circus" rather than writing about the circus.

Past performances, though, are not entirely lost because the circus skills and modes of staging have been sustained over time by robust traditions which are transmitted from generation to generation, usually in the context of professional families or through selective apprenticeship usually exclusively reserved to the closed groups formed by extended families. It is, however, a relatively risky insurance against eventual extinction as the permanence of these traditions depends on complex social, cultural, and political circumstances, which are only relatively stable over long periods of time. They are narrowly connected to family structures and modes of existence which have been the object of continuing legal and ethical scrutiny by the authorities of nation-states during the past two centuries, and whose most extreme forms have survived mostly thanks to the geographic mobility of the nomadic groups which foster them. Until the emergence of a sophisticated technology of surveillance, the circus has proved to be remarkably elusive and highly adaptable to the various languages and customs that map the Euro-Asian continent and beyond. The ethnic background of traditional circus lineages and the nature of their trades have contributed to make this mode of survival a resilient fluid institution, which is now bound to be increasingly confronted by the enforceable demands of global legislative powers. It is hard to know how long the principle of cultural exception will prevent children born in the circus from being trained at a very early age in physically and psychologically limiting acrobatic disciplines, thus denying them the right to a lawful education.

But, in such difficult contexts, the circus remains somewhat immune to various forms of assimilation to the societies in which it performs. It seems that its existence is protected by a kind of mystic, a sort of cult of the circus that prevails in the general population and has generated a following of influential devotees who persistently endeavor to protect its trade. Where does this unparalleled fascination with the circus come from? Does the circus have some implied affinities with religious rituals? This is a question which will be encountered as we progress through the chapters of this book but addressing it at the outset is in order as it might sound at first paradoxical.

Circus as ritual

A recurring theme in the following chapters will be that the circus qualifies as a form of secular ritual. The term ritual has often been used in a metaphorical sense in modern sociological literature to designate forms of interaction which follow set patterns and convey meanings attached to the forms themselves rather than particular individualized contents. Greeting formulas such as "how are you?" or "have a nice day," accompanied by stereotyped gesture and facial expressions, do not imply that one asks a question or cares about someone else's day. It is a quasiautomatic maintenance of the functionality of a network, the reassurance that we are on speaking terms, a kind of social glue. Shaking hands in some cultures is a strong performative gesture which makes a contract effective. But in other cultures, this is a form of greeting gesture which is a mere perfunctory reassertion of a pervasive social contract, the sign that we are linked as part of a network of friends and acquaintances or when it is performed in order to acknowledge a mutual introduction, that we become a part of a group in which we can claim membership, people who keep in touch, literally speaking. In animal behavior, ritual refers to stereotyped interactions such as courtship, threat, or submission. In medical jargon, it categorizes repetitive movements associated with anxiety and other dysfunctions. Repetition is the feature which all these significations share in common. But the origin of the term is to be found in the religious sphere in the Latin word *ritus*, which refers to a sequence of actions prescribed by a cult. This word is related to a more ancient Indo-European root "*h rei," whose sense is "number," "counting," "payment," perhaps "giving the gods their due."

A ritual, in the proper sense of the term, carries a religious meaning. It is a prescribed performance involving action, gesture, objects, and words, whose purpose is to interact with supernatural entities. An extreme form of ritual is a human sacrifice, the staged killing of a human being by priests who perform this action according to precise rules with an assortment of props, chants, and incense. It is supposed to enforce a contract with a divine power, to secure its protection, or to appease its destructive anger. Such acts are well documented in history and are still occasionally performed underground in the context of religions such as Voodoo and Tantric Hinduism. But a more common form of ritual is animal sacrifice or the presentation of fruit and flowers. It often involves accomplishing specific actions on the part of the priests or the faithful. What counts as ritual is the formal accomplishment of stereotyped actions as exactly as possible as traditions prescribe them. They cause awe in as much as they are framed by transcendent narratives and believed to be counterproductive if they are not executed scrupulously according to the rules. They may or may not be accompanied by conscious meanings and emotions. They must be set apart, remain unquestioned, and require a radical suspension of disbelief. They are believed to bind humans and gods alike. The age of Enlightenment has deflated the claims of rituals as ways of relating to the sacred. They have, however, proved to be resilient as if there was a ritual imperative in the human psyche, a deep need to transcend individual rationality and circumstances through relating to more general defining forces and break away, at least periodically, from the social grid and its prescribed behaviors. But, in general, a ritual exceeds its rational justification, even its symbolic value. It transcends the sphere of the individual.

Students of religious rituals (e.g. Driver 1991; de Coppet 1992; Bell 1997; Kyriakidis 2007) have emphasized the role of a universal requirement: the delimitation of a portion of space within which a ritual can be performed. Temples, a word whose Indo-European etymology simply means "cut out from a spatial continuum," are bounded places which set out well-defined sacred spaces clearly separated from the profane outside territory surrounding them. The marking of such a space is the founding gesture through which a sacred place is established as an appropriate template for a sacrifice, a divination, or any kind of prescribed religious action. This founding can be conceived as temporary—for instance, in a nomadic context—or permanent when it is a part of a definitive settlement such as the building of a temple.

Another constant formal property of rituals, as was noted above, is that they include the performance of sets of actions which follow compulsory patterns. There is no practical rationale for these constraints except that they must be obeyed for the rituals to be effective. They carry the symbolic seal of a transcendent order. They are meant to be reiterated periodically without significant variations.

The third characteristic of rituals is that they are transformative. They perform a change of status, either permanent or temporary, in their participants. They unfold in time through stages. Their temporal structure is as marked as their spatial template with respect to the ordinary open-ended duration of individual and social life. The transformation can take the form of an emotional surge or simply the mere satisfaction of having met the requirements of a superior rule or the expectations of the social group to which one belongs. Rituals of exclusion and reintegration have been described by anthropologists (e.g. Douglas 1966; Turner 1969).

Religions tend to punctuate the solar, lunar, or seasonal cycles with regular rituals to the extent that the cosmological context they promote is saturated by the meaningful return of the same patterned actions and emotions.

These universal properties of rituals can be abstractly summarized as: (1) delimitation of a special space; (2) periodicity; (3) stereotypy; (4) repetitiveness; (5) transformative impact mostly in the sense of group integration. All these properties entail that religious rituals are social, live events which require the physical presence of the participants and that, as a necessary consequence, they are multimodal phenomena.

> *Mumbai, December 1984. This is the first day of my second visit to India. This time, it is after the monsoon, when circuses start performing again all over India. In spite of the jet lag, I do not want to waste any time. The local newspapers advertise the performances twice a day of Apollo Circus which has set up its camp at Church Gate, steps from my hotel in Kolaba. From the banners painted in front of the monumental*

entrance, I recognize all the regular staples of the circus programs I am used to in Europe and America: jugglers, magicians, lion trainers, flying trapeze acrobats, clowns, horses, and elephants. The big top is monumental. I have better to quickly learn how to use my elbows in a crowd to access the wicket where the best seats are sold. Beyond the gate, I find myself in a huge tent through which the public proceeds to enter the circus. Oriental carpets are spread on the ground; five glittering chandeliers are hanging above our heads; incense is burning in shiny copper vases; twenty elephants are lined up on one side, at a safe distance; a few horses and camels are kept in low enclosures of decorated red canvass on the other side. I am aroused by this unexpected transition from chaos to ceremonial order. The show has started when I claim my seat. A young girl spins high close to the top hanging by her teeth from a rope. She now descends to the ground as men slowly release their grip on the rope that runs over a pulley. The spotlights are dimmed; a black, elongated object is brought to the center of the ring; a bell is hooked to a hanging rope; the music is the kind of chants I heard in movies showing Hindu temples; five elephants enter the ring; I cannot see any trainer among them; one after the other they ring the bell by pulling the rope with their trunk as faithful do before stepping in a temple; now, one pours some water on the dark object, another follows by breaking a coconut on it and spilling the liquid content which run to the platform; the third one blows some red powder; the fourth one places a garland of flowers around the statue; the last one holds a small plate on which some incense is burning and walks around while swinging its trunk to disperse the fumes. They all now proceed on their front knees around the object which, as I will learn later, is a Shiva Lingam, an icon of the divine penis of the god of dance and destruction, which is worshiped in countless temples all over India.

In all the circuses I visited in India during two decades of sporadic research, I witnessed this circus act, sometimes involving a single animal. The elephants are supposed to perform a *puja*, a ritual which all Hindus accomplish daily or occasionally when they visit a temple. The second time I witnessed this act, I realized that the trainer was discretely standing close to the ring, cueing the animals with verbal orders. Again and again, I observed the circus elephants' *puja*. It was obviously appropriate for the audience to see a religious ritual accomplished by animals in a circus ring. Often, I heard some members in the audience humming the sacred chant which the loud speakers were blasting during this performance. Of course, elephants are sacred animals in the Hindu cosmology, like cows and monkeys. I am told that it would be scandalous to have dogs trained to perform this act. The point is that the circus space is compatible with the accomplishment of a religious ritual.

We might conclude that this is unique to Indian culture. But it does not seem to be the case. Circus performances in Europe have for a long time been associated with Christmas in a capacity which is not restricted to the modern secular festivities at this time of the year. Catholic Midnight Masses have often been celebrated in circus rings after the show on Christmas Eve. On December 24, 2011, for instance, Mgr Renaud de Dinechin, the Auxiliary Bishop of Paris, officiated under the big top of French Circus Alexis Gruss, which was set up for the winter season in the Bois de Boulogne in Paris. This was the thirty-fifth time that Midnight Mass had been celebrated in this circus.

Figure 1.1 This elephant is performing in the circus ring the ritual honoring the Hindu God Shiva. (Rendering by David Blostein from photographs of this act taken by the author in 1985.)

The daily *Le Monde* reported that the circus was packed and that more people attended this ceremony than the one which was held at the same time in Notre Dame Cathedral. This has become a common feature in Europe. Other circuses commonly schedule Catholic masses even for other liturgical celebrations than Christmas such as Easter. On November 1, 2011, Father Etienne Guillet celebrated All Saints Mass at Cirque Joseph Bouglione in Mantes La Jolie. Baptisms, weddings, blessings of the animals and human performers, are often performed by priest or pastors in circus rings. It appears that the properties of circus space and the nature of the performances which take place within its confines are congruent with the characteristics and requirements of religious rituals. Quite significantly, on January 23, 2012, at the conclusion of the Thirty-Sixth International Circus Festival of Monte Carlo, an ecumenical ceremony was held under the big top. Photographs documenting this event were published online in www.aucirque.com on February 3. Several denominations are represented among which we can see several Catholic priests in liturgical garments accompanied by choir boys, saying prayers and giving blessings. Two acrobatic couples and a male juggler are shown to take part in the ceremony by performing their acts. One of the priests plays clarinet with circus musicians in the final procession which follows a pattern typical of both circus and religion.

But there is more. If we review the formal properties of rituals which were listed above, we can see that circus acts indeed share in common most of these properties with religious rituals. Circus is indeed very repetitive. Horses may come in various colors and breeds, but all the categories of equestrian acts unfold with minimal variations. Cage acts may include lions, tigers, leopards, or bears, and they may be staged differently but the core of the action is doubly constrained by the natural behavior of the animals and the millenary tradition of training techniques. Tumbling, balancing, somersaulting, rope walking, funambulism, and juggling can truly differ only in degrees of perfection. We discover that the antics of clowns are based on a finite set of gags and props once they are abstractly analyzed. Artists, like priests, can be more or less charismatic but their performances boil down to sequences of distinct actions they repeat day after day for long periods of time until other, younger artists and priests take over and continue the tradition. These actions are executed with the formality of ceremonies, in a highly predictive manner. Periodically, once or twice a year, people go to the circus knowing what they will see but anticipating an experience which the circus alone can offer them, an overwhelming empathy with heroes who risk their lives in extreme situations they usually survive although the outcome remains ambiguously open to a sudden tragic end. These heroes, like willing victims of a sacrifice, do so by their own will, gratuitously, for the sake of these actions which have no other purpose than themselves. The audience feels the kind of fusion which only religious rituals can create, an unanimity quite alien to the divisive emotions caused by sport events when separate groups rout for their own teams or champions in competitive contests.

Religious rituals are loaded with symbolic contents. They deal with serious matters involving pollution and purification, survival and redemption, life and death. So does the circus. In the following chapters we will deepen our understanding of the meaning of circus performances which are staged as open-ended games where the public can see a lion trainer or an acrobat make a sign of the cross, or kiss the medal he or she wears as a talisman before entering the cage, or taking the first step on the high wire. After succeeding in a daring trick, some tilt their head toward the sky with a hand gesture of gratitude before acknowledging the applause of the public, thus retroactively endowing their action with a religious significance. The specter of death is indeed always present in these sawdust rituals. Mortal accidents are rare but real. On Sunday, December 21, 2008, 24-year-old Rafshan Alimov, a member of the Russian Puzanov Troupe fell on his head in the ring of the Blackpool Tower Circus and died shortly after on his way to the hospital. He had missed the padded chair in which he was supposed to land after being propelled from the ground in a teeter board act. He had succeeded countless times since his late teens in safely reaching this landing position after performing a somersault on his graceful aerial trajectory. In the very same ring, Neville Campbell had lost his life in 1994 when he lost his balance on a revolving apparatus called "the wheel of death" or "the wheel of destiny." We will encounter other such tragic cases as we proceed through the chapters of this book. Circus rituals are intensely entertaining. They capture our attention and stir our emotions. But they are deadly serious games.

2

The "Textility" of Circus Acts: Disentangling Cognition and Pleasure

Writing circus: From performance to text

How to transform the multimodal experience of a performance into a linear verbal account and eventually into a text? How much trust can we place in this process for producing a reliable written equivalent of a circus spectacle? An acrobatic act, for instance, seems to offer multiple strands of events in parallel sensorial modalities, which are woven into a holistic, complex set as the performance unfolds. It is endowed with dynamic consistency and a bounded identity. By contrast, its description is a linear string of words and sentences enclosed within the rectangular frame of a page or a computer screen. The apparent gap between the two media—the performance and the written text—raises a challenge for the ethnographer of the circus arts. This chapter will address this issue from both theoretical and practical points of view.

The metaphorical use of the notion of text to characterize cultural objects and events was introduced in the semiotics of the twentieth century by Russian Juri Lotman (1977). It was meant to express the abstract notion of static or dynamic cultural objects as finite sets of relations among signs and their transformations within some spatial and temporal templates. This intuitive metaphor foregrounded the notion of system. This general model was cast upon a great variety of nonlinguistic phenomena which were analyzed as if they were essentially of the same nature as literary works. The notion of primary and secondary modeling systems was proposed in order to extend to nonverbal cultural objects the relationship that existed between languages and texts, the latter systems using the former as the basic materials for their creation. Thus, the concepts of textuality and literariness which had been the cornerstones of structural poetics could be applied to the analysis of all kinds of performances. The etymologies of the terms "text" and "structure," which are derived respectively from the Latin verbs meaning "to weave" and "to construct," show that both "text" and "structure" in their literacy sense are themselves ultimately metaphorical.

The neologism *textility* is designed to bypass the loaded legacy of the structuralist assumptions. It is coined on the model of *ductility*, a term from physics, which refers to the capacity of some metals to be stretched into a wire. We will explore in this chapter the methodological productivity of this new metaphor and we will attempt to justify it as we endeavor to establish circus ethnography on sound theoretical grounds.

Circus performances, though, are essentially visual and acoustic events. "Writing the circus" cannot merely consist of producing reliable verbal narratives of circus acts. Even if these translations into a written language can achieve some degree of completeness when they are supported by exhaustive analyzes of the components and dynamic of the multimodal processes of these acts, the visual information will always be missing. This volume offers snapshots of gestures, postures, and situations which will clarify some descriptions or exemplify some typical gestures. Reliable visual documentations of circus performances, though, are extremely difficult to obtain because a deep understanding of the "logic of the acts," so to speak, is a necessary prerequisite for actually seeing what is happening and expertly capturing it on film. This is why some illustrations in this book are in the form of line drawings which make it possible to abstract the most relevant relations, which define, for instance, the exact nature of an acrobatic act.

It is impossible not to mention here that there exists an invaluable trove of visual and written archives concerning the circuses which performed in France during the first half of the twentieth century. We mentioned in the previous chapter the legacy of Marthe and Juliette Vesque, two sisters who made an artistic career in Versailles and Paris where they worked as illustrators. Their passionate love for the circus and their tragic sense of its ephemeral beauty led them to devote all their free time to make visual recordings in the form of colored drawings of the acts they admired. This iconography is unique because it is not based on pure visual impressions, as is the case for many painters, but on the precise understanding of the body techniques involved in the acts they documented. Their method consisted of repeatedly watching circus programs while covering their working pads with sketches which they processed into first drafts at home before returning to the same spectacles in order to feed details into their rendering of the acts until they obtained a set of finished images. They usually submitted the results of their artistic labor to the artists themselves who often corrected technical errors or even, in some rare cases, invited them to observe their movements at close range while they were rehearsing. At their death, they donated tens of thousands of documents to the French Museum of Popular Arts and Traditions where I had the privilege of examining and classifying a part of these archives between 1967 and 1975. Although most remain unpublished to date, a 200-page book of drawings in black and white was published under the title *Le cirque en images* (Mauriange and Bouissac 1977) and a large number of documents was made available in two sets of microfiches (Bouissac 1976b). A luxury book featuring 90 colored drawings appeared in 1992 (Boustany 1992). A sizeable part of the Vesque collection is now accessible online at www.circopedia.org/index.php/Marthe_and_Juliette_Vesque

Examining the Vesque legacy, leafing through their notebooks and diaries, and finding countless evidence of their passionate determination not to let all the wonders they were witnessing in the ring disappear totally in the abyss of time, could only be an inspiration for anyone who would undertake a historiography or an ethnography of the circus. I always considered them as my virtual guides as I traveled the world in search of circuses to document and as I endeavored to record in writing as precisely as possible the circus of my time. One of the most remarkable lessons to draw from perusing their work is how little change there has been in the nature and appearance of the acts they froze in time compared to those we can admire today, a century later. How similar too, are the emotions which are felt when the juggler keeps eight balls alight; the acrobat maintains a delicate balance on top of a tower of chairs; the trainer embraces a lion; the horse makes fun of its master; and the clown surprises us by making us laugh when we thought that we were blasé. Such a capacity to reactualize itself by producing meaningful experience is indeed the hallmark of a resilient ritual.

Events and their verbal accounts

Natural happenings, for instance, a snowstorm or an earthquake, and complex social events, such as street protests or multiple car accidents, confront their human witnesses with multisensorial chaos. In these circumstances, it is often hard to make sense of what is taking place, let alone provide a coherent account in the form of a verbal narrative. For a single and same event, inconsistent, even conflicting reports are common occurrences. The nature of such experiences depends indeed on the position of the witness and his or her mental disposition at the time these events happened. These dynamic moments of the surrounding environment can be encapsulated in semantic categories such as "snowstorm," "earthquake," "protest," or "car accident" but there is no compelling order according to which they should unfold or the exact form their description should take. Various physical laws or spontaneous social behaviors are at play to create a set of chain reactions that no single vantage point can possibly attend in their totality. As a result witnesses have a sensibly different experience to report and if they are asked to provide a written text describing these events they tend to fill the blanks in their perceptual memory with virtually consistent information based on assumptions or delusions rather than actual remembered experience. From this perspective, the events which are transformed into texts can be said to be *malleable* to a great extent because so many factors and dimensions are involved in the events themselves that the resulting texts are necessarily selective and can be forced into various narrative consistencies which are all equally valid within some limits. This suggestive metaphor, the *malleability* of experience when it is represented in written forms, is derived from the property of some metals to take a great variety of shapes under appropriate physical conditions, for example, when they are heated, hammered, or bent. It is markedly distinct from the metallurgic property of *ductility* which was described earlier as a felicitous model for the notion of *textility*.

As opposed to a natural or spontaneous social event, a circus performance implements a preestablished program. It obeys two sets of constraints: cultural norms and biological laws. The training of an acrobat, a juggler, or a magician develops to some extreme limits natural skills which are based on the abilities of the human body. This potential is comprised within lower and upper thresholds which cannot be transgressed if the body is to maintain its integrity. Moreover, the body is ruled by the laws of gravity, which further restrain the range of movements if it is to keep or restore its balance. It ensues that only one state of the system of the body can be achieved at a single moment. From this point of view, the building blocks of an acrobatic act are dynamic configurations governed by biological constraints which determine the successful outcome of each trick and for which there are no alternative paths. The observer is presented with a necessarily linear dynamic which can be described adequately as only one string of events whatever the level of resolution of the description. Naturally, each acrobatic moment is a complex set of complementary biological factors but they form a vector which leads to the conclusion of the act. In acts which involve more than one actor, such as those performed by acrobatic duos and teams, trainers and their animals, or clown dyads or triads, the complexity of the combined constraints does not alter the linear, hierarchical unfolding of the acts. All the threads are integrated into a unified dynamic process and they all converge toward the same end point.

The second set of constraints which govern a circus act originates in the cultural norms which prescribe the artistic form of the performance. A circus act is a set of routines ordered according to their real or apparent difficulty along a time line whose duration is predetermined by the producer of the program. The clusters of signs carried by the actors are constant qualities which have been selected in view of the staging of particular acts. The music and the lighting, whatever may be the connotations they bring to the act, narrowly follow the bodies' dynamic. All these semiotic components result from deliberate choices to produce some anticipated effects in the audience. Except in the rare cases of genuine accidents, there is no chaotic randomness in the multimodal stream of a circus act which could justify diverging descriptions based on attentive observation. Some spectacular failures are carefully staged in order to enhance the difficulty of some tricks and may convey an impression of an open-ended event to onetime viewers of the show but they can be as precisely described by the ethnographer as any other moment in a program because they are located at preset junctures in the articulation of the acts. In some acts, an artistic impression of chaos is crafted according to a rigorous choreography which becomes apparent after several viewings of the performance.

Therefore, if a circus act or a circus program can be reliably transformed into a linear verbal text, it is because it is an artifact which has been constructed as a linear sequence of events in the first place. It is a preprocessed experience in which surprises and chaotic moments are part of the script or the score. In fact, an apt image could be to consider the circus ring like the eye of a needle through which the circus acts proceed as braided multithread strings which any attentive observer is bound to describe in basically the same manner once the finite sets of the components of the acts have been technically categorized and identified. This, of course, requires several successive viewings of the acts and some degree of reflexivity on the part of the ethnographer who must acquire a definite level of technical awareness so that he or she can perceive the individual threads that are woven, so to speak, in the apparently seamless fabric of the performance.

However, as we pointed out in the previous chapter, the nature of a circus act implies the potential risk of a tragic outcome. On rare occasions, true chaos erupts in the ring and confronts us with so confused an experience that it gives rise to multiple accounts, a property I have dubbed the *malleability* of happenstance. The death of a trainer during a performance is such an unfortunate occurrence.

On May 5, 1978, Circus Gatini was performing in a suburb of Sherbrooke, in the Canadian Province of Québec. Eloïse Berchtold, a well-known American wild-animal trainer, was the star of the show. She presented her impressive cage act of fourteen lions, tigers, jaguars, cougars, and bears, which opened the program. Her second act concluded it. She entered the ring to the sound of a fanfare with her two male Asian elephants, Teak and Thai, which were solemnly announced by the presenter as the "Giants from Thailand."

The act starts. After a fast walk around the ring, the two tuskers are led to the center and ordered to rise on their hind legs thus displaying their impressive height. The trainer faces them, closer to the larger of the two which needs extra prompting to keep the pose. She turns toward the audience to acknowledge the applause. She trips and falls flat to the ground. She quickly rolls over to face the elephants. In no time, Teak hits her with its trunk. She shouts: "Get him out!" No time to react. Still lying on the ground she raises her arms. The elephant crushes her to death by pushing one of his tusks through her body in front of the horrified audience. The other elephant panics and rushes out of the tent. The presenter urges the audience to remain calm. There is confusion around and in the ring. The public starts leaving the tent. Some experienced spectators spontaneously act as marshals and guide the crowd toward the emergency exits. In the center of the ring, Teak lifts the lifeless, bleeding body and shakes its massive head to let it drop from its tusk. It smells it and rolls it on the ground with its trunk. The tent is slowly emptying. Nobody else, here, is familiar with this elephant act. Someone has to do something but there is no contingency plan. This circus is run by entrepreneurs who simply hired the acts of the program. It will take more than two hours to resolve the drama.

There was only one man present with circus animal experience, the head of an equestrian troupe, Napoléon Zamperla. He was watching Eloïse Berchtold's act that evening. When he saw her trip, he instantly assessed the seriousness of the situation and quickly fetched an iron bar to confront the elephant and try to save her. But it was too late. His priority immediately changed to protecting her body from further indignity and he managed to drive the animal away. A wooden panel was brought to hide the corpse from the elephant's sight and someone threw his jacket on it to cut the smell of blood which seemed to excite the tusker. The elephant was now on the side of the ring, standing still but out of control. The public had safely left the tent. Pictures which were taken at this moment show that about eight individuals remained in the circus, most staying at a safe distance. Among them was the organist, Rick Rosio, a close friend of Eloïse Berchtold. He was in shock but remembered that they had discussed once what could be done if something went wrong in her act. She had said: "try to distract the animal, take the hook and the whip, and give it orders." Without thinking Rick rushed toward Teak, picked up the hook and whip on the way, stood on its left side and shouted with the intonation he remembered from the previous shows: "Give me foot," "give me leg." The animal obeyed and was thus maintained for a while in a state of relative submission, alternately lifting its front and hind legs. But the animal was giving signs of restlessness. Rick did not know how to lead it outside to its truck and it was obvious that Teak was increasingly nervous. It made several mock charges. This suspense had lasted almost 2 hours when Rick panicked, rushed away and collapsed. Someone else attempted to take over without success. Apples were thrown in front of the elephant to keep it busy eating for a while but, now, nobody could approach it without triggering a charge. From second to second it was impossible to anticipate the animal's next move.

In the meantime, an emergency response to the situation was being organized outside the tent. A zoo veterinarian with pachyderm experience was woken up and transported by helicopter to the lot. Known big game hunters and paramilitary sharpshooters were rounded up in the vicinity and were strategically placed in case the tranquilizer would fail to act fast enough. "Any way, the vet had said, it normally takes 20 to 30 minutes." The elephant reacted aggressively to the first shot and proceeded toward the gunman it had quickly identified among the seats, crushing the chairs on its way. Then the execution started, hardly slowing down the animal until a fatal shot at a fairly close range put an end to Teak's life.

A few photos were taken on the spur of the moment. In the following days multiple accounts of the event appeared in the press and in radio interviews, mixing snippets of truth and unbridled fantasy. From what I heard at the time, I formed the image that a female elephant had seized the trainer with its trunk and thrown her to the ground before crushing her with its foot, and that the other animal had dashed through the audience to flee the ring. Twenty-four years later, an eyewitness to the event, Giovanni Iuliani, collaborated on a book designed to set the record straight because he was shocked to hear so many versions of what had become a legend, none of them conforming to what he had experienced firsthand. The book was written in collaboration with someone who, although not present at the time of the attack, was working as press agent for Circus Gatini and knew well those who were in and around the ring that fatal evening. Some photos illustrate the book. None of them captures any sense of drama: we can see a massive elephant in the distance near the border of the ring with half a dozen men either standing at a safe distance or walking away. One of them, though, remains close to the animal, holding the hook and making what seems to be a commanding gesture. Two pictures show the massive animal lying dead in the ring.

This detailed, factual account of a tragic circus accident was not produced by a single witness. It is a meticulous reconstruction based on the memories of some 20 persons who were present when the event took place and contributed, in a way or another, to its development and eventual resolution (Bordez and Iuliani 2002). Not all witnesses had the same direct information because the crisis was totally unexpected and nobody knew how to react to a situation for which there was no backup script. Its novelty precluded any form of anticipation. Decisions had to be made on the spur of the moment in a highly volatile and unpredictable context. The presenter, Pierre Jean, who was the closest to the ring when the trainer fell and the elephant attacked her, did not actually see what happened because he was standing at a distance behind the animal and, as he confessed later, was not paying attention at this particular moment, probably scanning the first row of the audience in search of eye contacts. He quickly understood that something was amiss when he noticed that the trainer was on the ground and that a member of the cast started rushing toward the animal with an iron bar. He automatically shifted to the default behavior in such cases: urging the public not to panic. When the second elephant tried to escape through the artist entrance, Pierre Jean first remained in place holding his microphone, briefly and unwittingly preventing the animal from fleeing until he realized the danger and accidentally disconnected the microphone in his haste. That elephant was scared but not aggressive and switched to an alternative sideway route. The only witness who had a clear view of the accident was the drummer in the band because he had to time his beats with precise moments in the act and constantly focused his attention on the trainer.

Once the routine of the act was abruptly derailed and the animal got out of control, every move had to be riskily improvised in response to the unknown. The attempts to restore some form of order could not follow a script and, as a consequence, the possibility of an ethnographic description collapsed. The historical account by Bordez and Iuliani is to a large extent an artifact based on an arbitrary selection and combination of points of view. Admittedly conceived as a tribute to Eloïse Berchtold's memory, the narrative is grounded in the circus ethos. Whatever happened is cast into the pattern of a heroic and tragic tale in which the killer elephant plays the role of destiny. Evidence for the *malleability* of experience comes from the fact that a decision must be made regarding the starting point of the chain of events and the aspects which are foregrounded. The authors first sketch a virtuous portrait of the trainer in order to exonerate her of any wrongdoing or error of judgment. They do not raise questions about the wisdom of training an act which initially included five male elephants nor do they report the actual methods which had been used to train them. They chose to start the story with the arrival on the lot of the act which had been reduced to three animals for this contract, and with the peculiar circumstances which had prompted her to present only two of them in the ring because the other, Tonga, had started a dominance fight with Teak. They cautiously assign ultimate responsibility to inexperienced circus ring boys who had not properly flattened the rough carpet that had been placed in the ring and which, in the authors' opinion, caused her to trip. Other, less flattering explanations had been put forward and, as it was mentioned, undocumented versions of the event had been circulated over the years. Backstage accidents are relatively frequent with circus elephants but there is almost no record of mishaps occurring during a performance. Elephant acts are usually uneventful, somewhat slowly unfolding under the firm direction of a trainer who shouts orders and holds a hook, and does not let his or her charges forget who is in control. These acts can be described with ethnographic precision because they can be repeatedly observed without noticeable variations. Naturally, the expert will see more details than meets the eyes of the naïve spectators. He or she will sense how readily individual animals comply with the orders of the trainer and how much prompting some of them need to accomplish their routines. Obvious wars of wills at times take place in the ring, in which bluffing plays a great part. But even in a smooth elephant performance there is a constant mutual testing of resolve which belongs to the subtext as does the past history of the act, a dimension all the more relevant as elephants are endowed with exceptional memory. This, however, is irrelevant to the ethnography of circus performances which pertains to the way acts are perceived as meaningful and pleasurable by their audience.

> *Circus Krone rightly advertises itself as the largest in Europe. It travels with seventy horses and nine adult elephants including a spectacularly huge male. As I watched the show for the second time in May 2011, I decided to take some notes during the*

elephant performance which was presented as the second item in that year's show. The act was announced in the program as an "oriental fantasy" titled "Holly-Bollywood":

As the Chinese acrobats who opened the show take a bow and leave the ring, the music suddenly changes to an exotic mode. Lightly clad dancers, eight women and two men, true to the "orientalist" imagery move their pelvis in suggestive rhythms while a Hindu princess is carried to the center of the ring on a gilded throne. The dimmed light lends an air of dangerous mystery to the scene. Two banners representing the elephant-head god Ganesh drop in front of the stage which stands at the artists entrance. As the dancers vanish through the right side of the stage, a monumental elephant appears from the left side followed by five others. The front of their heads is decorated by triangular panels studded with golden spheres on red, yellow, and black backgrounds which increase their height. The act starts.

The six massive animals, four Indian and two African females, fill the ring. Four girls are seated on the neck of the Indian elephants. A short man in exotic attire shouts orders which are mostly drowned out by the music. He walks fast from one animal to the other, holding his hook as discreetly as he can. A woman assists him but pays attention mostly to the African elephants. In the meantime the circus hands have quickly rolled six heavy stools they placed at equal distance around the ring. Each elephant stops in front of one, puts its right foot on top and moves around the stool in this position as if pivoting on one leg. Sneaking between the animals the circus hands roll the stools away. The two Africans are led to the back while the four Indians execute a "mount": three elephants rise and rest their front legs for a brief moment on the back of the elephant in front of them. The Africans are brought back and the six animals now move around the ring three by three. They stop and are ordered to lift their right leg in synchrony. They are quickly led to form a line facing the trainers across the ring, and lift one leg and their trunk in parallel. As the music fades into slow, relaxing jazz, they all pace once around the ring. The Africans are made to walk backward toward the artists' entrance and the woman keeps them interested in some small bits of food she offers them while the man makes the four remaining animals lie down on their sides, a process which is spectacular but requires some insistent prompting and occasional prodding. As they eventually all lower themselves toward the ground, the dancers who were on their necks jump down and, as soon as the trainer signals to the animals, the girls retake their initial place. As the elephants start rising again, they are stopped midway and are left seating on the ground, a position they hold for a short while during which the dancers strike graceful poses. The Africans rejoin the group. All in a line again they bend a front leg, performing a curtsy, then walk around and pirouette three times in a row as they proceed around the ring. They stop and form a line while one of the Indians is called to the front and raises its hind legs, resting on its head. A new walk-around takes place. Six taller stools are now rolled along the curb of the ring in the back so that maximum visibility is ensured for all the audience. The six elephants, one after the other, ascend the first stool and move from stool to stool, clearing the gap with a long stride as if they were proceeding on a bridge. The effect is monumental because of the relative height of the stools. They are made to lift a leg, then to sit down on these stools, and hold the pose with their front legs raised. A concluding walk-around follows and the animals leave the ring after a final pirouette.

Scripts, skills, and algorithms: The birth of a circus act

The continuous flow of a circus act is an artistic construction. The smooth way in which one exercise leads to the next, sometimes ushered in by a brief pause during which the acrobats seem to acknowledge the public's appreciation while in fact they catch their breath, masks the fact that a complete act is technically a discontinuous process. The observant ethnographer can discern the script or the score which is the backbone of the performance. It is a succession of routines (or tricks) which can be variously combined to create particular effects. The techniques and the style can be distinguished as two independent variables because a single and same routine can be implemented in different styles from one year to the next. In the 2011 performance which was described earlier, the six elephants were wearing head ornaments typical of the ceremonial elephants which can be seen in Kerala, the Southern Indian state. The visual and musical theme was "exotic India" with a touch of combined sacredness (the Ganesh images) and modern Bollywood (the suggestive dances which introduced the act). From the cultural point of view, there was total semiotic consistency from beginning to end and all the material signs could be exhaustively listed as it was done in the course of the verbal account. These material objects endowed with symbolic values (the elephants' forehead decorations, the costumes, the props) are directly observable since they are all stored in good order in circus wagons between the performances and reassembled shortly before the act starts. The same is true of the musical scores and the choreography which could be examined by an inquisitive ethnographer. Actually, the archives and the storage rooms at the Circus Krone's headquarters in Munich undoubtedly contain the valuable props and scripts of decades of performances and would provide the whole paradigm of the themes used in past programs for the staging of elephant acts. Most are probably recycled and recombined periodically. Let us note that in the 2011 staging of the act, the head gear of the animals contribute to visually integrate the two African bush elephants into the Indian mode by toning down their markedly different morphology.

Similarly, the trained behavior of the performing elephants is based on a finite set which can be precisely described. From year to year, the particular structure of the acts combines the elements of this set in an original manner. The 2011 program included: (1) walking forward; (2) walking backward; (3) walking in line clockwise around the ring; (4) turning around and walking counter clockwise; (4) making a pirouette; (5) climbing and standing on stools of various heights; (6) raising the left front leg; (7) bending the right front leg (curtsy); (8) raising the trunk; (9) sitting on stools and on the ground; (10) raising on hind legs; (11) raising on hind legs and putting the front legs on the back of another elephant; (12) lying down on the ground on one side; (13) putting one foot on a stool and pivoting on it; (14) lowering the head and raising the hind legs to make a headstand. This gestural lexicon can be combined to create spectacular visual discourses which progress at a rather slow but continuous pace dramatized by appropriate musical rhythms. The order in which these movements were staged in the 2011 program will be examined in the next section of this chapter. The repertory of trained movements of circus elephants is not limited to the ones which were selected for this particular act. In subsequent years, it can be safely predicted that both the style and combination of movements will change to produce different performances and meanings.

These movements are elicited from the animals through verbal commands—elephants can readily distinguish more than 100 such orders—which are often supported by gestures of the hand holding the hook or, even, at times, by prodding the elephants behind the ears. Let us note in passing that the tip of the hook is blunt and is not meant to create an open wound. It stimulates a sensitive part of the animal and calls it to order. In India, mahouts, who control their charges from above as they ride astride on their neck, keep putting pressure with their feet on the skin behind the animals' ears as they direct their mount through the chores of the day. Circus trainers, like James Puydebois and Jana Mandana at Circus Krone, have the challenging task of implementing the choreography of the act from the ground by making sure that they remain the exclusive focus of the elephants' attention. As long as the act unfolds as planned, it can be described in a linear manner using all the resources provided by the lexicon and syntax of natural language to construct a reliable, exhaustive representation of the controlled multimodal events which interpret the score of the performance. Comparing the implementation of a circus act to the actualization of a memorized list of musical notations is indeed an appropriate metaphor. But as in music not all interpretations are equally felicitous, mainly when some of the actors are animals which are far from being automata. Incidentally, this is why, when circus performers compete for a prize (like in the International Circus Festival of Monte Carlo), animal acts are usually given two chances. They indeed imply a potential for unplanned malleability which does not exist to the same extent in human acts.

Description and explanation

An analysis of the intended meaning of the elephant act which was summarily described in the preceding section consists of engaging in a kind of reverse semiotic engineering. Producing and directing a circus act is a creative process which uses a limited number of patterned movements as the basic blocks of a construction game and combines these with cultural symbols in order to form a coherent and consistent visual discourse. The rhetoric of this discourse aims at achieving a progression from simple to complex tasks, or from relatively safe to more dangerous behavior so that the audience's interest is sustained by their expectation that the next trick will be more difficult and spectacular. The gradation is usually a matter of appearance, a semiotic effect, rather than an increase in the actual difficulty of the exercises because no performer would take the risk of ending an act on a failure even if this possibility is built into the staging of the act. In flying trapeze acts, for example, the most difficult trick of the repertory is the triple somersault but its outcome is often uncertain and flyers may have to try once or twice again if they miss the catcher the first time, with no assurance that they will succeed on the second or third attempt. This is why the concluding segment of this type of act is usually a "pass over" in which a flyer is caught by the catcher and waits until another flyer leaves the platform then passes over the one who is released by the catcher and eventually joins the first flyer on the trapeze to return with him or her to the platform. This exercise requires perfect timing and acrobatic skill but is much less demanding than a triple somersault. The odds of its successful outcome are very high while its visual complexity achieves an effect of extreme danger since two flyers are at the same time in the air and may run the risk of collision. Whenever the triple is actually the last trick of a flying trapeze act, this means that the flyer has reached a complete mastery of the required skill.

With this in mind, let us consider the construction of the Krone elephant act. It is formed of two basic sets: four Asian animals and two African ones. First, the six elephants take part in five collective routines. Then, the four Asians perform the lying down and sitting up trick while the two Africans are kept aside. The latter join again the former for five more routines. The whole act is framed by two exercises on stools: the first one consists of having the elephants put a foot on fairly low pedestals and pivoting around; the last one involves higher stools placed along the ring curb on which the elephants climb and progress as if it were a discontinuous bridge, and eventually each one stands on its stools and they all perform synchronous movements before sitting down on these elevated platforms. The progression between these two collective exercises is obvious: in the first one, the animals remain in contact with the ground; in the last one, they are all well above ground and they tower above the trainers who cannot reach their ears with the hooks, thus asserting the power of their voice on these formidable animals. During the act, more demanding tricks are performed by the Asian elephants, concluding with one doing a headstand, alternating with the choreographies of the whole group which frame the Asian subset's routines. The composition is governed by a concern for balance and symmetry as well as by the rhetorical imperative that leads to a climax and a coda. The latter consists of having each elephant leave the ring in good order after performing a pirouette.

This is not, of course, a chance composition. The trainers have brought together two different species but they don't play out their distinctive features in the staging of the act since they are all made to look alike through identical decorative headgears. However, the two subsets are characterized by their own specific psychologies and behaviors, and keeping them together may test their tolerance for each other. In the act, the female trainer closely monitors the two African elephants when the male trainer is busy putting the Asians through their paces. More is going on in elephant acts than meets the eye. These animals are highly social and, if let alone, they constantly test and reinforce their relationships with each other. They have friends and foes. They tussle for ranking in the group. They hold grudges. Trainers have to keep all these urges and emotions in check lest the animals' priorities take over, and they must pay attention to any changes of mood which could tip the delicate sociobiological balance, including periodically sex-driven behavior. In brief, trainers have to be permanently on their toes as, they all agree, elephants are unpredictable. The poetic structure of the 2011 Krone elephant act, as I have outlined it above, resulted from the deliberate choices of the trainers and it is daily imposed upon animals which necessarily perceive the situation from their own biological points of view. Humans and animals in the circus, however, do not live in totally separate worlds ruled by indifference and violence. Social animals often adopt humans as social partners and react positively to their voice, gestures, and smell. They also respond to the names which were bestowed on them by humans. Men and women, conversely, develop emotional attitudes which can bias their evaluation of situations and generate anthropomorphic understandings. This can apply also to people who only occasionally witness animal performances.

Indeed, circus audiences always include a fair number of spectators who are regular visitors since some companies have often visited the same cities over several generations as was the case for French Cirque Bureau, mentioned in Chapter 1, and as it is true nowadays for Zirkus Krone in Germany which was founded over a century ago. Many people develop a personal feeling toward the trainers and their animals. Both are known by their stage names which thus become a component of the performance. In many circuses the names of horses and elephants are indicated on panels close to their individual quarters, either posted on their stalls for the former, or hanging on the back canvas wall for the latter. Both kinds of animals are sometimes even introduced by their names in the printed program or verbally when they enter the ring. Regarding elephants, there exists an internet database in which informative details about each captive animal in the world are recorded: www.elephant.se/elephant_database. It is possible to learn, for instance, that Circus Krone currently owns four Asian females as well as their names and ages (Mala, 48; Delhi, 39; Bara, 36; Burma, 36), three African bush females (Kenia, 29; Aischa 28; Sandrin, 28), and a 47-year-old castrated Asian male, Colonel Joe, who was previously known as Dillinger when, as a younger bull, he was owned by American Circus Vargas. These web identity kits contain the essential elements of individual elephants' story lives which are also often spread through circus fans literature or simply word of mouth, and contribute to the symbolic integration of circus animals into culture and society. Such information adds personal dimensions to the reception of the acts and reinforces the illusion of complicity that many trainers convey through performing human interactive gestures directly toward the animals but intended for the public.

With these considerations, we approach a level of interpretation which goes beyond the mere reverse semiotic engineering through which we can uncover the generative algorithm of typical and particular acts. Formal descriptions cannot count as explanations. The challenge for the ethnographer is to attempt to proceed from the former to the latter.

Disentangling meanings, emotions, and pleasure: Textility and cognitive malleability

Observing and describing a circus performance so that its relative objectivity can be supported by a significant consensus is a demanding but achievable task. Attempting to understand the meaning which this performance produces in the audience is a true challenge because audiences are not socially and psychologically homogeneous. There is nevertheless strong evidence that acts can trigger unanimous appreciation and emotion. Let us reflect on this issue by examining an example.

> *The eighth act in the 2011 program of the Circus Charles Knie is a solo performance by "sixteen year old René Sperlich," as announced in the printed program. When the*

spotlights reveal the young acrobat who has taken position in the ring, I recognize the immature face of the adolescent who served me an espresso at the circus bar while I was waiting for the gates to open. In the semidarkness which succeeded the preceding act, some props had been carried in the center. The music had changed to a more serious mood. Now he is smiling, his arms raised as a welcoming gesture, standing at the top of a transparent chair whose legs rest on four champagne bottles which have been placed on a fairly high pedestal, artistically curved and made of the same material as the chair. An attendant brings a second chair identical to the first one and hands it to the acrobat who puts it upside down on the first chair while cautiously moving his body in order to keep his balance. Then he ascends the second chair on which he takes a pose. His white costume bears some irregular red patterns and is widely lacerated to let his naked torso appear and reveal the muscles of his arms, thighs, and calves. A third and a fourth chair are pulled up by a rope so that he can grab them from the height at which he now precariously balances while making sure that the legs of the new chairs are aligned with those which are below.

At every stage, after adding a new chair and securing his balance, he ascends to the next level and performs a different acrobatic exercise: handstand elevations and change of direction, blending muscular strength and balancing skill at the top of what has become quite a high tower. The transparent plastic lends to this narrow construction the fragile appearance of glass and when this tower oscillates, as René Sperlich moves up, I cannot forget that the first chair rests on four glass bottles. A glance at the public around me shows anxious faces intently focused on the acrobat as well as a few spectators who have lowered their heads and brought their hands in front of their eyes. The live rock music suggests tension and suspense. Suddenly, the attendant enters the ring with a sixth chair. The tower seems to oscillate still more dangerously. The acrobat freezes and slowly adjusts his body to the center of gravity. The last chair is now in place and he balances on one hand only. The audience cannot help clapping their hands vigorously. There seems to be a feeling of relief that this must be the end and he has survived the challenge.

But no, it is not the end. The attendant removes one of the four champagne bottles which are the basis of this extraordinary game of construction. The whole tower rests now on three bottles only and René Sperlich gets ready for an ultimate daring feat: he balances on one arm while lowering his body to extend it horizontally. Returning to the initial position, then descending chair after chair and handing them to the attendant is the final challenge which must be met for the act to conclude. He is now, at long last, standing safely on the pedestal, like a sculpted hero on the base of a statue. The audience literally explodes in thunderous applause and very quickly synchronizes the clapping to produce a long rhythmic sound of glorious consecration. The acrobat acknowledges the homage with modesty and an angelic smile while I can see the intense perspiration which runs along his face. Some spectators rise from their seat. Some wipe tears from their eyes. Blackout. The horses of Marek Jama are already cantering in the light-flooded ring as the orchestra starts playing joyous tunes from Bizet's Carmen.

The "Textility" of Circus Acts 41

Figure 2.1 René Sperlich starts building the tower of chairs upon which he will balance and perform daring acrobatics. (Photo Credit: Zbigniew Roguszka, 2011.)

Figure 2.2 He has now reached the highest level. Note how carefully he distributes his weight in order to remain within the gravity perimeter. (Photo Credit: Zbigniew Roguszka, 2011.)

Figure 2.3 Performing a handstand on top of the tower of chairs requires the absolute control of the trajectory of the body during the elevation. (Photo Credit: Zbigniew Roguszka, 2011.)

Figure 2.4 The acrobatic figure is achieved and maintained with perfection while the tower oscillates as a result of the change of position of the acrobat's body. (Photo Credit: Zbigniew Roguszka, 2011.)

Figure 2.5 Regaining the initial position requires some amount of contortion in order for the body to stay within the critical perimeter of the towering structure. (Photo Credit: Zbigniew Roguszka, 2011.)

There is no doubt that every single component in that act results from a choice. The acrobat was trained to master every move in view of the particular situations which he himself constructs as an essential part of his act. It illustrates perfectly the linearity of the series of actions which ensure his survival. All his movements are logically linked and must be contained within the restricted perimeter formed by the four bottles in order for the acrobat to remain in control of gravity. However, ascending from one chair to the other requires that parts of the body briefly extend beyond this perimeter. This is possible as long as the body's weight is judiciously distributed. The contact between the first chair and the bottles as well as between the successive chairs is not artificially secured but relies entirely on the principle of gravity. Any significant margin of error would cause the collapse of the tower of chairs. At times, the slow displacement of the body transfers to the fragile structure an oscillation which is all the more dramatic as the acrobat is higher above the ground. The acrobat's behavior must be as exact and rigorous as the algorithm which expresses the constructed situation in terms of physics. The rendering I attempted above conveys, through a narrative using literary means, the development of the act while taking into account its interface with the audience but it should be obvious that this act, as most acts, could be described in the mathematic language of equations. There is only one path to survival. Minimal variations are unavoidable, of course, but they are constrained by the strictest law of all: universal gravitation.

Figure 2.6 The acrobat can now safely acknowledge the applause of the audience but he will have to deconstruct the tower chair after chair while descending toward the position from which he started. (Photo Credit: Zbigniew Roguszka, 2011.)

44 Circus as Multimodal Discourse

Figure 2.7 The last feat is a one-handstand balancing on the back of a chair whose legs rest on only three bottles. (Photo Credit: Zbigniew Roguszka, 2011.)

Figure 2.8 Finally, René Sperlich enjoys with a modest smile a well-deserved triumph. (Photo Credit: Zbigniew Roguszka, 2011.)

Reflecting now on the properly semiotic components of the act, we will understand that more is involved in the reception of the audience than a mere appreciation of the acrobat's skill. An innocent looking adolescent undertakes to meet a life-threatening challenge. His demeanor is modest. He is dressed in white but the lacerations on his tights and the irregular red patterns cannot fail to evoke death. The connotation of the music verges on the tragic mode, or at least the seriousness of destiny: successively Queen's "We are the champions," "The show must go on," and "Who wants to live forever." The naked body which appears through the irregular gaps in his tightly fitting costume contributes to merging the erotic and the lethal into the powerful theme of fatality. The apparent fragility of the transparent material and the brash provocation of building a tower of common objects which rest on the narrow necks of glass bottles without any apparent hooking device convey a sense of real danger. Moreover, the acrobat is not secured by a safety lunge that would prevent a mortal fall nor is there any net that could catch him before he crashes on the ground should the column of chairs collapse. His performance belongs to the paradigm of death-defying acts, a category which is explicitly represented in most circus programs. This is actually the only such act in which risk is emphatically staged in the 2011 program of Circus Charles Knie.

The act, however, is based on a combination of balance and strength, and has been rehearsed repeatedly step by step and with all the safety measures required until the performance could be considered safe. The acrobat is not suicidal and the parents or friends who trained him are not murderers. The risk is both controlled and staged, including occasional oscillations of the tower of chairs which make most spectators clench their hands and hold their breath. The rhetoric of the circus nevertheless classifies it as a death-defying act and thus introduces a specific narrative whose discursive modalities result from the semiotic engineering which was analyzed in the preceding section of this chapter. To defy death is to play a game in which each move leads to an outcome which is either winning or losing. The challenge for the acrobat is to beat death by putting himself in increasingly daring situations in which the odds for survival are decreasing until he throws an all or nothing bet: reducing the even number of the bottles which had secured the base of his construction so far to an odd number and performing in this unstable new context an extreme feat of balance. This performed multimodal discourse led to a climax but each stage was endowed with the same anxiety linked to the uncertainty of the outcome. The game is all the more intense as the player is very young and brings to the game the high-valued prize of a full life ahead of him. Betting one's life in old age is a greatly reduced pledge as insurance companies know all too well.

Let us now return to the reception of the act and let us try to explain in a nontrivial manner the intense cognitive and emotional participation of the audience. No other acts in this otherwise exceptionally good spectacle triggered the spontaneous rhythmic and lasting applause which I consistently observed in three successive performances. As an ethnographer who was attempting to document this act as precisely as possible, I was equally moved each time and had to return to this circus several months later to check visual details which had been drowned, so to speak, in the emotion I experienced in total communion with the public of which I was a part, irrespective of my research agenda. Understanding the meaning produced by this performance requires that we take some distance and analyze it in light of game theory. It also demands that we characterize the intense emotion it causes in terms of brain states.

> *September 11, 2011. I am back to Circus Charles Knie with my friend Zbigniew Roguszka who will photograph this act, trying to convey a sense of the height of the column of chairs and the precarious balance René Sperlich achieves at the top. Actually there seems to be only five chairs, not six as I had noted in my previous visit three months earlier. I feel humbled to discover that my ethnographic objectivity had proved to be unreliable. It is true that it is not easy to keep track of the number of chairs as the attention is captured by the empathic concern for the instability of the construction and the chairs are brought in rapid succession. In fact, after watching the act for the second time, I am so unsure about the exact number of chairs that I have to ask the acrobat himself during the intermission while he is selling coffees at a booth under the annex tent. He candidly confirms the number five. But there is more: when I reconstructed the act from my notes, I located the removal of the fourth bottle while he was still balancing on the fifth chair. In fact, this happens when there is only one chair left at the end of the act. It is still a remarkable feat but my memory of the act, in spite of precise, albeit cursory field notes, had transformed it substantially. Why point out this error now rather than correct my first account? Because it has been my constant experience that most spectators foster memories of circus acts which magnify their beauty and audacity. Undoubtedly, these biased memories are as much a part of the performances they have seen as the actual multimodal experience they processed under the big top. I have often noted this phenomenon but acknowledging that, to my surprise, I personally became subjected to such an illusion vividly bears witness to the interplay of perception and imagination which occurs during a circus performance and the way in which we remember it.*

Circus audiences are characterized by great social and psychological diversity. Children accompanied by their parents or grandparents, adolescents, and adults of all ages come from a variety of economic and cultural backgrounds. The range of the price of admission determines the distribution of the spectators under the tent but the spatial constraints of the circus impose a physical closeness which, under favorable circumstances, forms a continuous, undifferentiated mass through which contagious laughter or anxiety ebb and flow. Younger children, though, usually find it difficult to follow with interest the unfolding of the performance because its length and complexity challenge their attention span and their capacity for understanding the biological and semiotic subtleties of the acts. But the great majority in the audience shares a common appreciation of the situations which are created in the ring and react emotionally in similar fashion to the ordeals of the artists and their eventual triumphs. Phenomenological accounts rather confusedly point to mixed feelings of arousal, anxiety, elation, and relief which intensely color the experience of circus performances. This holistic impression can be disentangled by first considering the nature of the spectators' interest and, secondly, acknowledging that the emotional outcome is euphoria, a sense of reward, even a kind of "high" beyond reason.

The multimodal discourse of a circus act such as René Sperlich's tower of risks is structured as a narrative: a hero confronts a succession of tests and eventually succeeds in overcoming an extreme challenge to conclude the act. Continuous interest is triggered by the relative uncertainty of the outcome of each move of the game and the constant introduction of novelty in the initial situation. In that case, it consists of adding chairs to the height and, at the end, removing one of the four bottles which, so far, had formed the stable base of the construction. In the same manner, the disproportion between the formidable power of six adult elephants and the frailty of their trainers creates a challenging situation. To manipulate through voice and gesture the behavior of the animals according to a preset choreography achieves a succession of moves of increasing difficulty. The possibility of an accident such as the one which was reported earlier in this chapter always haunts the witnessing of wild-animal acts with more or less acuity. The chronicle of the circus, including its recent history, provides a sufficient number of deadly accidents to remind the public that not only the acts which are explicitly staged as death-defying but also most other acrobatically challenging performances involve real risks.

With the abstract representation of circus acts as instances of games which are ritualistically played in a manner that leaves the outcome relatively uncertain, as any live show does by nature, we can better understand the audience's emotional involvement. Empirical evidence has indeed accrued during the past few decades to demonstrate that the feeling of pleasure is consistently correlated with the release in the brain of chemicals secreted by specific neurons which respond to the organism's satisfaction of needs by releasing neurotransmitters. We will return to this issue at the conclusion of this book but let us consider the most likely explanation for the pleasure most humans draw from attending circus performances. Prominent among these neurotransmitters is dopamine, a molecule which stimulates the brain's so-called reward centers. Addictive drugs such as cocaine artificially stimulate these centers because their molecular structures mimic dopamine. The relevance of such data to the understanding of the pleasure which countless humans feel at the circus is that participants in, as well as witnesses to a game, get a dopamine high when they experience the outcome of a move. Gamblers ceaselessly seek this gratification. So do those who passionately watch sports competitions, matches, and televised games or reality shows. The famous slogan "Bread and Circus" which, since imperial Rome, purports to express the most essential needs of the populace is grounded in the way our brains process information and evaluate dynamic situations involving vital risks. The artificial construction of such situations is precisely what the circus offers. All circus acts indeed create the context for a challenge and stage the required moves in the real time and space of the ring. The outcome of these acts impacts our brains in a significant, transformative manner, which in many ways must be addictive since we return again and again to participate in circus rituals.

3

Magic in the Ring

Veils of illusion

Contemporary circus programs often feature magic acts. A typical performance usually unfolds as follows: a formally dressed man or woman, the magician, enters the ring with one or several assistants. Some objects such as scarves or ribbons are made to instantly change colors or bunches of flowers appear at the snap of a finger. Doves seem to materialize out of thin air when the magician waves his hands and the legendary rabbit is extracted from a top hat. Larger objects disappear in boxes which are puzzlingly shown to remain empty. Small fishbowls filled with water in which a goldfish is swimming materialize in succession in the hands of the magician as if they were caught in the air at the end of elegant gestures. A cabinet is rolled into the center of the ring. It seems to be just wide enough to allow one of the assistants to step inside. The door is closed. The magician thrusts a dozen swords through the cabinet from all sides and from top to bottom. Then the swords are extracted with apparent effort. The door opens and the assistant walks out with grace, displaying a cheerful look. A big trunk is brought in. The magician gets inside and is tied up with chains by an assistant. The trunk is locked by a spectator who has been called as a witness and is asked to keep the key. The assistant climbs on top of the trunk and spreads a large veil over herself and the trunk to form a kind of tent from the tip of her raised arms to the ground. The veil vibrates for a few seconds while the ring master counts to five and quickly pulls the veil. Wow! It is the magician who stands on top of the trunk. The helpful spectator is asked to bring the key and open the lock. It is the assistant, now bound in chains, who is rescued from the inside of the trunk. The music becomes more dramatic while a rectangular cage on wheels is placed in the center of the ring. The cage is empty. Two female assistants ascend the four-step stairs that lead to the entrance of the cage and they are locked in. A black drape is drawn over the cage. The magician walks around the cage and emphatically gestures for a few seconds before pulling the cloth and revealing a huge tiger which paces in the cage where the two girls were standing an instant ago. At the same time, the two girls appear among the audience and walk toward the ring from the top row of seats. They all bow to the befuddled audience as the cage is rolled out of the ring. Thus ends the act.

There are, of course, numerous variations in the staging and composition of this scenario. The above sketchy description is only one possibility among many. We will examine in details several other magic performances in this chapter. But this typical act implements a narrative and rhetorical pattern that can be frequently observed in contemporary circus programs. The unfolding of such magic acts can be expressed in a more abstract manner. For instance, we notice the definite progression from the appearance and disappearance of objects and small domestic animals to larger props in which humans vanish or from which they pop up. The mood has moved from playful fantasy to the evocation of death with confinement, chains, swords, and dangerous predators. A climax has been built up step by step to reach a sudden release of the anxiety through the happy ending which displays all the actors perfectly sound and safe, and smiling. The dynamic of the drama through its successive stages has been brought to its closure: everybody is accounted for and all is well which ends well. However, a kind of puzzlement lingers in the mind of the audience. A few tricks were quite obvious and only required perfect skills and clever props. The fast pace of the actions did not leave much time for observation and reflection. But how could the two girls who were locked in the cage suddenly come back from outside the ring? There remains in many spectators an after-taste of uncanny wonder. The stern rationalist dismisses this feeling: no such miracles are possible. Others, more impressionable, may keep wondering. Some may be simply truly scared mainly if they are prone to believe in magic or if they are too young to make the difference between truth and illusion, life and play.

> Blackpool Tower Circus, September 2009. The afternoon show is well attended. Many children have been brought there by their parents. Some have been brought here as their birthday treat. Before the intermission, the ring master has read their names aloud while the band was playing "Happy birthday to you." The second part of the show features a magician. This is a run-of-the-mill act which offers the classical repertory of tricks: scarves tie themselves to each other after they have been put separately in a top hat; bunches of artificial flowers emerge from a hollow cane; doves vanish from a cage and reappear in a box placed a few yards away. Then, an assistant girl is pushed into a basket and swords are thrust through it without causing her any harm as she soon emerges relaxed and smiling. It is nevertheless a display of violence and I cannot help wondering how the young children in the audience process this information, what kind of meaning they experience during their first exposure to these tricks. The magician now turns to a more serious business: a bejeweled woman in a formal evening gown has vanished from a tall box made of mirrors. The magician requires the help of a spectator for the next trick as a big trunk is being carried to the center of the ring. As no one volunteers, he grabs the hand of a man who is seated on the front row and pulls him gently but insistently toward the ring. The man is reluctant to fight back but warily glances at his son who was next to him. The boy may be 4- or 5-year-old. As his father is dragged toward the trunk, he suddenly shrieks and loudly cries. The magician seems amused. The boy is frantic, obviously in utter panic at the thought that his dad is going to disappear forever in that sinister trunk. It takes some time for the magician to realize that his act is not funny any longer. He releases the man who has no choice but to carry his son out of the circus to make him feel safe and secure again.

We may admire the cleverness of these sleight-of-hand artists and the inventiveness of their props which fool our attention and create illusions which defy our understanding. But we know that these magicians are skilled humans rather than special beings privy to supernatural powers. At least, we think we know and trust our modern rationality. But this is a relatively recent development in the understanding of magic as a human skill. Ancient priests and modern gurus, as we will see later in the chapter, could rely on techniques of illusion to impress their followers and convince them of their ability to control the forces of nature and perform miracles. In some contexts, though, our rationality proves to be vulnerable and we can happen to puzzle whether this rationality could itself be an illusion. The point to keep in mind as we consider circus magic acts is that not only sleight-of-hand knowledge but all the other circus skills were initially developed as body techniques and artifacts designed to create illusions and support the claim of some individuals that they could fly, walk on water, control fierce animals, and keep objects moving around or simply appear from nothing and vanish into thin air, as well as cast and remove spells, or tell the future. The magic acts we can still observe in circuses is a fragile remnant of the age of wonderment that is embedded in a secular form of mass entertainment.

Belief and disbelief

Indeed, modern, educated audiences look at magic as entertainment. They know that circus magicians are not endowed with unnatural powers but are gifted professionals who have submitted themselves to an exacting training. Fastness of hand movements and smart manipulation of their spectators' attention are the keys to the illusions they create. The staging of a trick in which two girls disappear in a cage and reappear from outside the cage has involved a distracting walk around the cage by the magician while the hollow wooden prop they had used to step up in the cage is rolled out of the ring. Nobody noticed that discreet change in the situation as it was done in a perfunctory manner by the circus hands that had previously brought the cage to the center of the ring. It helps that the assistants of magicians are also contortionists and can bend themselves into small containers.

But as we will see later in this chapter, the transformations actualized by the circus magicians are not purely physical and mechanistic events: they are biologically, cognitively, and culturally relevant. The emotional gratification they cause in their audience is beyond truth and deception, belief and disbelief. Even the most rational spectator may experience at times a brief instant of worrisome doubt.

In 1988, during a brief stay in Bombay—which had not yet recovered its erstwhile name Mumbai—I noticed that the snake charmers who displayed their antics in squares and along avenues were doing more than playing flute in front of erected cobras fanning out their hoods. They were performing complex magic shows of which the snake stunts were only a part. The following year, I received a small grant that allowed me to spend a week there, in Kolaba and Juhu Beach, observing closely with the help of hired interpreters the details of their performances. Those around the

Gate of India were there merely to attract the brief attention of tourists who were fascinated by the cobras the magicians "charmed" or repulsed by the bloody fights they were staging between a mongoose and a snake. Tourists were consuming an instant dose of exoticism and would quickly quit after making a photo and dropping a coin on the ground at a safe distance from the cobras. But in other parts of the city, such as Church Gate or Cuffe Parade, the shows were longer and more substantial. They were attended by small crowds of ordinary people which kept crowding around the performing areas which had been staked out in public squares or on large sidewalks by positioning snake baskets that kept the audience at bay. Whenever they identified foreigners among the crowd, they fiercely proclaimed in broken English: "Not film! Not picture!" I assumed that they would equally object to my small tape recorder—small for the time but huge compared to today's standards—and I kept it in a rag bag as I was scouting the streets for an opportunity to observe and record the patter of snake charmers in the full display of their art. The first time I used the recorder, I discreetly pressed the "start" button through the canvas of the bag when the magicians began the ranting which continuously accompanied their demonstrations. The progression was dramatic from conventional sleight-of-hand tricks to intriguing feats that genuinely puzzled me. For instance, a cursed pigeon started to run frantically on the ground in large circles on its wings, looking like anything but a pigeon, and causing the audience to step back. The word "uncanny" came to my mind as I could not explain to my satisfaction what was actually happening. Then came the cobras and it was increasingly obvious that I was in the middle of something which was more than a mere entertaining performance. The tone of voice, the drum beats and flute rhythms had changed, and the mood of the audience had switched to utter seriousness. I truly felt out of place, receding slightly within the crowd to become less visible, split between the urge to flee and the unholy desire to record "interesting ethnographic material," being acutely conscious at the same time of my transgressing an injunction that the performers would not take lightly if they discovered my tape recorder. At the end all of the cobras with their hoods deployed were carried around in their majestic baskets and the Hindus in the crowd touched them with awe, placed money in the containers, and joined their hands as a gesture of devotion to the God Shiva, the dancing master of death. I rushed to the hotel, anxious to check my clandestine recording. The tape was blank. "The cobra curse!" was my spontaneous first thought. I was surprised by the uneasy emotion I experienced at this very moment. My rational mind had been briefly defeated by the power of the context. Obviously, I had pushed the wrong button through the canvas of my bag. Nevertheless this rational explanation could not absolutely disprove the irrational hypothesis since the technical mistake had been merely a small part in a complex process.

The structure of the few performances by the snake charmers I observed was obviously bearing some similarities with the composition of the magic acts which can be watched in modern circuses. Lee Siegel's (1991) ethnographic and historical account of magic performances in India provides ample evidence for the resilience of this structure and the practical constraints which determine it. His participant observation of nomadic magicians and his historical investigation of the techniques and staging of their performances over at least the past two centuries show how this way of earning a living is transmitted across generations among the Maslets, a specialized ethnic group which is both despised and feared by the population at large.

How do they operate? The first imperative is to call the attention of passersby through playing drums and flute, then to cause them to stop and watch by performing some intriguing sleight-of-hand tricks such as small balls unexpectedly appearing or disappearing in goblets. The audience is captivated by still more puzzling feats: for instance, ropes transformed into snakes, snakes into pigeons, and so on; empty jugs from which water is poured; a bird killed and resuscitated. With the latter the theme of mutilation and death is evoked and will be the focus of the remaining of the performance which has thus moved from surprise and entertainment to the seriousness of a kind of dark ritual that generates anxiety and fear: blood will ooze from a sliced green lime; a disrespectful boy will have his tongue cut off through a realistic gimmick which impresses and frightens the gullible crowd; then, the tongue will be restored and the child will speak again; more gory tricks will follow with the purpose of convincing the audience that the magician is endowed with actual magic power. In due time, this will motivate them to give some money if only to avoid being cursed and they will purchase amulets and rings that are supposed to bring good luck and protect from dangers. The vivid descriptions found in Siegel's remarkable book are appropriately set in the context of Hinduism which is a fertile ground for the popular acceptance of magic at face value, all the more so since traveling magicians invoke the primordial God Indra who is claimed to be the originator of their art and the terrifying Goddess Kali whose cult is associated with a tradition of human sacrifices. I once witnessed a performance by the celebrated Bengali stage magician P. C. Sorcar Junior whose act started with religious invocations in front of an icon of this red-tongued deity which was prominently displayed on the stage. However, the *Maslets* are now all Muslims and can at will illustrate their patter with references to Koranic scriptures whenever they perform for mostly Muslim crowds in front of mosques on Fridays.

The snake charmers, I observed in Mumbai, were handling "deadly reptiles"—they have usually been defanged—for the amazement of Western tourists around the Gate of India but indulged in Hindu invocations of the God Shiva when they were displaying the same snakes as "sacred cobras" for their mostly Hindu audience in the business districts or near the temples. Siegel interestingly documents instances in which the magicians simultaneously played for Hindus and Muslims through engaging in clever syncretism or ecumenical rhetoric.

The relevance of this detour to India is grounded in the fact that it is generally accepted that nomads from the Asian subcontinent migrated to medieval European cities and villages where they eked out a living through performing most of the deceptive skills which form the repertory of modern circuses, including magic. There is a remarkable cultural continuity between the means of existence and expertise of these groups and the circus as we know it today. These nomads are still productive in modern Pakistan and India. Joseph Berland's ethnographic account of the way of life of the Qalandar (1982) is a unique window on the social and cultural origins of the arts we admire in the circus ring. These mountebanks were delivering wonders such as bear and monkey training, tightrope walking, acrobatics, juggling, comedy, and sleight-of-hand demonstrations. The borderline between genuine extraordinary accomplishments and exploitative deceptions was blurred. Fortune telling, medicinal herbs and powders, amulets and charms, curses and their removal were traded in the shadow of the shows and the carnival atmosphere of the fairs. These transient performers and magicians were accused of various crimes and often persecuted by the civil and church authorities but they kept fascinating the sedentary populations among which countless irrational beliefs and superstitions were flourishing. The rationale for the structure of traditional Indian magic performances as it has been outlined at the beginning of this chapter does not hold for contemporary circus magic acts, if only because the modern entertainment industry compels spectators to pay in advance and the performers are labeled as "illusionists." But the progression from bemusement to puzzlement, then extreme illusions involving various forms of dismemberment, decapitation, and disappearance coincides with the successive stages of the traditional display by Indian magicians. The magic act's modern rhetoric is nevertheless equally effective and even troublesome when it is implemented with realistic acting and staging.

Considering disbelief as the norm for modern Western spectators is indeed misleading. No audience is perfectly homogeneous and includes individuals who hold diverse beliefs and a range of cognitive capacities to reason about the methods used by the magician to achieve the wonders which are produced in the ring. There are those who believe in miracles; those who fear dark forces which can interfere with human affairs; those who believe in angels and demons; those who are impressionable; and those whose level of education or stage of mental development cannot handle the complexity of some of the tricks. The little boy we encountered earlier at the Blackpool Tower Circus had not yet reached the cognitive maturity that is necessary to put some distance between what we see and what we believe. Even if the determined skeptics were the majority, the makeup of any audience can include spectators surprisingly prone to suspend their disbelief in particular circumstances. The discourse of folktales, tabloids, and horror movies feeds a pervasive anxiety concerning black magic in the population at large. The circus as a whole is not totally immune to a range of interpretations which are at odds with the secular rationalism of our cultural officialdom. We will often point out in the chapters which follow how dormant irrationality can easily be wakened up and color our experience of those immemorial rituals we call the circus.

The mechanisms of miracles and the logic of illusions

The progressive disenchantment of magic which has taken place during the past two centuries has been thoroughly documented by cultural historians (e.g. During 2002; Mangan 2007; Coppa et al. 2008; Hass 2008), but the capacity of conjurors to puzzle and enchant has proved to be very resilient. Secular magic, notably in its staged version, remains a prosperous industry. Its mystical potential is far for being totally absent. A couple of decades ago, André Kole's magic show, World of Illusion, was performed on university campuses where it was advertised as "A Dazzling Magical Musical and Spiritual Experience." It was officially sponsored by "Campus Crusade for Christ International." It included all the classics of conjuring from vanishing doves and appearing fires to dismemberments of women. But all was well which ended well, and a message of peace and love was conveyed in the form of a hymn which the audience was invited to sing in concluding the event.

We hear about the power of priests in ancient texts. For instance, in Homer's Iliad we read that the Greek navy which was on its way to fight the Trojans became stuck on the shore because the winds were not blowing. The king who was leading the expedition consulted the seers of the temple and was told that the gods would send back the winds if his young daughter Iphigenia was sacrificed. The king consented to this deal and the girl was taken to the altar. Fortunately, a miracle happened: as the priests were approaching to kill her, she was instantly replaced on the altar by a deer. This is, of course, a miracle that any trained circus magician can perform with the proper prop. When we refer nowadays to the secularization of magic, we must keep in mind that it is the state of mind of the population which has changed, not the mechanisms used to achieve such miracles.

Historian of religion Peter Jackson (2012) has shown the extent to which Vedic and ancient Greek religious rituals imply the existence of artifacts he calls "apparatus" which made illusions concrete for the believers. The magic in the circus ring perpetuates these mechanisms in a way which requires additional skills since magicians are almost totally surrounded by spectators and cannot take advantage of a backdrop as is the case on stage and in temples.

However, the ethnography of magic spectacles cannot foreground the mechanisms which are not perceived by the audience. It must remain focused on the interface between what the conjurors do and what the public perceives or rather misperceives. This visual discourse is endowed with a symbolic consistency, a kind of semiotic logic which is as culturally compelling as the perceptual delusions created by the magicians.

Let us look at what we take for granted when we watch a modern magic act: first, the utensils from which things appear and into which they disappear; second, the objects which are made to appear and to disappear. The former are household implements such as dishes, cloth items, pots and pans, vases, trunks, cabinets, and the like, which are made to look exactly like those we find in our domestic environment. The latter are representative of the products of cultivation, weaving skills, and animal husbandry: flowers, ribbons, ropes, scarves, doves, rabbits, eggs. These are typically from the domain of women in the contextual traditional cultures. Women are also the objects which are manipulated, even apparently dismembered. Magicians are traditionally males impersonating figures of authority. Over four decades of observations I encountered only a very small number of female magicians performing in circuses or on stage. One particularly interesting example was in a program of the Paris cabaret the *Lido* in the 1970s, of which I kept a record: the female magician concluded her act by making two young men disappear in a narrow box where they were transformed into two Afghan greyhounds. It could be argued that male dancers in cabarets tend to be thinner than their female counterparts and that greyhounds are among the flatter breeds of dogs. These are indeed very practical choices when the point is to make both fit into a narrow container. However, it may be significant from a systematic cultural perspective that switching from a male to a female magician might indeed have structural consequences on the kind of objects which are manipulated while maintaining some form of symbolic consistency: once the gender of the transformer is switched to its opposite, males instead of females are made to disappear and they are transformed into dogs rather than felines. To which extent the practicality of a trick determines the choice of the objects which are used by the magicians is not an easy problem to solve. Whether the choices are constrained by material consideration or symbolic consistency raises an interesting question, though: was the tradition of the magicians conditioned by the fact that their audiences were originally mostly made of males, notably in the fairgrounds and in the early circuses of the eighteenth and nineteenth centuries? And could it be the case that in this cultural context the status of women was so compatible with manipulation and objectification that their dismemberment and transformation into animals was somewhat acceptable, if not expected? The multimodal discourse of the circus is not merely a matter of performing skillful actions; its content is also meaningful with respect to the culture of its context. Circus makes sense in as much as it is perceived by audiences as relevant to their cosmologies and their values, even if these tacit dimensions of everyday life are ritualistically transgressed. Indian street magicians do not expose women to such indignities but use immature boys whose status is quite ambiguous in the ambient culture.

A double-edged skill

All circus skills are ambiguous by nature. They can be displayed as forms of entertainment or they can be used for deviant purposes. Acrobats, high-wire walkers, trapeze artists, for instance, could use their physical talents to cross fences and enter private properties; sharpshooters and knife throwers could engage in contract killing; trainers of elephants and other dangerous animals could channel their violence toward targeted persons or objects. The James Bond 007 film directed by John Glen, *Octopussy* (1983), which is set in the context of the Cold War, demonstrates how various circus specialties can become precious assets in fighting enemies. Such an ambiguity is particularly obvious in conjurors who are expert in sleight-of-hand techniques. In fact, the term pickpocket applies equally to thieves and to circus entertainers. It is one and the same skill which is used in both cases. It is common knowledge that, as I have witnessed in India, street magicians occasionally stop their performance to warn the audience that they should be careful with their money because they have learnt there were pickpockets in the crowd around them. Since the first gesture of someone who is thus warned is to check to make sure his or her cash has not disappeared, these warnings are designed to inform the pickpockets who have been strategically placed among the crowd about the exact location of the money they will endeavor to steal. But as a well-staged act in a reputable circus, a good pickpocket can be both puzzling and entertaining. It is indeed a category of "magic" performance since it is based on fooling our sense of touch as sleight-of-hand tricks deceive our visual perception.

> *The circus I decided to visit in April 2011 on my way to a conference on "live performance" in Belgium was advertising a pickpocket on the posters that were displayed in front of the train station. This is not for me an irresistible attraction*

because run-of-the-mill circus pickpockets usually carefully choose their victims so that their task is made easier. I have also strong reservations about using spectators, who have paid their admission tickets, as part of the performance. Moreover, the pickpockets usually target short older men, rather formally dressed with ties and old-fashioned watches. They are relatively easy to manipulate because they try to maintain a respectable composure when they are dragged from their seats to the center of the ring. The ethnographer, though, must overcome such reluctance on the grounds that even a bad performance can be an informative experience and a worthy source of reflections.

As I feel that I might fit the profile of a good target in the eyes of the pickpocket, I am careful to empty all my pockets and place the valuables in a safe at the hotel before leaving for the circus. In addition, I wear a tight leather jacket. I carry only a pen which I zip into one of my pockets, and I slip in the outside pocket a small and thin blank pad just in case I want to make some notes during the show. No wallet, no keys, no tie, no watch, in brief none of the things pickpockets love to snatch from you and return to you with a triumphant smile in the center of the ring where they have convinced you to join them as observers.

Sure enough, as soon as I step in the circus holding my admission ticket, a tall man dressed as an usher offers to guide me to my seat and places his hand on my shoulder as he escorts me toward the bleachers. I have no doubt that this is the pickpocket in disguise who distracts my attention through a very unusual gesture. I feel proud of having second-guessed him and I have a good inner laugh at the thought that he could not find any of the things he was expecting to discretely extract from my clothes. At least I will not be dragged to the ring when his act comes.

The performance is enjoyable. I will come back the next day to make some notes. But I want to quickly write down a reminder that I must check a detail. Well, my little notepad has gone! I still have my pen which I had tightly zipped in my inner pocket but nothing to write on. I feel truly frustrated and furious. When the pickpocket starts his act, a few minutes later, he zooms toward me probably with the intention of asking me if I have some paper on which he could write something. He expects me to say "yes" and look for my note pad. Then, he will hand me back that object! I am not in the mood to play. He does not insist. He is now a few rows below telling an old man that the parking attendant needs his car keys to temporarily move his car. The gentleman panics as he cannot find them in his pocket. Here they are, in the hands of this pickpocket artist!

Another skill closely associated to magic is ventriloquism (literally speaking with one's belly according to the Latin etymology of the term). This too forms the basis of some circus acts but is rooted in very ancient religious traditions. There have been stones and trees as well as animals which were supposed to deliver oracles. The audience of Circus Charles Knie does not think of this when they enjoy the act of Kenneth Huesca who can utter speech in various languages without moving his teeth and lips. He is able to impersonate male as well as female voices with a range of accents and intonations. Thanks to clever gestures, he disorients the attention of his public toward the expressive faces of the puppets he manipulates, apparently paying attention to what they say as if he were a mere witness to their arguing with each other. In the second part of his act, he invites some members of the audience to join him in the ring and convinces them to wear funny hats or wigs. As three or four of them are in line, he schools them into moving their lips whenever he presses their hands. Then, he creates hilarious effects by literally putting words which are out of character with their appearances in their mouths. This multiplies the effects he obtains with the puppets.

The spectators of such acts usually heartily laugh without realizing the dramatic potential of a technique of speech-producing which disconnects the voice from its source through a multimodal strategy. It can recombine at will spoken words and individuals. Making speechless persons produce articulate statements, as is done jokingly in Huesca's performance, can produce the illusion of miracles or even put incriminating statements in the mouths of the accused or witnesses. But the mere fact of dissociating one of the main tenets of civil society, that is, the value of one's words as the basis of one's identity, shows that the crucible of the circus ring is a place where, at the end of a millennial trajectory, more happens than meets the eyes or the ears.

The next chapter will pursue this approach by focusing on horses trained to perform tricks which for ages were considered to be the uncanny result of magic. The roots of the circus as we know it today are located in a remote time when nomads could carry with themselves the means of eking out a living. A single horse could be a source of regular income in addition to providing a means of transportation although, as we will see, this was not without risks.

4

Horses which Speak, Count, and Laugh

The cultured horse

Horses belong to a social species which has evolved a wide range of interactive signals in the same sensorial modalities as humans. They share in common with us visual, acoustic, tactile, gustatory, and olfactory information or, at least, there is a sufficient overlap between the range of perceptions in humans and horses for limited but meaningful communication to occur. Among domesticated animals, horses rank very high, possibly second only to dogs, in terms of the quantity and quality of the interactions with their keepers. Over the last few millennia—archaeological evidence of domestication points to 4,000 BP (Olsen et al. 2006)—there has been a mutual cultural molding between horses and humans as the selective breeding of horses has adapted them to various generic tasks whereas novel modes of trade and warfare have emerged in Euro-Asian societies thanks to the possibilities afforded by domesticated horses.

Communication between humans and their horses can be developed beyond the relatively crude conditioning required by husbandry and basic training. In one-to-one relationships, bonding may occur and mutual sensitivity to signaling repertoires can reach a degree of subtleties which may escape the attention of an outsider. The celebrated *Kluge Hans* (Clever Hans), the German horse which was credited with mathematical expertise at the beginning of the twentieth century, bears witness to this. We will examine, in the conclusion of this chapter, the semiotic foundations which sustained such human-equine spectacular interactions which were then submitted to scientific scrutiny.

But these controlled experiments were not dealing with a new phenomenon which would have been conceived and contrived for the sake of scientific knowledge. They were designed to put to the test a long-established claim by some horse trainers and performers that their charges could understand mathematics and competently handle calculations which involved additions, subtractions, multiplications, divisions, and even the extraction of square roots. They were also supposed to be conversant with the natural language spoken by their master. As we will see in the examples discussed in the next section, the tradition of the "educated horse" can be traced back for centuries, even millennia.

An equine performance on record

Testimonies concerning "educated" horses are indeed found in the historical record mostly in the form of allusions (Hachet-Souplet 1897: 93–8). But the most detailed and realistic account is found in the diary of a French nobleman, Pierre de L'Estoile (1546–1611) who recorded a witness's account of such a horse in Paris in March 1601 and wrote the following entry in his journal:

> This month, could be seen in Paris a horse which belonged to a Scotsman who had taught it many tricks for the greatest wonderment of all the spectators. This bay horse was an English breed, of medium height, about 12 years old. Its name was Moraco. It fetched whatever was thrown at a distance and brought it back in the manner of a dog. It jumped like a monkey. It could stand on its hind legs and walk both forward and backward. It could stoop and kneel down.
>
> A trusted friend of mine witnessed this performance on Thursday the 22nd of this month, at the Lyon d'Argent on rue Saint-Jacques: Its master ordered it to go and fetch a glove which he had thrown to the ground and to bring it to the spectator who was wearing glasses. The horse immediately complied and brought the glove to a bespectacled young man. He then asked the horse to take the glove to someone with a fur coat, and so did it.
>
> This horse had also been taught by its master to discriminate colors by means of a method that no one could understand. It was told to carry the glove to a girl wearing a green muff and the horse found such a girl in spite of the fact that she was far away at the end of the hall. After this it correctly located a woman wearing a purple one.
>
> The trainer then covered the horse's head with a coat and asked the audience to give him a few coins. He received one gold coin and two silver coins which he slipped inside the glove. After having removed the coat from the horse's head, he asked it how many coins were in the glove. The horse tapped the ground three times with its hoof. He asked how many gold coins and the horse answered likewise by stamping the ground once, and twice when it was asked how many silver coins were in the glove. [Then the questions became more sophisticated, bearing on the relative values of the various monetary units which were used in Paris. All were answered correctly.]
>
> For the next trick, the master got a card game and asked a spectator to pick a card. It was a five of spades which was shown to the horse. It was asked to tap the ground to give the number but to use the right hoof for a red card and the left one for a black card. Without hesitation the horse produced the number five with its left hoof.
>
> The horse was then instructed to proceed in a manner appropriate to carrying a maiden and immediately started ambling gently two or three times around the hall. After this, it was asked to walk as if it was ridden by a servant and it changed its gait to a rough and tumbling allure. When told to behave as if under the control of an expert rider, the horse made courbettes, jumps, and other figures and allures typical of the equestrian art.

Then, claiming that the horse said it did not want to work any longer, Banks scolded it and threatened to give it away as a work horse to a man who would beat it and make it pull heavy loads all day. Moraco protested by shaking its head and lay down on the ground as if it was sick with its legs straight up as a dead horse. Its master walked on him without triggering any reaction. However, he declared that he would forgive it if someone in the audience would agree to ask for mercy on its behalf. A young man with a red beard who was at the end of the hall begged the master to pardon the horse. Banks made the horse rise on its legs and asked it to go and thank the red haired person who had obtained its release. The horse dashed in the right direction without hesitation, found the man, and put its head under his coat as a way of expressing its gratitude. The crowd was amazed and many suspected that all this was achieved through magic.

Banks resumed his scolding of the horse because it did not want to work and said he would sell it as a coach horse. But Moraco lifted one of its forelegs and walked on three legs alone to show that he was too sick to work.

Now, the master told the horse first to sneeze three times, then to laugh. The horse complied by lifting its lips and showing off its teeth while agitating its ears as if it were laughing. After this, the horse was made to dance some popular steps [Canaries].

Banks gave a glove to a man and asked the horse to bring the man to him. Moraco went to this man, seized the man's coat with its teeth, and forcefully dragged him toward its master. Then Banks drew the figure 8 on the glove and asked the horse to stamp the ground with its hoof as many times as the figure indicated. So did the horse without hesitation by tapping eight times on the ground. (Pierre de L'Estoile 1978 [1601]; translation mine with minor adaptations)

This is a unique document because it is extremely rare that such popular performances have been so thoroughly recorded in the literature from beginning to end. The tricks mentioned in this text are corroborated by numerous allusions and partial descriptions in English documents of the time. The deep impression that Banks' educated horse had made on its audiences when they performed in London between 1595 and 1600 secured for it a place in chronicles and poems. Ben Jonson, Shakespeare, and Sir Walter Raleigh have devoted lines to this wonder horse to which they referred variously as Marroco, Morroco, and Moraco as Pierre de L'Estoile does. A poem published in 1598 in London provides information on this performance, which corresponds to some of the details reported in the 1601 Parisian diary albeit in a more concise and selective form:

>   Of Bankes' horse
> Bankes hath a horse of wondrous qualitie
> For he can fight, and pisse, and daunce, and lie,
> And finde your purse, and tell what coyne ye haue:
> But *Bankes*, who taught your horse to smel a knaue?

Circus bibliographer Raymond Toole-Stott (1910–82) lists ten items relevant to Bankes and his horse in the literature at the end of the sixteenth century, including a *Maroccus*

Horses which Speak, Count, and Laugh 61

Figure 4.1 An engraving of William Banks and Marocco, the performing horse, illustrating "Maroccus Extaticus" in Thomas Conser's Collectanea Anglo-poetica (1860).

Extaticus (1595) that celebrates Marocco and its master, and features a wood engraving of a horse standing on its hind legs with a stick in its mouth, ostensibly counting the pips on a pair of dice on the ground while his master watches with a stick in his hands (Toole-Stott 1958: 30–1).

The feats of this "educated" horse came to us through the channel of literati and historiographers because it performed in the main cultural centers of its times, and because the religious authorities were prompt to accuse the man and his horse of sorcery, thus dangerously contributing to their celebrity. Banks once escaped condemnation by having his horse kneel down in front of a crucifix held by a priest. In France, he managed to counter the charge of magic by disclosing to the judges the method by which he had trained his animal and claimed that he could thus educate any horse in one year. But, if Ben Jonson is to be believed, both were eventually burnt in Rome as two magicians when the Inquisition construed the evidence given by Banks as mere ruses of the Devil. Other chroniclers traced to 1641 the natural death of Banks who had then become an innkeeper in London. In the world of nomadic performers, acts are so commonly imitated that it is practically impossible to assign historical beginnings to any of them. It is difficult to know how many Banks and Maroco, by any other names, might have exhibited their tricks in courts and fairs. Some might have indeed perished at the Church's hands. But for one man and his horse reaching such tragic fame, how many similar equine displays have been performed in the deep past of popular entertainment? Banks was not the last one, as we will see below, because this kind of circus acts can still be witnessed nowadays.

A multimodal dialogic discourse

I observed such an act in 1978 and, after the first show I attended, I decided to note down during the next two performances the "dialogue" between Derrick Rosaire, a British circus trainer, and his wonder horse Tony. The term "dialogue" is appropriate here because the trainer constantly appeared to address the horse which "replied" by complying with the polite injunctions of its master while, at times, demonstrating some measure of calculated insubordination. The microphone which was held by the trainer allowed the audience to follow the interactions which unfolded in this manner:

As a soft, fast, and cheerful music starts, a formally dressed man enters the ring with a vivacious Palomino horse in his wake. The behavior of the horse can be easily inferred from the words of the man and supplementary information will be provided only when necessary. The act lasted exactly 12 minutes and 30 seconds. There were no letdowns, repairs, or pauses which would have broken the fast momentum. The transcript, which was handwritten on a pad as the act proceeded, attempts to reflect the actual rhythm of this performance:

> Hello! Good evening!
> Where is he?
> Oh! There he is.
> Ha! Ha!
> Here he goes,
> my friend Tony.
> I say: Tony, go this way.
> Now, this way.
> Across this way,
> And back this way.
> Stop here.
> Stand up!
> Down!
> Thank you!
> And a dance!
> A little waltz.
> A WALTZ, Tony.

Is that not relaxing?
They love you.
Once more!
All right.
Tony, that was very, very nice!
Now, stand like a rocking horse.
If you please.
[the horse extends both its fore and hind legs by about a feet in each direction]
That is good.
Here we are:
One rocking horse.
Now, rock a little!
[the horse moves its body back and forth without changing the position of its hooves]
That was a rather skinny rock.
Remember! We are getting paid for this, weekly.
Very, very WEAKLY.
[the audience laughs]
He is going to do a nice big rock
this time, I believe.
A little further!
That is beautiful! (applause)
[the horse walks with the allure known as the "Spanish step" by extending its forelegs alternatively]
Stop!
He stopped!
This time, I want you to stand absolutely straight.
You are not straight like that.
Back up a little bit.
Put this one back.
Put the back legs together.
Good!
Well, that is not good enough!
Put the other back a little bit.
That is VERY good.
Now, the right forearm.
The left forearm.
The right one again.
And the left one.
I am supposed to be the trainer!
The right one again.
That is the left! Put that back!
Now, the right one.
Thank you very much!
[he tickles the horse]
Tony, you are a good boy and I love you very much.

Now, what do we do? Show me!
[the horse kisses the man on the mouth and receive some treat]
[the horse extends his forearm toward the man]
A nice hug! Straighten up a little!
Now, we are going to take out your harness.
A little striptease. Not me! The horse!
Good boy! [a girl comes to carry the harness away]. Good girl! [the audience laughs]
Now, when I take off your bridle, please don't move!
You won't move?
Good!
[the horse shakes its head as if saying "no"]
Say "no" again!
Thank you.
[the horse says "no" again]
Thanks again!
Thank you very much!
Now, move your lips, talk a little. Now, just move the top one.
What's that? You want to whisper?
OK, whisper!
[the horse puts its mouth near the man's ear]
He says he cannot talk tonight: *he* is a little hoarse.
[the audience laughs]
What do you say? You want some sugar.
Oh! I don't know.
Shall I give Tony some sugar?
[the horse says "yes" with its head]
I cannot hear you.
[the horse vigorously shakes its head up and down]
[it receives some sugar]
Tony, what do I get for the sugar?
[the horse brings its lips close to the man's mouth while the latter produces the sound of a noisy kiss in the microphone]
Good boy! That was a wet one!
[the man throws a piece of white cloth to the horse]
Catch this! Now, waive good-bye to the boys and girls!
Good boy!
[the man ties the cloth around the horse's forearm and the horse unties the knot with its teeth]
[the Master of Ceremony intervenes:]
Do you think that Tony could do that on one of its hind legs?
You hear that, Tony?
Let me ask the boys and girls if they want you to do that.
They said "yes." I suppose you better try.
[he ties the cloth to one hind leg and the horse unties the knot]

Thank you!
Now, Tony, lie down!
Lay here while I take a little nap. [Tony lies down on its side and Rosaire sits down on the ground and briefly rest his head on the horse's flank. The horse moves its neck toward its master and gives him a kiss.]
Thank you. Now, I am going to sleep.
I am tired.
I have been breathing all day!
Tony is tired too.
Good boy!
I like that. I could do that for ever. That, and 2,000 dollars a day.
I am going to give Tony another sugar. And he is going to give me another kiss.
[Rosaire tickles the horse]
Now give me a kiss right on the lips.
Thank you.
[they both rise]
Now shake your head to acknowledge the applause.
[but the horse chases the man as it wanted all the applause for itself only]
OK, you win. A big applause for jealous Tony!
Thank you.
Stop.
You are very clever.
And so am I.
[the music changes to a faster pace]
Now Tony will give you an imitation of a wild stallion.
[the horse runs, rears, and bucks. And leaves the ring with the man]

Derrick Rosaire's monologue is structured like a dialogue because he pauses just long enough between his orders, acknowledgments, and witty asides in order for the audience to construe the movements of the horse as its answers to its master's requests. He also, at times, engages the audience by directing some remarks to them or asking for their advice. The shortness of the utterances and their colloquial syntax, the friendly, often even affectionate tone, the occasional emotional outburst of impatience, and the almost intimate behavior the man and the horse display, combine to create a personal profile for Tony. The obvious playfulness of the horse, which moves freely and willfully approaches its master, suggests a symmetrical relationship. The illusion of an intelligent dialogue comes from the foregrounding of language interactions and the clever blending of gestural cues with rhetorical and indexical movements of the hands as well as the variations in the distance which is maintained between the trainer and his charge. The role of some pieces of carrots which are discreetly manipulated as rewards prompting the behavior of the horse are referred to as "sugar," a treat which children can relate to better than carrots. The act managed to build a remarkable empathy between the trainer and his friend Tony as well as between the audience and both the horse and its trainer because there was not the slightest sign of constraints and coercion. In the concluding part of this chapter, we will analyze in more detail the multimodal discourse which this circus act displayed for the greatest enjoyment of its audience and we will compare it to other examples of "educated" horses in order to further explore this paradigm of equine performance.

Bringing Derrick Rosaire and Tony into focus after having discussed the feats of Banks and Moraco over four centuries earlier is indeed all the more in order as it bears witness to the resilience of the training methods and staging of this kind of circus act. Rosaire and his horse reached in the 1970s a celebrity status comparable to the fame of their predecessors as they were featured in countless television talk shows, were solidly booked for circus programs, and were even commissioned to perform at the White House under President Richard Nixon. However, they were not the only "educated horse act" which was performing at the time.

There are indeed countless variations on the theme of the "educated horse," including parodies. The following act was observed on April 3, 1982, in a small family circus, Cirque Arizona, which had pitched its yellow tent at Porte Chaumont on the periphery of Paris. The equine displays included four black mares which were cued to their routine by an elegant equestrian who also acted as MC and announcer. After the mares came a Palomino gelding, introduced as a "stallion," which waltzed, jumped, and reared on command.

"And now, ladies and gentlemen, boys and girls, we are proud to welcome Popaul and his mule Saccharine!" Popaul is a young clown with a red nose, shaggy hair, and an ill-fitting gaudy suit. A playful mule enters the ring and canters around several times. It jumps over a bar held by an attendant. The MC intervenes and tells Popaul that his mule does not jump very high. "Well, believe me, it jumped seven meters next week [sic]! It is because it fell in a deep hole." The MC bets that he can make the mule jump higher than Popaul can and he commands it to do so. But the clown orders the mule not to jump and indeed, when it arrives in front of the bar, it makes a detour to avoid it. The MC insists but the mule again refuses to jump.

The MC bets again that the mule will not avoid the obstacle this time and loudly tells it to jump. But Popaul gives her another order and the mule stoops and passes under the bar.

The clown has demonstrated his perfect verbal control of the mule which can thus be credited for understanding language and taking orders only from its friend Popaul. But the MC now demands that they both leave the ring and refuses to honor the payment of the two bets he lost. Popaul protests. The MC promises to pay the next morning. "OK, says Popaul, we will stay here until tomorrow." The MC then tries to remove the mule by pulling it out of the ring by the tail but it does not budge. Popaul asks the mule to follow him instead and it complies, thus demonstrating that it is very obedient with him as it walks and stops on mere verbal cues. The MC tries to make the mule leave by chasing it but the mule keeps trotting around the ring and refuses to leave through the exit. It even starts aggressively chasing the MC. Eventually, the MC agrees to pay the bets he lost and Popaul leaves the ring with the mule which willingly follows him.

Examples of reverse training—animals which are trained not to do what they are asked to do or simply to do nothing at all—are an important part of circus displays.

They mirror the transgressive behavior of the clowns. Chapter 6 will be entirely devoted to this kind of narrative and its rhetoric. We will look in detail at the dynamics of the performance of "Popaul and his mule" in the concluding section of this chapter when we attempt to set forth the circus matrix which generates "educated horse" acts and their ironic complement.

Themes and variations: A cowboy and his horse

The educated horse act is a rich paradigm in the circus tradition. This theme, however, has been observed in countless variations at least, as we have seen, for the past few hundred years. Circus routines are nomadic by necessity and must be adapted to the cultural contexts in which those who inherited them perform for a living. Artists exploit the semiotic resources provided by the milieu as a way to constantly reinvent their cultural relevance. With the popularity of the cinematic epics of the American conquest of the West, the theme of "the cowboy and his horse" spread to the circus imagery of the twentieth century. It foregrounded male bonding, loyalty, cooperation, even self-sacrifice between a man and a horse. Feats happened on the screen in narratives which would be impossible to achieve through the deceits of training. These images nevertheless biased the perception of circus acts and fed the emotional imagination of spectators. In the 1950s I often witnessed both some training sessions and occasional performances of such an act by Julio Hani and his wife Brenda. But at the time circus was for me a matter of existential experience far from any form of ethnographic preoccupation. The best way to recover a detailed account of this act was to interview one of its surviving actors, Brenda Hani.

> *It is always a pleasure to have lunch with Brenda whenever I visit Blackpool where she now lives. I met her with her husband Julio in the 1950s at the Cirque Bouglione. I was then a student who had run away to the circus and had been quickly adopted by the folks. Julio was the elephant trainer and Brenda one of the girls who paraded on top of the animals and took part in the act with a great split between two elephant heads and a walk around the ring hanging upside down from the mouth of one of the animals which was holding her leg between its jaws. Julio was also a horse trainer and after they moved to England in the 1960s, I kept visiting them at the Sir Robert Fossett Circus wherever it happened to be when I traveled there. This is where I saw Julio's cowboy act several times, enjoying it without noting down its details.*
>
> *September 10, 2011. Brenda is expecting me for lunch. We shed tears evoking those who are no more. But soon we reminisce the good old days at the circus in France. Baby, Jenny, Taboo, Puncho, Maboc, and Taki are still vividly present in our memory. These were the six elephants which Julio trained. And there was also Trigger and Panthera, the horses of the cowboy act. Brenda was a part of the act. She relives step by step the successive episodes. I will now be able to document this performance as precisely as if I had taken notes 40 years ago in Dundee or Manchester.*

The initial inspiration was the popular media stars Roy Rogers and his horse Trigger. The Robert Fossett circus horse, a Palomino, had been given the same name. Julio was dressed in a fantasy cowboy outfit and entered the ring riding Trigger which galloped around for a short while as Julio was shooting balloons which had been placed on the ground, and cracked his whip with thundering energy. Then Brenda entered on an Appaloosa horse called Panthera. She was scantily dressed but wore the imposing feather headgear of an Indian chief and held a large American flag which was floating in the air as the horse speeded up around the ring. The flag was caught by an attendant and removed from the ring. In the meantime, Julio had unrolled the lasso which was hooked to his saddle and started demonstrating his skill first by catching the head of Panthera, then its fore hoof, and eventually Brenda herself whose arms were tied up by the rope. Julio pulled her and her horse next to his own horse, released the lasso, and stood up on top of the saddle while Trigger kept immobile. He started spinning the rope, making a big circle around both himself and Brenda, and their horses. Brenda and Panthera could exit as they were not needed until the end of the act to take their bow with Julio.

Now side by side, the man and the horse engaged in a series of tricks. The saddle and reins were removed, and the horse was free of all restraints except for its light bridle. Trigger pulled a white scarf from the chest of its trainer who tied the scarf to one of its fore legs. The horse untied the knot. The same trick was repeated with one of the hind legs. Then an attendant brought a candle to the center of the ring and the horse was given a kind of long ladle which it held in its mouth. A small flame was burning at the tip of the utensil. The horse lit the candle by itself, dropped the ladle, and stomped the ground to extinguish the fire. It then galloped three times around the ring, came back to the center, and blew out the candle. The time to sleep had come since the light was dimmed as soon as the candle was extinguished. Julio unrolled a carpet, lied down on it, and Trigger lied down next to him. Julio covered his body with a blanket but the horse bent its neck over its trainer, caught a corner of the blanket in its teeth and pulled it upon its own body. Julio reclaimed it. The horse repeated the move three times, causing the public to laugh. They both rose from their brief "sleep" and engaged in a few bits of comedy with the horse being called "naughty boy" and trying to retaliate with a bite. But Trigger soon displayed some other kinds of skills by walking on its hind legs around the ring both forward and backward. This concluded the act and Julio was starting to take his bow when Trigger shoved him away, showing its teeth, and behaving aggressively. This, of course, was construed as a joke on the part of the horse. All was well. Brenda and her horse joined them and the four of them acknowledged the applause while the horses kneeled down then walked backward waving good-bye with scarves they were holding with their teeth.

Brenda relives every moments of the act. Looking in the distance, she tells me again how, on Saturday December 22, 1973, in Bournemouth, during an afternoon Christmas show, Julio collapsed during the act after the candle trick. Trigger immediately lay down next to him as it had done on cue countless times, expecting to catch the blanket. But nothing happened. Julio had passed away.

Figure 4.2 shows Julio and Brenda Hani posing for a photographer after the act.

Figure 4.2 Julio and Brenda Hani strike a relaxed pose with their horse Trigger after their performance at the Robert Fossett Circus (ca 1972). The costumes were designed, cut, and sewn by Brenda. Note the semiotic *bricolage* which freely blends chorus girl outfit, Indian warrior ceremony headgear, and imaginary cowboy outfit to produce a semantically consistent effect with respect to the contextual popular culture of the time. (Photograph from the archives of Mrs. Brenda Hani reproduced here with her kind permission.)

Pragmatics of the "educated" horse act: A biosemiotic perspective

The purpose of this section is not to expose in detail the secret of the trade: how to train a horse to perform circus tricks of the sort which have been recorded in the previous section. The celebrated Banks purportedly disclosed his method on several occasions (Markham 1607). There exists an abundant literature on this topic mainly since the late nineteenth and early twentieth century. Pierre Hachet-Souplet for instance, a French psychologist of the late nineteenth century, provided reasoned explanations concerning the methods used to train both wild and domestic animals, in particular circus horses for the kind of acts we have examined so far (1895: 110–12). Hippisley Coxe's *A Seat at the Circus* (1951) offers also a wealth of information. Focusing on this latter period is particularly interesting because it will show how the nature of the meaning generated by circus acts shifted over time in synchrony with broader cultural changes. Moving from sixteenth-century England, a time when magic reigned both as a political force and an uncanny threat, to nineteenth-century post-Darwinian and scientific enlightenment, the meaning of "educated horses" was bound to take on a new significance. A symptomatic case is the Clever Hans affair. Some horses which were located in Elberfeld, a small town close to Wuppertal in Germany, became famous in the popular and scientific literature at the turn of the twentieth century because they were displaying what appeared to be the mental capacity for performing correct calculations and solving mathematical problems which were presented to them verbally and in writing. This was well beyond the simpler operations which for ages had made Moraco and its kind wonders of the fairgrounds. Nevertheless, these Elberfeld horses were performing under the supervision of their trainers in a setting which was formally quite similar to a circus. The only difference was that the context was science rather than entertainment and magic although the horses were occasionally toured in German cities and featured as stars in front of audiences. Their mathematical prowess soon became the object of philosophical debates. The issue was whether animals such as horses could have mental powers approaching humans in some capacities. The owner of one of these horses, Wilhelm von Osten, a secondary-school teacher and amateur horse trainer, was apparently convinced that human intelligence was in part shared in common with some advanced animals. A photograph of one of the demonstrations shows a strikingly different context from the fairground: a rather small group of formally dressed middle-class men including a few women sporting summer hats surround the horse *Kluge Hans* in front of its stable with his trainer at its side close to the rear of the animal. There is an obvious effort made to convey the impossibility for the man to give gestural cues to the horse whose understanding of the German language and mental ability are thus credited for producing correct answers in response to verbal questions (http://en.wikipedia.org/wiki/Clever_hans). Other horses from the same stable were also performing in the same manner. The competence of Clever Hans was truly stunning: when it was asked "what is the date of the following Friday if the 8th day of the month comes on a Tuesday?" the horse would tap the ground 11 times. These horses were also commonly spelling words by tapping the correct order of each letter in the alphabet.

These demonstrations became public performances when von Osten freely exhibited his horse in halls and theatres elsewhere in Germany, and gained such fame that the Ministry of Education appointed a scientific commission to investigate this phenomenon. Under psychologist Carl Stumps, the committee included a veterinarian, a Cavalry officer, a circus manager, several school teachers and the Director of the Berlin Zoo. In September 1904, the committee delivered its conclusion: no tricks were involved in Clever Hans' performances. But two years later, a more formal investigation was conducted by psychologist Oskar Pfungst who developed controlled experiments and demonstrated that the horse would provide the right answer only if the trainer (or someone in the immediate surroundings) knew what the correct answer was. It turned out that the horse was able to pick up subtle cues from the body signs of the trainer and observers which signaled him to stop tapping on the ground. Apparently, von Osten himself was deceived in believing that the horse was genuinely calculating because the cues indicating to the horse that the right number had been reached could be as simple as a small change in the breathing rhythm of the trainer. It was eventually demonstrated that the cues were unwittingly leaked to the horse (Pfungst 1911). If nobody knew the correct answer or if the horse was wearing blinkers, it would fail to tap the correct answer.

This phenomenon can be easily explained by considering the constraints under which equine vision has evolved. For a steppe animal, predators can surge from any side. A mostly frontal rather than lateral vision would not be adaptive. Horse vision may be lacking in acuity, accommodation, and color discrimination compared to humans but the size and position of their eyes provide them with almost panoramic vision. A horse can detect minute movements from anywhere in its periphery except for two blind spots at both extremities of its body. Its survival in the wild depends on this hypersensitivity to information coming from all sides (Murphy et al. 2009). But monitoring their surroundings to locate potential predators is not the only evolutionary constraint which has molded the visual system of horses. Their social mode of living in herds provides them with a 100 percent panoramic scanning power since, contrary to individual animals, a herd has no blind spots. Their escape strategy consists of dashing together in the same direction when one individual responds to danger by the flight reflex. The greatest liability for stampeding animals is to bump into each other and create a fatal chaos, hence the advantage of being able to monitor the position of the full length of one's own body on both sides and to adjust instantly to each other's movements. This double evolutionary constraint endowed all horses with a robust almost panoramic vision which is exploited at its most by circus trainers. Horses which are prone to tap the ground with their hoofs—a behavior related to the search for roots and water—can be prompted to start and stop on cues given by someone standing back. This is all that it takes to train a calculating or spelling horse. The cues can come, deliberately or possibly at times unwittingly, from a trainer who stands on, or moves around any of his horse's sides.

Such a biosemiotic explanation is necessary but not sufficient to account for the meaning produced by a circus act which exploits this natural affordance in order to transform it into a cultural object. The ethnography of performance focuses on the interface between the performers and their audience rather than on backstage processes and their biosemiotic foundation. We will focus in this concluding section on the communication dynamic which I adumbrated in an earlier work (Bouissac 1976a: 59–63). When the performance involves animals, circus artists must maintain simultaneously two dynamic interfaces, the one with the audience and the one with the animals. Both have to be semiotically integrated.

This is very obvious if we further analyze Derrick Rosaire's act. His discourse is supposed to be addressed to the horse which, of course, does not understand the English language but responds instead to the gestures of the trainer and the movements of his whip. The actual mechanics of the spectacular interaction that takes place in this act escapes the attention of the audience because humans assume that horses see like humans, that is, they see better what is in front of them. Face-to-face interaction is the model the audience transfers to the situation they witness in the ring. We can communicate through gesture as long as we can focus frontally, possibly by orienting our head appropriately. By contrast verbal communication is perceived peripherally with a sense of directionality which is indeed very adaptive for an organism like us which does not enjoy a wide field of vision. The fact that Rosaire addresses his horse from its side, or even at times from behind, reinforces the illusion that Tony indeed responds to articulate language whereas the small gestures that Rosaire makes and which are blended with the repertory of audience-oriented human kinesics are what is the most salient for the horse.

Keeping all this in mind, let us reconsider the spoken component of this act which frames and confers meaning to the horse's behavior. Technically, Rosaire recites a monologue while gesturing and moving around expressively. His first words ("Hello! Good evening!") are pronounced with a sweeping motion of the head that clearly indicates that he is addressing the audience. But the people's attention is captured by the beautiful horse which followed Rosaire and playfully wandered around behind him. The second utterance ("Where is he?") is a question Rosaire asks to himself as much as to the public. It construes the horse as an autonomous agent which can escape its trainer's control and may go wherever it wants. If Rosaire suddenly pretends to find it ("Oh! Here he is!"), it means that the horse is not trying to avoid him but was only hiding playfully. The interjections ("Ha! Ha!") can be understood as "I found you!" and the following remark ("Here he goes") is a mere state of affairs statement, describing what the horse does as if Rosaire had no part in its behavior. Let us note that Rosaire does not use the neutral pronoun "it" usually assigned to animals but the personal "he." Then comes the social introduction directed to the audience with a proper hand gesture ("My friend Tony"). Rosaire's next step consists of asserting his own position as the trainer albeit in a subdued manner which de-emphasizes coercion. Rather than using the direct style by commanding the horse, he transposes the grammatical injunction into a semi-indirect form ("I say Tony go this way, now this way, across this way, and back this way"), then he switches to direct orders ("Stop here! Stand up! Down!"). To obtain such behavior as rearing on command the trainer needs to communicate to the horse a strong impulsion and uses the whip he holds in his right hand not to hit the horse but to suggest a confronting signal which prompts the horse to rise on its hind legs, a posture which belongs to the fighting behavior of stallions. The command "down" is superfluous since the horse cannot keep the erect position for long. The latter order is actually intended for the audience as a redundant proof of the trainer's competence and is opportunistically uttered only when Rosaire senses that the horse is about to come down. Timing is here of the essence. Finally, Rosaire plays down the brief coercive episode during which the horse reared by thanking it ("Thank you!") with a warm intonation of gratitude which implies that the horse had willingly complied and could have refused to do so. It retroactively transforms the results of a long training into an almost spontaneous behavior which was socially motivated by the desire of the horse to please its master.

The analysis of the first few minutes of the act shows that Rosaire's monologue is construed as a dialogue through being framed by the behavior of the horse which is elicited by the trainer by means of visual cues. The gestures which are interpreted by the audience as mere rhetorical supports for the verbal commands are the only cues the horse actually perceives as relevant. Semiotically, the multimodal interface between the perceptions of the horse and the perceptions of the audience is analogous to the positive and the negative of a photograph. Rosaire generates the two modalities simultaneously within a tempo which contributes to their seamless integration and gives the audience a sense of witnessing a meaningful dialogue between a man and his horse.

If we review the rest of the act, we can see that the same well-tempered semiotic entanglement is repeated throughout the next 11 segments which follow the first episode. But they all presuppose the information which was fed to the audience in this introductory segment through which the two characters, their competencies, and their mutual rapport have been defined for the public. Depending on the time slot allotted to this act in the program, some of the following episodes can be dropped or some others can be added without altering the meaning of this act. The subparts which were observed include: (1) the introduction, (2) the dance, (3) the rocking horse, (4) the Spanish step, (5) standing straight, (6) the kiss, (7) the whisper and the laugh, (8) saying yes and no, (9) untying knots, (10) lying down together, (11) imitating a wild stallion. These are the labels which Rosaire assigns to the patterned behaviors he elicits from the horse and which provide the audience with interpretation keys for movements which might be otherwise visually ambiguous. Let us note the nature of these episodes and the order in which they are introduced as the act unfolds: (2) to (6) refer to things circus horses do and after "the kiss" we progress toward more and more human behaviors (6) to (10). The climax of this progression (11) represents the capacity for a fully cultured horse to *imitate* a wild horse, that is, engage in art (*mimesis*).

The general theme of the exit reveals that the horse eventually claims full credit for what he has accomplished since he prevents the trainer from acknowledging the applause. It suggests that "in the horse's opinion" only he, Tony the wonder horse, deserves the appreciation of the audience. This is, of course, on the part of the trainer, an elegant way to suggest that his training has been so successful that the student has surpassed the master.

5

Steeds and Symbols: Multimodal Metaphors

Circus horses: From the steppe to the ring

The preceding chapter has examined a rich circus paradigm in which the staged interactions between a horse and a man suggest a commonality of abilities, purposes, and values. It foregrounds the horse's apparent capability for some of the defining properties of humans: understanding a natural language, possessing reckoning skills, having a robust sense of humor, and even appropriately producing (visual) laughter through a suggestive pulling up of the upper lip. It also brings to the audience a convincing display of unfailing connivance, even intimacy, through the metaphors of whispering in each other's ears, exchanging kisses, or even sharing a bed. As we saw, such performances strongly evoked witchcraft in pre-Enlightenment societies, and still feed nowadays the irrational beliefs which can be encapsulated in expressions such as the "mystics of the horse." Horse whisperers, therapy through horses, and the like prove to be popular themes for books which often make best-seller lists (e.g. Grandin and Johnson 2005). In brief, the educated or comedy horse acts we experience in circus spectacles blur the border between animals and humans as do myths and fairy tales. This kind of horse act shows that the circus ring is the crucible in which nature is transmuted into culture with all the force and conviction carried by the synergy of all our senses. The rhetoric of the multimodal discourse of the circus is put in the service of a delusional but extremely pleasurable ontology which expands the range of the achievable and mends the gaps between species. Derrick Rosaire and his "friend" Tony, after and concomitantly with many other such acts, have personified this ritualistic process of symbolic integration for full generations of circus and television spectators.

But the paradigm of the "educated" or "comedy" horse represents the equine species in the most unnatural manner or, in other words, as a pure cultural construct since all the natural components of horse behavior which are elicited by the trainer are framed in a way which drives the spectators to misconstrue them as evidence of cultural competencies. It is all the more so since the natural horse is in the first place a social animal which is observed in the wild only as part of herds which are structured by strict, albeit constantly contested, hierarchies. The mere fact of producing a solo act with a horse who acts as an individual agent endowed with subjectivity is a radical cultural move which denies the nature of the horse.

The circus displays two additional paradigms of the horse in many inventive forms: the mounted horse and the liberty horse acts. This chapter will explore the complexity and richness of this visual discourse by focusing on a single program which offered the whole array of horse acts which have been produced by centuries of circus traditions. This will provide us with an opportunity to discuss further the theoretical foundations of our approach to performance as discourse, an approach that presupposes that circus can be construed as a language.

A semiotic perspective: Making sense of things

One aspect of human creative intelligence is the capacity to decipher natural objects as meaningful signs or to invent languages, that is, to assign in a more or less systematic manner, meanings to forms in order to achieve some cosmological analogical consistency through categorical interpretations, and to create representational mapping of reality or communicational tools. The availability in any modality of a set of differential entities that can be related through similarities and differences, or which can be combined according to some conventional rules is a prerequisite for the construction of even the most elementary languages. These entities may be artificially created for a semiotic purpose by human inventiveness (for instance, glyphs, dashes and dots, 0 and 1) or chosen from among existing ecological or crafted objects forming series of interrelated patterns endowed with clean perceptual and relational definition such as flowers, birds, the lines of the human palm, the configuration of the tea leaves left at the bottom of a cup, the combinatory power of playing cards, and so on. Any such natural or artificial repertory of differentiated forms, existing in nature or manufactured by humans independently of any semiotic purpose, may be construed as a language in a more or less spontaneous, more or less deliberate manner, with varying degrees of formal constraints, design sophistication and semantic complexity depending on the functions it is destined to serve. One could use the concept of "natural calculus" to refer to any range of patterns satisfying basic calculus requirements: that is, patterns that can be (1) abstracted from available natural objects or artifacts, (2) subjected to combinatory rules, and (3) adapted to the construction of a language, that is, used for interpretive, representational, or communicational purposes without having been developed for such purposes, but nevertheless possessing features well suited to such functions. This process has been amply described using various terminologies in the early semiotic literature when the principles of functional linguistics were commonly extrapolated to other modalities (e.g. Eco 1976), but the extent to which the term "language" is technically appropriate for the description of this phenomenon remains an object of controversy.

In the early semiotic literature of the mid-twentieth century, some did propose the term "code" to designate the systematic pairing of perceptual and semantic categories across the range of the sensorial modalities and with respect to particular uses (e.g. Prieto 1966; Eco 1976). It nevertheless seems preferable to use, metaphorically, the term "language," because it preserves the fuzziness and the ambiguities attached to this notion at least at the pragmatic level, whereas the term "code" conveys the ideas of exactness and unequivocal formal constraints, which are not found in most semiotic processes. Two reasons may explain this state of affairs: first, each "exapted" object remains somewhat ambiguous inasmuch as it may function both as a cultural object and as a functional term in one or even several "languages." Because it belongs to an active network of associative configurations, all its functional occurrences as tokens in a text of a language can trigger connotative effects—that is, can activate other languages or codes—which interfere with the intended message or representation. For instance, red as symbol of passionate love in the language of flower-giving, or as a sign of danger in the traffic light code, must be neutralized or inhibited if the color is used in some other semiotic capacity, such as highlighting a word or a passage in a printed text. In the first case it operates by opposition to white (as the color of sexual innocence in the Western tradition), in the second by opposition to green (as the signal for *go*), and in the third by its simple contrast with the black ink of the printed text. But there is, in all cases, a spillover of meaning, so to speak, through the general value of arresting intensity. Birds, which comprise a great variety of forms from both a morphological and an ethological point of view, provide another illustrative example. As Lévi-Strauss noted (1962: 270–2), they offer features which are particularly apt at metaphorically representing human societies. On the other hand, associations between some migratory species and the seasons of the year—for instance, in Europe, the metonymic link of swallows and storks with spring, or of wild geese with autumn—may endow some occurrences in analogical "languages" with supplementary values, which may or may not be functionally integrated into these "languages." Moreover, the survival in contemporary societies of ancient interpretive systems construing birds as ominous signs may also interfere with their other representative functions. Sinister connotations attached to the sighting of the huppa or the cry of the owl or the whippoorwill are examples of this. There must indeed be a good reason why human semiosis developed artificial languages relatively immune to such unwanted noise derived from the use of "natural calculi" which are, moreover, ecologically and culturally bound. In spite of these safeguards, some of our contemporaries find it difficult to conceive of the binary opposition 0/1 independently of the metaphysical and numerical values attached to the zero and to the unity, which, so to speak, stand in the way of their computer literacy.

The second problem encountered in the construction of a "language" from a preexisting natural array of differences is that the selected set of objects, once it is intellectually isolated from its ecological context, may develop a dynamic of its own which interferes with the combinatorial rules of the calculus; the user's attention or fancy may indeed be caught by nonfunctional formal associations. The phenomenon was once called "the logic of the signifier," and its role in poetic creativity has been well documented quite early in the semiotic movement of the past century (e.g. Kristeva 1974). To return to the former example, birds whose morphological and ethological differences have been selected as adequate representations of human social differences may be reclassified into "irrelevant" categories such as size, color, the kind of eggs they lay, and so on, just as concrete poetry may concern itself with shapes of typographic characters irrespective of their linguistic forms.

The language of the horse: How do horses mean?

The above considerations must be kept in mind when examining equine displays in circus performances. The *Equidae* offer a great variety of sizes, shapes, and colors as well as social systems (Rubenstein 1986). Thousands of years of domestication and selective breeding have further enhanced the diversity exhibited by this family, which comprises only seven species but which includes two culturally interesting fringes: zebras on the one side, donkeys on the other. The former are situated at the wilder and at the more exotic pole of the current Western popular classification axis, the latter at the more tame and trivial pole. Between these two extremes the fairly large number of horse breeds can be subdivided into several subgroups by taking into consideration physical features; cultural connotations; geographic origins; color and patterns of the coat; technical use such as farm, racing, hunting, or dressage horses, and so on. The intracategorical configurations created by the interplay of oppositions and affinities vary with time and space, and cannot be considered as absolute but relative to a given culture. Take, for instance, a Clydesdale—this strong, heavy horse originating in Scotland was once a fearsome war horse before becoming the iconic draft horse. It can be perceived simply as a giant, monstrous animal in a culture unfamiliar with the breed; but it appears, on the contrary, to be ordinary and utilitarian in a traditional culture used to seeing this type of horse working in the fields or pulling cartloads of logs or beer barrels. To a modern American audience these horses are colloquially referred to as "Budweiser horses," from the name of a popular brand of beer which uses them in parades and television advertisements. The particular associations triggered by their appearance in a circus performance have to be taken into consideration in any attempt to describe the cognitive dimension of an audience's appreciation. Similarly, common farm horses from Norway have become popular in England and Southern Europe as circus horses because their shape and color (short, rounded body; light beige coat; blackish mane and tail) are strikingly different from these countries' most common horses to the extent that they are endowed with exotic (Nordic) connotations. In at least two documented instances (Durkheim 1955: 52; Ramirez and Rolot 1977: 78), they have been mixed with zebras in acts which emphasized the compatibility of their exotic connotations, rather than their diametrical opposition as wild savannah animals compared to the staple of European farms. Undoubtedly, a different effect was created when these mixed group acts appeared in Scandinavia. In the same vein, massive Belgium horses are often featured in Brazilian circuses with an effect of exotic strangeness. The point here is that horses and their congeners provide the formal basis for a calculus, but that the terms of this calculus are already connoted by the place they occupy in the classificatory systems of the culture to which they belong. However, far from being a liability for the semiotic potential of the calculus, this state of affairs provides greater combinatory power because connotative values and physical features can be abstracted and recombined for the purpose of producing specially meaningful effects; this is what happened in the case of Canestrelli's black Shetland pony, which performed the high-class routine of a Lipizzaner stallion (Bouissac 1977: 150), or in the case of the *Percheron*—a typically heavy French farm horse—trained in all the *haute-école* airs by the equestrian Willy Meyer, who performed in the 1960s at Cirque Amar in France. In this latter example, the contrast was so great that it had to be tempered by the use of traditional folk tunes and a medieval costume for the rider, since this sort of horse in the context could be neither aristocratic nor exotic, and had to be staged as traditional and historical lest it produce a grotesque, comic effect.

The tension between the dynamics of the formal properties of the calculus provided by the *Equidae* and the partial use of this calculus in other "languages," such as the possibility of conveying the opposition between working class and aristocracy, or urban life and country life, by juxtaposing two different breeds of horses, is fairly similar to the tension often observed in poetry, with the subtle interplay of alliterations and connotations in the production of poetic meaning.

The social contract and the birth of the arts

The focus of this chapter will be on the four horse acts presented in Switzerland by Circus Knie in its 1985 program, which included a total of thirteen acts and five comic interludes. The initial two are liberty horse acts and were presented in the first part, respectively in the first and fourth position. The last pair belong to two other circus equestrian specialties: balancing on horseback and *haute-école* (i.e. mounted dancing horses), which came respectively in second and fourth position in the second part of the program.

Let us examine first the most complex of these acts, the second liberty act presented by Freddy Knie, Junior. The printed program announced the act as "Lipizzaner and Friesian horses in the latest liberty training of Freddy Knie, Jr."

The trainer, dressed in an elegant formal suit with a yellow tailcoat, enters the ring, bows to the audience, and from the center of the ring turns toward the ring's entrance as six black horses make their entrance, one after the other, and begin to canter around the arena; they are followed by six white Lipizzaners, who come and place themselves as they trot among the Friesian horses in such a way that within a few seconds the twelve horses, black and white alternating, proceed in good order around the ring. The harnesses (i.e. bridle, martingale, surcingle, and side reins) are blue and yellow combined to form identical geometric patterns which stand in striking contrast to the white and black coats of the horses—all the more so since for the former the patterns are yellow on a blue background, whereas they are the reverse for the latter. The chromatic juxtaposition is white-blue-yellow in the first case, and black-yellow-blue in the second, thus enhancing both the visibility of the harnesses and the contrasting qualities of the two sets of horses. A few dots of red on each harness enhance their chromatic contrasts. The horses do not wear plumes on their heads or backs.

They first canter counterclockwise; the trainer then makes them change rein to canter clockwise, and then back to counterclockwise, before forming six black-and-white pairs, heads to tails, which whirl according to a pattern of displacement, technically called the *valse à deux*, which may indeed look like waltzing dancers if the music is a waltz, but appears as a complex maneuver if the music does not thus determine the meaning of the movements. In this particular case, the tunes played do not call to mind ballet or Viennese dances, but rather cheerful parade music closer to sport or military events than to formal romantic occasions. The movements performed by the horses are actually identical to the drill patterns of mounted horses in traditional military equestrian displays, themselves being a stylized enactment of cavalry fighting. During this particular routine, the trainer stands at the top of the ring enclosure, thus demonstrating his control over the animals since his distance to them is alternately proximal and distal as they proceed around the arena.

This general theme of the act is further emphasized by the next exercise, consisting of the horses being separated and aligned side by side in two rows, the white facing the black; as they are stallions, who try to take advantage of this relative freedom of movement to challenge each other, the alignment and spacing are not easy. When eventually the six white horses and their black counterparts are facing each other across the ring, they move forward on a signal from the trainer and exchange positions in good order; the blacks are now aligned and spaced where the white were, and vice versa. Note that when they cross over they are required to pass alternately through the opposite row—that is, the colors alternate at the point of crossing. This is repeated four times. The horses are then driven back along the ring in their original order (i.e. black and white alternating), and they all walk backward until they have made a full circle. All are then called to face the trainer, who makes them rear three times simultaneously and in a sustained manner. The black horses and one of the whites leave the ring, and the remaining five white horses stand in the center of the ring while attendants bring in collars to which horse bells are attached, fix them around the horses' necks, and release the martingales which have constrained their head movements. While this is being done the orchestra starts playing the French tune "Frère Jacques" in a subdued, relaxed mood. The trainer spaces the Lipizzaners equally around the ring and makes them sit down on their hind quarters. Since each one of the bell collars represents a musical note, he causes the horses to shake their heads in turn in an appropriate order so that they appear to play "Frère Jacques." Upon completion of the tune, the orchestra replays the tune as the horses leave the ring. This is necessary to make sure that the melody is unmistakably identified (albeit retrospectively) by the audience because the equine musical execution is often uneven, the horses being at times slow to react to the trainer's prompting, at other times shaking their heads outside of the cuing frame.

The ring attendants bring four wooden bars, which they hold on one end, laying the other end upon the ring enclosure. The bars are spaced so as to enable a horse to stand between two of them. As they are positioned, the bars form four obstacles on the peripheral track of the ring. The trainer now stands in the center of the ring, facing the entrance. Three Lipizzaner horses enter at a fairly high speed. They do not wear any harness, and the only bridle they have is unnoticeable because it is of approximately the same color as their coat. They canter around the ring stepping over the obstacles in succession. On their third passage, as each horse happens to be between two bars, the trainer shouts "stop," and the horses abruptly freeze between the bars for a short while before resuming their movement on a signal from the trainer. This is repeated three times. The third time, instead of resuming their canter, they rise on the hind legs and, facing the trainer who walks backward, they proceed in this upright position toward the ring's exit. The bars are then removed. Two horses similar to the last three appear, and rise on their hind legs facing each other. The trainer then makes them proceed diametrically in the ring, one walking backward and the other forward, repeating the back and forth displacement once before sending them back; then he bows to the audience.

This act is clearly divided into two parts: the first consists of a series of collective evolutions; the second is characterized by several feats of sophisticated competence accomplished by selected individual horses. In the first part, by choosing to present together an equal number of white and black horses, the trainer posits a relationship of maximal chromatic difference, actually an instance of logical contrariness, the relationship of black and white being indeed the most frequent example given to illustrate the notion of contraries. However, the extreme chromatic opposition is mediated not only by the use of the three complementary colors in the harnesses, but further by the systematic variation of the order of the colors according to the coat of the horses. This is designed not only to enhance the visibility of the *cultural* outfits which both decorate and constrain the *natural* animals, but also to underline the theme of complementarity.

It is therefore clear from the beginning that the two sets will be played against each other not in a mode of confrontation (like, for instance, the pieces on a chess board), but rather in a mode of integration of differences in a collective organization. This implies the necessity for the members of the two subgroups to allow the members of the other subgroup to penetrate their ranks and to dissociate their homogeneity in a uniform manner. Through the successive configurations they perform, the horses dissociate their chromatic homogeneity in favor of a harmonious visual complementarity; the strongest moment in this process is the mutual penetration of the two groups, frontally, several times, as the centerpiece of the first part of the act. Let us not forget that all the features which have been reviewed so far are the object of a deliberate choice by the trainer. Given this particular group of horses, they could have been adorned with identical harnesses, red for instance; or the contrariness could have been enhanced by putting white harnesses on the black horses and black ones on the white horses. In the first case the integration would have been presented as a deal, because all the horses would have worn the same uniform, so to speak, irrespective of their group difference. On the other hand, the second case would have asserted the difference as positive versus negative, or as inverted symmetry, making any mediating effort irrelevant. The type and decoration of the harnesses used in the act suggest integration while preserving a sense of difference; in other words, they suggest a conception of collective integration as a mediating process aimed at complementarity. These considerations should be kept in mind as the successive phases of the act are now reexamined.

(1) Two separate sets of individuals in a relationship of contrariness are first introduced: six black horses enter the ring followed by six white horses.

(2) They are made to combine evenly, as a member of each group alternates with a member of the other, and to engage in collective, synchronized activities; progressing in good order in a single line. It should be remembered at this point that this type of behavior is a sign of social integration on two accounts: first, *Equidae* belonging to the same social unit proceed in this manner when they change location and each individual

occupies a position related to its social status in the group (Zeeb 1976; Klingel 1977); second, human societies have developed analogous features of progression in good order which indicate maximal social integration under a leader's authority. In such cases, the individual characteristics of the members of the troupe are neutralized as much as possible by the use of uniforms, strictly codified gestures, and synchronization of movements. Attention is also paid to sizes, which are matched so as to exclude random variations. Modern paradigmatic examples of this phenomenon are military parades and chorus lines.

(3) In this act, the even integration of the group does not go smoothly because all the individuals are stallions; even for an audience which is not familiar with the details of the socioethological code of *Equidae*—position of the ears, curvature of the neck, and movements of the head, nostrils, and mouth (Schäfer 1975; Klingel 1977)—the mutually aggressive behavior the horses display conveys a sense of tension and resistance, and the directing role of the trainer is much in evidence at particular moments when the situation briefly appears to get out of hand. But, on the whole, the man appears as a benign coordinator and displays the familiar bare teeth smile (Van Hooff 1972; Eibl-Eibesfeldt 1975) of entertainers and campaigning politicians. Master of the horses, the equestrian director is a triumphant cultural hero. He would disqualify himself, semiotically, if he were to exhibit anger, tension, exertion, or excessive coercion—all forms of behavior which are perfectly acceptable (i.e. semiotically desirable) on the part of a trainer of wild felines, irrespective of the real danger involved; this is because the trainer of felines deals with the cognitive category of "wildness," whereas the horses are already within the cultural framework in spite of the existence, on the fringe of the system, of wild *Equidae* and untamed horses. This is why, on the one hand, horses are so well suited for providing metaphors of the socializing process and the problems it entails; while, on the other hand, they can generate comic performances when they appear purposely to disobey orders, and even to outsmart their supposed trainer and master—a capacity, incidentally, in which they are not used in the particular program examined in this chapter.

(4) The trainer makes the horses change the direction of their progression. If we consider the ring entrance as noon, they are now made to run clockwise. Determining the direction in which the group proceeds is indeed the task of the leader (be it a horse or a human). This is usually the first item featured in a liberty horse act, as it undoubtedly constitutes the "qualifying test" through which the trainer's competence is asserted. At the same time, in this particular act, it confirms not only that the 12 horses are now visually integrated, but that they also act (not simply run) as if a common will were overriding individual resistances, since they are able to perform synchronized collective movements.

(5) Six pairs are then formed, each including a black and a white horse. The pairs whirl in a head-to-tail position—that is, the two horses are side by side but facing opposite directions and move toward each other, thus causing the pair to rotate. This behavior signifies group integration on several semiotic levels: ethologically, this is a common position of mutual grooming, a strong bond-forming ritual among *Equidae*; it is also an unmounted version of a classical figure of the equestrian quadrille; finally, the technical term *valse à deux* (two animals pirouetting side by side but head to tail)

which designates this term of liberty horse training definitely suggests harmonious integration of both will and movement. However, this item is not without ambiguities because the mutual position of the two horses can also evoke a fighting pass between stallions, each trying to reach the lower flank of the other. This is more congruent with what the two horses are actually experiencing and attempting to do than with mutual friendly nibbling positions—after all, most of the horses in the act wear muzzles to prevent them from wounding each other, but the muzzles are painted so that they unobtrusively blend with the color of the coat, thus making them hardly noticeable. In acts in which the ballet theme is activated by luxurious plumes, glittering harnesses and Viennese waltz tunes, the aggressive behavior of the stallions is semiotically overpowered and can pass for graceful energy and enthusiasm, particularly if the trainer, while keeping close watch, waltzes in the center of the ring by himself or herself or with a partner, as Mrs Trude Stosch-Sarrasani used to do at her circus in the early 1970s. Two further factors of ambiguity must be noted: first, this joint movement by the two horses evokes not only a quadrille, but also an unmounted version of a military maneuver consisting of training the war horse to maintain contact with the adversary while the mounted soldiers face each other and fight; second, from a purely formal point of view, the head-to-tail situation can be a positional equivalence of the black-and-white relationship, and functions in the visual text as a redundant expression of contrariness, a sort of Yin-Yang figure.

In view of all the potential ambiguities of this segment of the act, it is interesting to note how its creator has neutralized some possible interpretations and, conversely, enhanced the desired ones. Emphasis is put on the complementarity of the animals' actions, the drill nature of the movements, and the background of tension and resistance against which all this is achieved. The "waltzing" theme and its undertone of sexual complementarity is obliterated by the absence of typical music and by the fact that the trainer directs the horses for a while not from the center of the ring, but from the top of the ring enclosure, like a military instructor rather than a musical conductor. The interpretation is, therefore, channeled toward the notion of visual and social integration through functional complementarity.

(6) Both the military and the integrative themes continue to be reinforced in the following phase, in which the two groups are first sorted, then made to cross each other evenly several times in succession. This exercise represents a considerable triumph over antagonistic confrontations, as the stallions are marching toward each other and must overcome either their aggressive drive or their fear. The military aspect of the drill completes the effect of cultural integration. There are no clashes, simply opposition has been superseded by the socialization of the individuals within a system which transcends contraries and absorbs differences—something like the founding of a culture that succeeds in mediating destructive oppositions through a kind of social contract.

(7) The next phase is highly symbolic of the transformation which has occurred. The horses get back to their alternate positions along the ring's periphery and are made to walk backward full circle. This *unnatural* behavior consecrates, so to speak, their *enculturation*, inasmuch as culture can be asserted through an inversion of the natural order. Although walking backward is not an unnatural movement in itself (notably in

confrontational situations), it is definitely so if it is performed collectively in a single line formation.

(8) Finally, when they all come to stand side by side in line across the ring, facing the trainer who makes them rear three times simultaneously and in a sustained manner, the change signified in the previous segment is reaffirmed, because rearing—which is the typical behavior of fighting stallions—is now reoriented toward an audience *in order to produce* an aesthetic and semiotic effect: the sign of individual distinction is generalized in the group; the process through which natural hierarchies are established is transformed into simultaneous collective behavior whose original function has been reassigned in a radically modified social order.

(9) During the second part of the act, comprising three segments, further progress in the cultural transformation of the horses will be achieved through the introduction of three human competencies in their behavioral repertoire: first, music played in a humanlike seated position; then the understanding of speech and its semiotic capacity of controlling behavior. Note that in this latter item three horses perform what amounts to the opposite of a stampede: a stampede is an uncontrollable flight, whereas in this sequence they abruptly interrupt their galloping upon hearing a verbal command, and do so several times in succession, so that there can be no doubt for the audience that they really control themselves and understand human verbal commands. Finally, walking on their hind legs toward the exit, and the finale with two rearing stallions facing each other but not fighting, and walking in the typically human erect position, both forward and backward, brilliantly demonstrate the integration of these chosen individuals into the highest forms of cultural anthropomorphism.

This act illustrates the hypothesis I developed earlier (Bouissac 1976a)—namely, that liberty horse acts create metaphors for human social patterns and address various problematic aspects attached to the sociocultural process. This theoretical approach takes the view that conceptual problems generated by the constraints and paradoxes of social life—such as the contradiction between individualistic drives and social harmony, perceived incompatibilities between the laws of nature and the laws of culture, and so on—are abstracted and expressed using the equine calculus. Such a notion may sound far-fetched, but how otherwise to account for the deep interest general audiences take again and again in these spectacular displays, whose organizational complexity and semiotic sophistication obviously follow some rules? The recursive structure of liberty horse acts which makes parsing and prediction possible articulates a meaning relevant to human affairs. Undoubtedly, the master or mistress of the horses celebrates and reasserts the advent of the domestication of an animal which, put to the service of human goals, literally changed the face of the earth and accelerated history. But the process of domestication—that is, the passage from nature to culture—can provide a very apt metaphor for the advent of culture itself. From this it ensues, quite naturally it seems, that a system of expression can develop using the organized variety of horses to articulate sociocultural issues of a general sort.

This development is made all the easier by the way in which *Equidae* are conceptually treated in our culture. Like humans, they are categorized into subgroups defined by a mixture of physical features and geographical regions (Arabians, Andalusians, Shetlands, Friesians, Norwegians, Fjord ponies, etc.). Horses are also classified according to their technological functions, such as plowing, mining, hauling, racing, hunting, sporting, and so on; finally, they are identified by names which distinguish a specialized "aristocracy," the "pure breed" animals, whose genealogy is known, from a common stock for which naming rules are less strictly regulated. In the former, proper names are indeed constrained by traditional explicit rules underlying the uniqueness of each individual, whereas the latter may receive any names that their owners fancy or which refer to some physical characteristic or particular circumstance. As a result, the identification of a horse is remarkably similar to the identification of a human, inasmuch as each individual's identity is determined on the one hand by its position in a sociogeographical structure, and on the other hand by a proper name carrying some indications of social status.

It is not clear when humans started to conceptually organize the horse population in a manner akin to human societies, but it seems that nineteenth-century Europe focused a good deal of attention on equine taxonomies in relation to the systematic development of new breeds offering desirable physical or psychological characteristics with respect to particular uses. It is precisely at this time that liberty horse acts appeared in circus programs. It is important to note that an act like the one examined above cannot be fully understood independent of well over a century of intense production of similar acts, and that during the year in which this act was performed, hundreds if not thousand of other liberty horse acts were also presented to audiences throughout the world. The hypothesis proposed here is based not only on the detailed analysis of a single act, but also on a large sampling of such acts. It can be assumed that average circus audiences have past experiences of such acts and their variations.

Once upon a time: A play of nature and culture

In order to show how different liberty horse acts can be systematically related to each other from the point of view of our theoretical approach, we will now focus on the first equine act of the Circus Knie program of 1985. This act, which opened the show, unfolded as follows:

When the spectators enter the circus tent and are led to their seats by the ushers, they notice three piebald Shetland pony mares with their young foals, roaming freely in the ring. The ring exit has been fenced so that the animals cannot wander outside, but apart from this constraint, there is no human intervention. The mares and their foals spontaneously display their gamut of natural behavior: sniffing the ground in search of blades of grass under the thick layer of sawdust and woodchips, keeping an eye on their progeny who occasionally suckle, threatening the other mares and kicking at them when they come too close to their foals; begging for tidbits of food from the first row of spectators. The foals engage in circular galloping, playful fights, and short naps when they are tired of cavorting around. All this is exactly what can be observed in paddock and pasture or free-ranging herds. The lighting is dimmed, but the color changes from time to time, blue light like a night of full moon, red and orange like sunset or sunrise. As the time for the spectacle to begin draws near, the mares and their foals are removed from the ring and twelve Shetland ponies are herded in. There are eleven piebald-bay mares and a completely black one. Left to themselves, they walk, fight, reach for some blades of grass, and groom each other, and so on. Suddenly a 12-year-old girl holding a whip enters the ring, full floodlight illuminates the ring, and she gently drives the ponies to their positions as they start trotting counterclockwise around the ring, the black pony last. There is a change of rein (i.e. the ponies do an S-turn and now canter clockwise around the girl); they form successively a double line and then three groups of four; after this they all proceed abreast, thus reversing their initial position. They now climb on the top of the ring enclosure and walk slowly the full circle, but the black pony follows the rest of the group on the ground at the edge of the ring without objection on the part of the trainer. A dwarf comes in and holds a bar over which all the animals jump in turn—except, again, the black pony, who runs around the obstacle. Then a "giant" (a clown on stilts) joins the dwarf and makes an arch with his two legs. The ponies proceed under it and form a small circle around the leg nearer the center of the ring. Every time the ponies go under the legs, the black one climbs on the top of the ring and bypasses the arch. After this item the ponies leave the ring, except for the black, which comes to the center and sits down. The dwarf attempts to push and pull it to make it leave the ring, but the animal stubbornly refuses until the girl speaks to it politely and gives it a piece of carrot. The black pony then makes a voluntary and graceful exit.

The next item is the sudden and noisy arrival of a white pony, larger than the Shetlands, pulling a sort of low cart upon which a wheel carrying two clowns gyrates at high speed. This cart, guided by the MC, makes two full circles and leaves. It is succeeded by an Appaloosa pony which rises on his hind legs and walks all around the ring following the girl, who runs in front of him along the top of the ring enclosure.

Let us now return to the successive episodes of this act to examine the categories of individual qualities and actions which were sequentially displayed.

(1) At first, free-roaming animals display spontaneous natural behavior. This naturalness is emphasized by the fact that in the first instance they are mares with foals; in the second they appear as a disorderly herd. Note that they do not wear any harness, not even bridles. The choice of piebald animals, with the irregular patterns of their coats and their association in the contextual culture with wildness and marginality, underlines their initial position on the margins of culture. Countless American Western films have indeed led several generations of European moviegoers to associate such a coat—albeit not on animals of this diminutive size—with the ferocious bands of American Indians who attacked settlers and soldiers; the horses of the latter are generally of a solid color. In Europe piebald horses are also associated with marginality for another reason: small nomadic troupes of gypsies have indeed trodden the roads for generations with such horses pulling their caravans and sometimes performing circus tricks.

(2) The human agency which intervenes and puts the animals through their paces is a 12-year-old child, and the general mood conveyed by the music and the demeanor of the participants is relaxed and playful. Moreover, the smallness of the Shetland ponies and their neotenic features, irrespective of their actual age, reinforce the playground atmosphere of the scene, as do the fanciful costumes—mostly bright red and yellow—of the girl, the "giant," and the dwarf who, interestingly, wears a fool's cap. All this creates an "Alice in Wonderland" flavor.

But this is only the mood, not the focus of the action, which is clearly articulated. From the apparent initial unruliness of the ponies who are behaving freely in the dimly lit arena, a cultural order emerges when all the spotlights are turned on as the small girl enters the ring and gently herds the animals toward the ring enclosure until they form a single line, trotting around and changing direction on command. The collective movements they execute without any visible resistance take them each time a degree higher on the scale of culture: the walk on the ring enclosure's top, the jump over obstacles, the "round" under the giant's legs, the latter explicitly evoking a children's folkdance.

(3) However, from the beginning, tension is introduced between collective uniformity and individualism—first on the mere chromatic level (eleven piebald bay animals vs a single black one), then on the behavioral level: the black pony does not conform to the others' actions. The "black sheep" of the group, the animal sets itself apart not so much through disobedience as through unconventionality. This is a recurring feature of liberty horse acts (Bouissac 1976a: 141; 1977: 150), and evokes the potential designation of marked individuals as scapegoats, but never pushes the tension between the group and the transgressor to an extreme: having demonstrated its individual particularity, the norm-breaking animal then rejoins the common herd. For instance, in this act, the black pony's rebellious innovativeness leads it to attain the human sphere, as it refuses to leave the ring with the others, and remains *sitting* at the very center of the ring stubbornly resisting force. It yields only to the kindness expressed by the little girl as she offers it some tasty food, murmurs sweet words in its ear, and treats it with consideration. The "primitive" herd has thus gone through several stages of acculturation, concluding with three instances of individual performance in which each one displays a particular human attribute: the black pony manipulates its trainer and claims a form of social status; the white pony is a cart animal (this is, a useful, domestic animal integrated in culture as a partner for some specific tasks); the Appaloosa pony walks a fairly long distance upright on its hind legs, like a human, and does so apparently of its own will, since there is no obvious coercion by the girl. The pony indeed follows her as she runs on the top of the ring enclosure toward the exit with a joyful, carefree gait. This stands in stark contrast to the usual demeanor of a trainer facing the horse, prompting it with his whip, and moving backward as the horse advances upright on its hind legs in a brief, tense, confrontational situation.

(4) This remarkable progression from a state of nature, represented by the free-roaming ponies, to a distinctive level of anthropomorphic acculturation is implemented in the play mode, which is preserved with great consistency until the end of the act. It is significant, for instance, that the cart pulled by the white pony resembles a toy rather than a functional vehicle and, moreover, carries two clowns madly gyrating on a large wheel.

The ascent of the horse

The whole act clearly enunciates a theme which will be deployed in a more serious mode in the second liberty act, in which, as has been shown earlier, the Friesian and

Lipizzaner horses enter the ring with the full trappings of cultural integration. The contrariness they represent through the striking visual contrast of their coats appears as a problem to be negotiated within the framework of a given social order. Once this stage has been completed, higher forms of cultural competence can emerge in the guise of patterns of anthropomorphism.

Interestingly, this "ascent of the horse" is picked up in the second part of the program at the point where it has been left in the first. Only a few individual horses are involved in this second part, and they exhibit at the outset very specialized competencies of a higher kind. The first is a French mare named Nadia, as we learn from the caption of the photograph in the program booklet; it belongs to a female equestrian who performs acrobatic ballet steps on its back while it trots smoothly around the ring. Through the even, regular flow of her movements the mare enters into a partnership with the daring and graceful equestrian, who must rely on the predictability of the horse's movements in order to perform her routine safely. During this act a trainer stands in the center of the ring, monitoring the gait of the animal, making sure that her speed is constant and that she does not reduce the radius of her circular path. This person usually holds a long whip pointed toward the horse, its tip close to the ground, to ensure that the proper distance from the center is maintained, but its presence is not obtrusive, since under normal circumstances no obvious coercion is involved. Rather, the impression conveyed is one of a harmony of will and perfect cooperation between the three partners—at least this is the effect produced when this sort of act is implemented according to the best training and artistic standards, as was the case in this program.

As noted above, the animal is individualized through a proper name in the written commentary of the act, where we also learn that the equestrian is the wife of one of the circus owner's sons. The same feature is prominent in the fourth equine act, which is presented by one of the owners of the circus and his elder son. Both humans and animals are verbally introduced by their proper names in a formal way as the act starts. *Haute école* dressage stands highest among the various specialties of horse training. The riders take their mounts through intricate patterns in a manner so regular and predictable that the music can be adjusted to the rhythm of the animals' movements and thus produce the illusion that the horses are actually dancing. The illusion is still more compelling if two or more horses are simultaneously performing, since the synchronization of the animals' steps suggests a convergence of intentions and commonality of musical appreciation on their parts. All depends, of course, on the ability and subtlety of the riders, who discreetly prompt their mounts according to a predetermined script and achieve, in the best cases, a convincing effect. The overall result is the realization of a perfect integration of horses into the cultural world of humans, not only because they seemingly give evidence of their sensitivity to music, but also because the melody played usually belongs to the repertoire of classical music. Such an association between animals and higher artistic forms is culturally relevant as long as the animals concerned are horses—that is, an animal which is considered the noblest of all domestic animals and which, moreover, is credited in folk zoology with *quasi*human, if not superhuman intelligence. The cultural attitude which formed the ground upon which the mathematical reputation of Clever Hans, Wilhelm von

Osten's horse, could be built during the first decade of the past century is still alive to an extent, as witnessed by Blake (1975) and Hearne (1983, 1986). There is little doubt indeed that any other domestic animal, such as cows or pigs, trained to perform dance steps to the tune of classical melodies would appear grotesque and comical and would trigger laughter or even protest in the audience. By virtue of its intrinsic beauty and elegance, and because of its long-standing association with sculpture and painting as a privileged aesthetic object, the horse's involvement with classical music is not perceived as a degrading transgression.

Textualizing the horse

The use of horses of various sizes, breeds, and coats for creating meaningful effects such as those described above does not necessarily follow similar patterns in all circus programs. The same set of horses can be combined differently in successive years. For instance, the 1986 program of Circus Knie featured as its opening act a complex equine composition with a Spanish theme, in which human dancers, mounted horses, and liberty horses were combined in the following order:

(1) Two Andalusian horses performing a *haute école* routine; (2) a four-person ballet troupe from Madrid; (3) a liberty horse act including twelve white horses (Lipizzaner) and four white Shetland ponies; (4) another dance by the Spanish ballet; (5) two Friesian horses in a *haute école* routine, later joined by the two Andalusians to present a final display involving the four riders and their mounts. The liberty horses which were presented bare—that is, without harness or trappings—were thus framed by two acts involving human dancers alone and two acts achieving the integration of humans and animals in a sophisticated choreography. The whole program itself was embedded in equine displays, since the only other horse act concluded the last part of the program. It consisted of eight Lipizzaners and eight Friesians, all wearing identical red harnesses and trappings. Both musical accompaniment and costumes evoked a Hungarian theme. The two subsets of horses—which incidentally included the same animals involved in the previous year's program—this time performed in parallel fashion, without any attempt to mediate the color contrast through the staging of the act. Two pairs of horses of the same color were ridden Roman style by a man and a woman (i.e. the riders stood with one foot on each horse, holding the reins tightly in their hands). After performing some patterns in the arena, the other horses were sent one at a time to canter under the arches formed by the two pairs of horses and their riders. Eventually the riders caught the long reins of the horses of the same color as their own as they passed under the arch and, eventually, each held six horses at a time like a team running before them. Introduced as the Hungarian Post, the display suggested a race between two teams—albeit an inconclusive one, because of the circularity of the track. The emphasis was rather on the mastery of the riders, given the number of horses involved and the speed at which they were moving, as well as on the integrated collective effort of each group, an impression reinforced by the homogeneity of their color.

Figure 5.1 As the liberty horses canter around the ring, two of them come to the center at the prompting of the trainer and, first, face each other; then, each one places its head on the other's neck thus forming an intertwined symmetrical figure. They hold this posture for a moment before rejoining the group. Note that the horses' position is based on a natural behavior which consists of mutual grooming. But fighting stallions also take this position when they attempt to bite each other's neck. The trainer has exploited the form of these ethologically based modules of interaction and obtained from the animals that they hold the pose for a while. He has thus transformed a natural behavior into an aesthetic formal configuration briefly frozen in time. (Drawing by David Blostein made after photographs taken by the author at National Swiss Circus Knie in 1986.)

Without going into further detail regarding the 1986 program, it should be obvious that the semiotic outcome of using essentially the same horses as the year before was quite different in its themes and organization. The principle of the overall construction of the equine part within the semiotic economy of this program was poetic—in the formal sense of Roman Jakobson (e.g. 1968, 1970)—rather than narrative, as was the case for the preceding program. Instead of symbolically retracing the ascent of the horse to the human sphere through domestication and acculturation, the whole 1986 program was embedded within two equine displays: the dancing horses at the beginning, and the spectacular acrobatic riding with an institutional theme (the Post) at the end. Note that both Spain and Hungary, which provided the themes for the acts, belong to a rich paradigm of horsemanship cultures. More important, the figuration of the wild horses (the white horses and ponies presented bare in the liberty act) is itself embedded in the first equine display as if equine wildness were bracketed, so to speak, by domestication and acculturation—a way of expressing in the formal, structural, static mode the same relationship that was expressed in the 1985 program in the transformative, linear, narrative mode.

The point made in this chapter—namely that *Equidae*, like any series of differential patterns, can be used for the construction of a language—is corroborated by Elizabeth Atwood Lawrence's brilliant analyzes of the rodeo and more generally of the symbolic role of the horse in North American culture (1982, 1985, 1989). For instance, she has described a particular sequence which she characterizes as "a pertinent rodeo variation" in which the speaker emphatically announces that the audience will be treated to a display of "the world-famous Lipizzaner stallions." Instead, a clown makes his entrance riding two mules "Roman style" (i.e. as explained above in a standing position with one foot on the back of each), and performs some comical tricks with the mules. As Lawrence notes:

> Here the lowly and ungainly mules provide an ironic contrast to the vision conjured up in the minds of observers of the precise and intricate manoeuvre exhibited by the Lipizzaners. For the celebrated horses are paragons of equine expertise, and as such symbolize a high degree of human culture being extended over the natural realm. The Lipizzaners, of course, would be as out of place at a rodeo as a cowboy in a tuxedo. The message in the act just described is that such sophisticated performances are all right for urbanites and Easterners, but, as for Westerners, give us the simple life. Let us cling to rural values, lowly creatures, and down-to-earth attitudes. *The anti-intellectual, anti-aesthetic strain of the frontier is clearly framed in the language ranch and rodeo people understand—through the use of horses.* (my emphasis) (Lawrence 1982: 234)

Notwithstanding the obvious overlap between the circus and the rodeo, the equine calculus is used to create two distinct languages whose semiosis is constrained by the particular cultures within which these languages are productive: European traditional societies and the American West. Naturally the training techniques are generally similar, but the staging of their results—that is, the construction of their spectacular display with all the cultural relevance it implies—brings into play different frameworks, connotative dimensions, and systems of values. Both languages—the circus and the rodeo—may occasionally "quote" each other, and they become functional parts of the consistent discourse to whose articulation they contribute. The transformations which take place in such instances are a precious source of information regarding both semiotic systems.

Equestrians as cultural heroes

Human agencies are also involved in these displays. The horses are indeed only half of the picture; their correlate is the human subjugator and educator. It takes force and some degree of violence to "break" a horse whether in the circus or on a ranch, but the circus equestrian conceals this aspect of the trade as much as possible, whereas it is emphasized in the rodeo. Lawrence (1982) has exhaustively described the ethos expressed in the latter. The former is well documented in various commentaries spanning the past 200 years or so. Most equestrians are supposed to be serene, calm, and poised while they put their charges through their paces. This applies both to the rider and to the presenter of a liberty act in which the horses are controlled from a distance through voice and gesture. The latter's long, thin, and elegant whip has often been compared to a music conductor's baton. Domination through force, with obvious exertion, resistance, and coercion—which is the rule in rodeo and in one of the two styles of large feline acts in the circus—is excluded from the public displays of equine acts. Whatever the archaeology and history of this type of outward relationship between circus trainer and horse may be, it remains a contemporary productive rule. In the context of the circus, the master of the horses is a prototypical figure who, in the form of the traditional MC, often appears as the "donator" and "director" of the whole spectacle. Most major European circus families are also renowned equestrians. An oft-quoted saying claims that the circus started with horses. As masters of the horse, endowed with a power which in appearance does not rely on brute force, the circus equestrians also impersonate the masters of culture, whose power they mimic through their stage costumes and demeanor. The equestrian directors usually perform in the formal garb which characterizes special occasions in the high society of their time (tailcoat, tuxedo, evening dress). For mounted exercises they may use sport or semiformal garments similar to those worn by the gentry. They use allusively only uniforms of the contemporary military establishment, but they relish replicating the parade uniforms of high-ranking officers of a more or less distant past. When they choose to stage exotic displays, the equestrian directors will impersonate figures of authority belonging to other cultures, such as a Maharajah, an Inca priest or warrior, an Arab sheik, and an Indian chief, and so on. They are cultural heroes whose claim to symbolic status comes from their alleged power before an audience which, in the nineteenth- and twentieth-century European tradition, includes the social elite, for whom high-priced seats are reserved—a tradition perpetuated nowadays by the yearly Monte Carlo Circus Festival and other events for socialites linked with the circus.

As has been shown earlier, the masters of the horse as cultural heroes train and stage equine acts through which deep-seated cultural problems are symbolically articulated. Having almost overnight lost its pragmatic relevance to the technologies of transportation, mechanization, and automation, the horse remains a luxury commodity, a status symbol, a sport and leisure animal. Formerly the keystone of civilization in the vast area of Eurasia, the horse has become a cultural object whose survival is determined almost entirely by the social structures of the population which foster an interest in perpetuating its species. To a large extent its modern function is purely symbolic and ritualistic. It has no significant biological reserves in the wild; its wildness is a *simulacrum* which is staged and performed in spectacles and is, as such, the paradoxical result of special training. This condition makes the horse a natural calculus doubly suitable to represent the algorithms of culture. After all, this suitability is indeed largely based on the horse's morphological diversity, which is itself the result of selective breeding (i.e. an intensive cultural processing of nature). On the other hand, the conquest of the horse was a turning point, a founding event of the culture within which it now survives as a haunting symbol. Both the familiarity and strangeness of the horse, its liminal and mediating position between nature and culture, pervade the circus experience with, it would seem, the persistence of a ritualistic theme endlessly reformulated in the circus ring. *War Horse* is the latest literary avatar of "that long-lost archaic companionship" which Edwin Muir movingly celebrated in his poem "The Horses" (1976). As the poem's last line proclaims, "Our life is changed: their coming our beginning."

6

The Staging of Actions: Heroes, Antiheroes, and Animal Actors

A theory of action

A circus act is a set of actions, that is, a succession of implemented plans which are ordered according to an overall rhetorical structure. This progression is determined by the amount of apparent or real uncertainty attached to the completion of the goal. These actions are *represented* in the sense that they demonstrate various competences to overcome well-defined challenges rather than being spontaneous responses to the ongoing vagaries of life. Circus actions are not part of open-ended processes although the situations are real and the outcome is always uncertain to a degree. The situations which circus artists negotiate are constructed by the actors themselves. These actions are reiterated day after day in front of an audience or as part of training and rehearsal sessions. When a minor failure occurs during a performance, the action which failed to achieve its goal is repaired by returning to its starting point. Rarely does a serious accident happen but even the best-trained performers can be victims of a physical setback or a technical malfunction.

There is no shortage of theories of actions. Logicians, linguists, and semioticians have debated for decades how to define an action because the phenomenology of real life does not provide clear-cut boundaries between actions and between action, reaction, motivation, intention, competence, planning, implementation, context, and consequences. Physical survival and the negotiation of social situations constantly require that we act or abstain to act. The latter can be, of course, construed as a form of action. As was pointed out in Chapter 2, reporting witnessed events or accounting for what we have done in the past is often confused and inconsistent because remembering actions is a challenging task which implies the selective processing of a mass of information and the construction of improvised narratives. By contrast, formal narratives in all their forms (folktales, novels, dramas, comics, films) can be neatly analyzed as sequences of actions which have been organized along the trajectory (the "story line") of a plot. Of course, these actions are *represented* by literary or theatrical means. Even when stories are complex and convoluted, they can be parsed as series of situations, actions, and consequences. In the second half of the previous century, the French semiotician Algirdas J. Greimas (1967) and his followers elaborated theoretical models in the form of algorithms which were meant to account for all forms of narratives in whatever medium they could be expressed. These models were inspired by earlier works done in Russia by Vladimir Propp (1968 [1928]) who had identified a limited number of stereotyped functions in Slavic folktales. From this point of view, actions could be classified in terms of the functions they were implementing with respect to the completion of the narrative. Greimas pushed further the degree of abstraction of this approach and proposed a canonical narrative structure which, he contended, was a universal form of meaning, a sort of a priori form of the human mind which accounted for every single instance of meaningful experience and its articulation in any kind of language. This is not the place to discuss in detail this insightful, albeit controversial theory but some aspects of it seem to be particularly relevant to the understanding of circus acts. After summarizing Greimas's model we will endeavor to apply this analytical grid to an analysis of the staging of acrobatic acts. We will then show how it can also help to understand acts involving trained animals. In so doing, we will focus on a type of dog act which can be ironically characterized as "the dog which is trained to do nothing." This paradoxical description is all the more interesting as it generates numerous such acts with canines and other species, and thus constitutes evidence of the capacity of the circus's multimodal discourse to reflect upon itself by means of performance.

According to Greimas, the general narrative structure is framed as a communication act within which a transformative process occurs. The starting point is a negative value: the subject lacks or has lost an object which will be acquired or found at the end of the process. This process consists of a series of tests which require the clearing of obstacles encountered on the way to achieve the goal. The subject is helped or hindered in this quest by actors (which Greimas called *actants* to indicate that he meant to coin a generic term to designate abstract narrative functions rather than actual actors in the usual sense of the word). It may be rendered in English by the term "agency" which can be endowed with a more abstract value than "agent." Objects such as a magic wand or a storm can be such agencies in as much as they perform respectively the functions of helping or hindering the progress of the hero toward his or her goal. It may be useful, though, to keep using the neologism "actant" to preserve its usefulness as a metanarrative analytic tool without any hint of ambiguity. In previous works (Bouissac 1976a, 2010), I have shown that circus acts mostly conform to this schematic organization of the actions they represent. Indeed, an artist in whatever specialty has to prove what he or she can do before enjoying the recognition by the audience of the status which has been acquired through the performance of exceptional feats. This narrative kernel is sometimes presented in a minimalist form. For instance, a single individual balances on a trapeze in increasingly difficult postures until an ultimate action appears to make the impossible possible such as keeping one's balance standing on the bar without holding the ropes while the trapeze is swinging. But most acts involve complex compositions with two or more acrobats, animals, and elaborate props. These acts can nevertheless be laid out as combinations of this basic narrative lexicon and syntax. Because of the abstract value of the functional terms of the elementary narrative structure, the *actant* subject can apply to a couple or a team, and the *actant* object (the purpose of the quest) can be construed as "life," that is, the eventual survival of the performing individuals. Note, though, that this life which asserts itself at the end of the act has the added value of having triumphed over a major challenge through which the subject has acquired a heroic status. This fundamental narrative structure which generates all circus acts is what ultimately accounts for their meaning, or, rather, articulates this meaning through a multimodal signifying discourse.

Another tenet of Greimas's theory is that no single term has meaning in itself but only in its relation with other terms. Signification is grounded on systems of opposition which determine the values of the terms. Expressions such as "domestic animals" or "possible actions" logically imply that there are other animals which are not domesticated and actions which are not possible respectively. The translation of these intuitive semantic relations into the idiom of the formal sciences led Greimas to import into this model the distinction made by logicians between contradiction and contrariness. He then asserted the axiomatic proposition that all terms have meaning only through their relations to contrary and contradictory terms, the latter term being also necessarily related to its own contradictory. Therefore, a term A relates to its contrary B and both relate to non-A and non-B, their respective contradictories. For instance, the semantic domain of social rules can be articulated into four related and mutually defining values: (1) what is compulsory; (2) what is prohibited; (3) what is not prohibited; (4) what is not compulsory. It is with respect to this set of relations that terms such as *obligation, prohibition, permission*, and *option* derive their differential meanings. As we will see below, such a semiological grid can be used to categorize the represented actions which are displayed in circus acts with respect to our perception of the degree of feasibility of the tasks that the artists set for themselves and the ways in which these tasks are implemented or not in their performance.

Whether or not this theoretical view, which was formulated in the wake of structuralism, can survive the test of systematic testing is not our concern here. Probing intuitively its elementary algorithms in confrontation with cultural objects in any medium quickly leads to unmanageable complexity. But, in practical terms, it provides a heuristic point of entry into meaningful complex objects such as literary texts and circus acts. We will see that once actions are categorized in this manner some unifying patterns of meaning emerge from the multimodal discourse of the circus. These recurring patterns open interesting perspectives regarding the semantic relationships which hold together the diverse acts in a circus program to form a consistent system of represented actions as will be shown in the last section of this chapter with respect to acts which involve animals as actors.

The modalities of actions: From doing to making another do

The abstract definition of a circus act as the completion of a series of actions which consist of implementing successive plans does not take into consideration that these actions are not simply performed but are staged as being easy, difficult, dangerous, or even insane with respect to normal standards. These perceived qualities which determine the emotional impact of circus acts on their audience can be made formally explicit through modal categories organized according to a single semiological grid.

All actions performed are obviously possible. But their staging can make their goal appear more or less within the reach of a normal human being. As we saw in Chapter 2, when we analyzed the act of equilibrist René Sperlich, a performance can be construed as an increasingly risky game. Let us examine now how actions are "modalized," that is, how they are made to rank on the scale of feasibility in the eyes of the spectators. Two sets of opposite values are correlated: doing versus not-doing, and possible versus impossible. A circus program usually displays the whole range of combinations of these values: (1) doing the possible; (2) not-doing the possible; (3) doing the impossible; (4) not-doing the impossible. These are intuitive categories from the point of view of an average circus audience which attends a spectacle: (1) there are skilful actions which are expected to be within the range of possibilities of a trained juggler or acrobat even though they could not be achieved by untrained persons; (2) on the other hand, a clown who fails to properly sit down on a chair and collapses in the ring or trips on a straw proves to be unable to do what everybody in the audience could achieve without effort; (3) but a wire walker who performs a somersault on a thin cable stretched high above the ground is perceived as achieving a goal which belongs within the realm of the impossible for the normal human condition; (4) this is why the risk of failure and death is ever present in the mind of the witnesses of such feats and lethal accidents occasionally occur as the annals of the circus amply document. This eventuality shadows the most extreme acts. The advantage of thus formalizing these intuitive categories of action is that it makes it possible to parse circus acts with reflexive precision rather than mere impression, and uncover the clever combinations their designs implement in order to achieve their ultimate goal which is to manipulate the emotions of their audience. Describing the ways in which these categories of action are constructed and transformed offers the most consistent and comprehensive approach to the multimodal discourse analysis of circus spectacles.

The kernel of a circus action is the implementation of a physically challenging plan but such actions are performed within a cluster of verbal, musical, and visual modifiers whose deliberate purpose is to make the actions appear easier or more difficult and dangerous than they actually are. Walking and dancing on a high wire is for an audience intuitively verging on the impossible. If the music is lighthearted and if the acrobat maintains on his or her face an easygoing smile or an expression of pleasure while cleverly merging his or her technical movements with seductive and affiliative social gestures, the act conveys an impression of wonder if not miracle. The distance from the spectators makes it possible for the performer to flash wide smiles which occult other facial signs of effort and anxiety. The bright white of the upper teeth which are uncovered in such performed smiles visually offsets the muscular contractions in the upper face, notably around the eyes, an area which is necessarily tense and focused during balancing acts. The same acrobatic feat can instead be displayed with dramatic music, dark costume, serious face, and exaggerated gestures which emphasize the instability of the process and the threat of a lethal failure. Some acrobats ostentatiously make a sign of the cross before performing a daring feat to indicate that they are prepared to confront death. Some, while the audience applauds at the end of their act, tilt up their face toward the sky and extend their arms in a gesture of gratitude to the divine power without which they would not have survived their ordeal, thus retroactively qualifying their last action as potentially fatal. Whether such signs of religious behavior are genuine—some acts are truly dangerous—or contrived is irrelevant from the point of view of the ethnography of circus performances. They are essential parts of processes in which clusters of multimodal signs consistently modify the meaning of the performed action. The artists always create a supplementary signification which consists of categorizing their act with respect to the system of modalities which was outlined at the beginning of this chapter.

Another kind of qualification of an action as quasi impossible is to stage a controlled failure before succeeding in implementing the plan. Such spectacular failures may require as much skill as the completion of the action itself. It also often involves the production of a cluster of signs of authentication such as mimicking fear or relief when the acrobat survives a staged loss of balance.

The attitudes and behavior of the assistants which monitor aerial acts from the ground play a significant part in construing the modality of an action as particularly dangerous. If they obviously follow with intense attention the development of the act, as if they were ready to intervene in case of a fall, the audience is entrained to empathize with them and the artist. In fact, in many acts, this staging is functional because in the absence of a safety net the best response to an accidental loss of grip or balance is to "break the fall," that is, to divert the body's trajectory by pushing it sideway in order to limit the severity of the impact on the ground without being oneself hurt by this free-falling crushing weight.

The inventories of gestures which have been produced over the past few decades in the context of nonverbal communication research provide means of analyzing the flow of facial expressions, postures, and hand movements which acrobats generate in parallel to the completion of their technical program of action. From this point of view, a circus act can be conceived as a multilinear score. The interpretation of such scores varies with the degree of professionalism or artistic sensibility of the performers. This total choreography constitutes the visual means by which the meaning of the represented actions is modified with respect to the system of categories which was outlined in the preceding section. Naturally, these deliberate signs are interpreted in the context of the physical situations as they are perceived by the audience and framed by the verbal text within which the acts are embedded. For all humans, stability on the ground is tantamount to safety. The sense of danger increases with instability and height, and the loss of contact with anything that can be gripped or grasped necessarily generates anxiety. The various apparatuses which are constructed in the circus space reproduce extreme situations which precisely create a range of typical risks as we saw when we analyzed the balancing act of René Sperlich. At the same time, the verbal discourse either written or spoken and the musical accompaniment provide information regarding the register in which an act must be interpreted. We have examined the role of the music as well as the lyrics in Chapter 2 when we noted that at the most daring moment of René Sperlich's balancing act the music of a song by Queen titled "The show must go on" was played by the band, thus adding a potentially tragic connotation to the performance. In some acts, a roll of drums is used to evoke the danger of death.

Occasionally, the staging of acrobatic acts includes the presence of a clown who performs spectacular failures and, thus, implements one of the poles of the semantic system of oppositions which was elaborated above concerning actions with respect to possibility and impossibility. This dimension of circus discourse is most interestingly represented in trained animal acts which, ironically, implement the inverse of the factitive verbal modality: "to make someone do something," which is one of the four semiological poles, the others being "not to make someone do something," "to make someone not do something," and "not to make someone not do something." We will see in the next section how this system plays out in some typical dog acts. The relationships between the semiological poles are figuratively expressed by the image of a square, thus transforming the fundamental algorithm into a graph formed by four equidistant points and their connecting lines.

Ironical discourse: A dog act in the semiotic square

Performing dogs are a regular item in circus programs. As domestic animals which are a part of everyday life in most modern societies, they serve useful functions as shepherds, sled dogs, search and rescue dogs, and police dogs, or provide their owners with interactive company as pets. They are familiar rather than exotic, and training them to do basic routines is within the competence of most people. However, more advanced training can make them behave as humanized actors in spectacular performances. Acrobat and comedian dogs are well documented in the annals of the circus. This section will review and discuss some dog acts in view of the theory of meaning which was outlined earlier in this chapter.

Vienna, September 21, 2011. Zirkus Roncalli has pitched its elegant dark blue tent in front of the city hall of the Austrian capital. I am queuing in front of the Rococo-inspired decorations of the circus entrance, readying my notebook and anticipating the acts I plan to document this evening. During the performance I watched the previous day, I had decided to focus, among others, on a dog act which appeared in the second part of the program. It was the last avatar of a series of such acts I witnessed over the past 50 years. Each one, though, had original variations both in the training of the dog and the staging of the performance.

After a breathtaking aerial demonstration, followed by thundering applause, a brief blackout signals the beginning of a new act. Soft background music seeps from the orchestra as a modestly costumed, humble looking man enters the ring followed by a phlegmatic female Boxer. "Hello, my name is Vitaly and this is my partner Klishko." The dog stands, motionless, next to the man. Boxers have very expressive faces with bulging eyes whose strong contrast between their dark pupil and light sclera makes the direction of their glance clearly visible from a distance. She looks intensely at him while he speaks and gesticulates. But all this excitement is met with a bland, almost judgmental expression on her face. He extends his leg high in front of her and orders: "Jump!" Instead, she lies down still looking at him in passive defiance. He lowers his extended leg in order to make the task easier but to no avail as she remains flat on the ground. He gives up the idea of a jump and lifts her on her fours and readies her for a walk between his legs as he makes the first big step. But she stops walking as soon as she is under him and lifts one of her back legs close to his trousers in the manner of a male dog which relieves itself against a tree trunk or a lamp post. Vitaly takes off his shoe and mimics that it is full of smelly urine. He wants to shame her by putting the shoe under her nose but she turns her face away. He carries her on a low table and orders: "sit down" and he pushes her back so that she sits down. "Smile!" and he lifts the two corners of her flabby Boxer's lips. The trainer announces that Klishko is going to imitate a butterfly and he moves her pending ears up and down. Then, she is going to imitate an elephant and he fixes on her nose a multicolor contraption which unfolds by itself and vaguely evokes the form of a trunk. Now she is going to balance a white billiard ball on her forehead, keeping perfectly still. But the first attempt is a failure: the ball rolls down. The second attempt is successful and the audience is requested to applaud. But the dog lowers her head and it becomes obvious that, this time, the ball had been stuck in place by the trainer because it stays on top of her head when she looks toward the ground. Finally, she lies on her back and he tries to have her keep one of her front legs up but it falls down along her body as soon as he releases his grip. After a series of apparent training failures, the man sheepishly bows to the audience when suddenly Klishko executes a perfect somersault and exits with her trainer as the star of the act.

This kind of act is of special interest for our inquiry because it foregrounds the discursive nature of circus performances. There is indeed not a single move which is not verbalized in parallel with what is done (or, in this case, not done) in the ring. Other acts are necessarily embedded within a text both printed in the program and uttered in the verbal introduction by the speaker: the name of the artists and their specialties, and various additional qualifications. The nature of some acts, such as clown acts or the one by Tony Rosaire and his horse Tony we analyzed in Chapter 4, involves real or fictive dialogues. But Vitaly's act, like the one we will discuss below, is continuously both verbal and nonverbal. The two strands unfold at the same time and the meaning of this multimodal discourse is produced by this very conjunction: a programmatic description of spectacular feats which do not occur. This results in the construction of the animal actor, in these cases a dog, as the manipulator of the trainer, a "trick" which reveals the semiotic negative, so to speak, of trained animal acts through an inversion of the signs.

Before going further into this analysis, let us consider an act which was presented for about three decades ago in the second part of the previous century. Douglas Kossmayer, under the stage name of Eddie Windsor, and his female Bassett Lola performed in many circuses and varieties. Dressed in a smart, flashy business suit, Eddie Windsor made his entry with self-assurance and great elegance. He eloquently introduced his partner, "Lola Bassett," suggesting by his words and gesture that she was a gorgeous girl, and kept looking toward the ring curtain or the theater wing in expectation of her arrival. To the audience's surprise and delight a long Bassett appeared from under the artists' entrance curtain whose bottom was lifted with its head (or from the wing in stage performances), slowly walking with an air of insouciance. Eddie Windsor kept describing her glamorous demeanor in terms which every move of the dog denied. With her long ears almost reaching the ground, Lola stopped beside her trainer, looking up at him with adoring eyes. Eddie Windsor then announced in the same emphatic tone of voice the extraordinary exercises that Lola was going to perform. First, she would sit down. But she kept the same position. He ordered, demanded, threatened, and even begged with no result. Eventually, he pushed down her back to make her sit and, with a triumphal gesture, acknowledged the laughter and applause of the audience. The act unfolded along the same line as the trainer was creating new situations and was giving new orders which the dog nonchalantly ignored. After a table was brought to the center of the ring, Lola was urged to jump upon it but Eddie Windsor had to lift her, put her front paws on the edge of the table, then, slowly pushed her up inch by inch until she was lying flat on the top. In midway, half her body was on the table while the other half was hanging down on the side. The same process was repeated with verbal variants when the trick consisted of jumping down from the table. Now on the floor she was presented with a hoop which the trainer was holding high. His emphatic command "Jump, tiger!" was met with laughter by the audience and indifference from the dog. The hoop was lowered by degree as the command was becoming a supplication until it touched the ground. Lola was then walking slowly through it and stopped. Eddie Windsor was perspiring and ostensibly wiped his forehead. He had lifted this heavy dog, pushed it, pulled it, and talked at a fast rate continuously. It was time for the act to come to an end. With his hands behind his back, holding the hoop at some distance from the ground, he bowed to the audience. Suddenly lively and alert, Lola trotted toward his back and made a fast jump through the hoop.

Comparing Kossmayer's and Vitaly's dog acts which were observed more than two decades apart shows that they were generated by the same formula, or algorithm, with variations in the selection of the breed and the staging of the tricks. They both rested upon identical training techniques and produced similar reactions from the public. The challenge is to understand with some precision the kind of meaning this type of act produces in the context of the circus because this meaning cannot be explained as the completion of remarkable actions. Their multimodal discourse is in fact a metadiscourse which offers ironic comments upon the whole paradigm of circus acts based on trained animals. This discourse is, as we will see below, a reflection on factitive actions since it is the dog which appears to manipulate the trainer while, at the same time, it is obvious that it is the trainer who has trained the dog to perform negatively.

But these acts have to be understood also in the context of the whole paradigm of circus dog acts. Such acts typically involve six to ten animals of the same kind or of mixed breeds which are made to sit on stools arranged in a row close to the artists' entrance in order to free most of the ring for performing their tricks. There are numerous thematic variations conveyed by the costume(s) of the trainer(s) and the way in which the dogs are decorated with fancy collars or hats and capes. They execute, usually one or two at a time, some acrobatics such as walking on their hind or front legs, jumping through hoops, climbing ladders, balancing a balloon on their head, somersaulting, and the like. Some are billed as educated in a higher sense and they perform the same tricks we encountered with educated horses: counting, dialoguing, identifying objects or persons on command.

Lynne and David Rosaire's dog act, which was observed several times in the 1970s and 1980s, will provide an interesting example in which the formal operations at work in both regular dog acts and acts which stage a dog "trained to do nothing" are complemented by the case of a dog which "does trick without being trained." This is, of course, the result of a training which actualizes one of the logical possibilities of the factitive grid which was not implemented in the dog acts we reviewed so far. Lynne and David Rosaire enter the ring each holding five Pekinese dogs in their arms. They bring them to a bench on the side of the ring and the dogs take their places on this elevated platform where they will stay until they are called in turn to the center and will return after their tricks are completed. At a distance from the bench, there is a small doghouse in which the audience can notice a little mutt of indistinct breed. The act unfolds as follows: the Pekinese, one or two at a time, perform tricks in succession under the vigilant eyes of the trainers and as soon as a trick is finished, while David or Lynne drive the dogs back to their place on the bench, the little fellow dashes out of the doghouse and quickly performs by itself behind their back the tricks which have just been performed by the Pekinese with much encouragement and occasional prompting. The trainers act out as if they were displeased by such insubordination and the mutt rushes back to his doghouse. This scenario is repeated several times and the mutt, called Sheba as we will learn below, steals the show. This act was presented in the program of the Swiss Circus Knie in 1977 and it was commented on in French as follows in the illustrated magazine featuring photographs of the acts which was for sale at the entrance of the tent:

> How elegant are the ten Pekinese dogs presented by David Rosaire! Their aristocratic look does not prevent them, though, from taking part in a most funny act. As they perform their serious tricks, an insolent little bastard of no pedigreed lineage dares to mingle with their games. Behind the trainer's back, she mischievously imitates the feats of her high class partners. She mocks her displeased master and, naturally, the public falls for her. [Translation mine]

This text, which most members of the audience are likely to have read as they were scanning the printed program before the show started, provides an interpretation of the action through articulating the difference between the two classes of actors in sociological terms: on the one hand, an elite group, the aristocratic pedigreed Pekinese; on the other hand, a commoner of the worst kind, a bastard or a "mutt" in the canine breeding language. The text also opposes two types of behavior characterizing the trainer: on the one hand, a technical competence which allows him to make the dogs do what he wants (implementing his plan); on the other hand, a lack of power to prevent an insubordinate individual dog from imitating them, thus undermining his plan while implementing the whole semantic array of the factitive semantic structure.

But we will find that there are more dimensions if we further explore deeper layers of cultural meanings by making explicit the categories of agents, actions, and names involved in this act. It activates indeed a powerful network of sociopolitical values. Domestic animals such as dogs can be categorized as useful or nonuseful. The former perform tasks such as guarding cattle, protecting their owners and their properties, pulling sleds, helping the blinds, hunting, rescuing, and so on; the latter are luxury objects which not only do not work but also are fed, pampered, and served by their masters who spend a part of their disposable income to maintain pets. Thus dogs are associated with social class distinction. As it was clearly expressed in the program's introductory text to this act, Pekinese symbolize not only the leisure class by association but also the aristocratic elite whose concern for genealogies they embody. Dogs are indeed classified as indigenous or exotic. The latter, such as the Pekinese as their name indicates, are redundantly luxurious artifacts. Their association with highbrow culture is confirmed by their trained behavior which evokes sports, dance, and other actions performed for the sake of it rather than some practical result. In addition, they are carried into the ring in the arms of their trainers and they sit on specially decorated circus stools when they do not execute their tricks.

By contrast, the mutt is sheltered in an undistinguished doghouse which is typical of a common household. This dog is not identifiable through its breed because it is the result of a free genetic mixing. Such dogs are valued for their individual qualities, for instance, loyalty and intelligence, instead of their genealogy. It bears all the signs of being indigenous: it is a common European female mutt. However, it embodies at the same time an apparent contradiction as its name is Sheba, a name marked as doubly exotic since it comes from the Old Testament (Book of Kings I, 8) and refers to the exotic country whose queen visited Solomon. The irony of the name outdoes the exoticism of the Pekinese like the mutt's actions outperform their exercises.

It is interesting to note that Sheba's persona and performance are the symmetrical inverse of those of Lola Bassett. Although the two acts were not part of the same program, we must keep in mind that dog trainers, like any other circus artists, are very much aware of the history of their trade and the contemporary productions of their colleagues. The equivalent of literary sources and intertextuality plays an important part in the creativity of these artists. The generation of an act may not be the deliberate twisting of another act but may spring from spontaneous variations in quest of originality. Novelty, in circus as in poetry, arises from tacit but consistent transformations. Innovations remain under semiotic constraints if they are to qualify as circus performances. Let us return for a moment to Douglas Kossmayer's act and compare it to the act of the Pekinese and Sheba. The general algorithm which generates the representation of the distinct modalities of actions is at work in both the Rosaire's and Kossmayer's acts. *Factitivity* is the common basis but it is deployed through different logical implementations. In David Rosaire's act, the trainer demonstrates his competence with respect to making the Pekinese do what he wants them to do. They behave like obedient pupils lined up on their benches. He and his partner use school masters' gestures. The dogs' good will is uniformly distributed. Rebel Sheba actualizes the three remaining modalities in her successive interventions: first, she instantiates the apparent incompetence of the trainer to make her do something since she does tricks by herself; second, she shows that he cannot make her not do the tricks since he unsuccessfully tries to prevent her from doing these tricks; finally, she forces him to accept her doing, thus not making her not do something since he eventually gives up and let her do what she wants. Parallel to the reiterated proofs of the trainer's competence with regard to the Pekinese, Sheba implements the other poles of the semiotic square and thus undoes, so to speak, the whole process of training which consists precisely of acquiring this competence by progressing from impotence to the control of an animal's behavior and the capacity of preventing an animal from doing something. This is the prerequisite for making this animal do something which the animal does not want to do. And, finally, the trainer makes the animal do what he wants it to do as is the case with the Pekinese. This process represents the transformation from total spontaneity to absolute control through intermediary stages.

Lola Bassett instantiates the same undoing of the competence of her trainer but from an inverted position since not only can he not make her do what he wants but she makes him do what he wants her to do by forcing on him her passive resistance instead of active rebellious actions. Her eventual display of competence implies that her whole behavior was deliberate. All this, of course, is the result of a sophisticated training which takes the very process of training as the topic of the act, thus producing what can be legitimately considered to be a metadiscursive discourse.

Finally, there is another layer of meaning in which the acts are contrastively related. The gender dimension is indeed played out in as much as the two dogs, Lola Bassett and Sheba, are introduced as females. However, the former is manipulative while the latter is competitive. Lola's femininity is marked by her makeup and her "diamond-stud" collar whereas Sheba is scruffy and jewel-free. Lola plays the role of a kept woman, the kind of *femme fatale* for whom a king would give up his kingdom. After all, Douglas Kossmayer's stage name was Windsor. Sheba outdoes both her trainer and the other dogs which are construed as males in the text which introduces the act. She achieves her goals through her own merits in a competitive and proactive way. She encapsulates at first in her persona three symbolic values: underdog, underclass, and "undergender," so to speak, and at the end she comes out on top by reversing these values.

But there is more. These two dogs perform through their actions a change in the status of their trainers whose factitive competencies are put in jeopardy. They transform them into the equivalents of clowns in as much as the two trainers eventually prove to be *unable to do the possible* since any dog owner can in theory make his or her dog obey. This opens an interesting window on a more complex semiotic system according to which all the circus icons: acrobats, clowns, and trainers are defined by their positions not only with respect to animals but, more to the point, to factitive categories in general. Indeed, the acrobats *make themselves do* what is necessary to achieve the impossible, that is, they implement a reflexive factitive category of action. However, this system would not be complete if the opposition between domestic and wild animals was not factored. Domestic animals are those animals which are made to do what we want. Wild animals can be defined as those animals which cannot be made to do what we want. Therefore, the clowns who usually deal with domestic animals of lower status (pigs, cows, donkeys, mules, and geese) remain in the sphere of the possible and even fall into negative values when they prove themselves unable to control these animals. Trainers belong to two different categories depending on whether they deal with domestic animals of higher status like dogs and horses or wild animals which qualify them as able to perform the impossible.

The multimodal discourse of the circus as a whole is sustained by a consistent system of action categories and displays. Under the apparent variety of its acts the full gamut of its combinatorial potential is actualized. Reaching goals and meeting challenges are such fundamental actions which define human life that it is no wonder the circus makes so much sense for its audience. The actions it represents in its rituals are the very mirrors of everybody's life and destiny. Heroes, antiheroes, and animal actors are mutually defined with respect to the system of the modalities of actions we have elaborated above. It is through this syntax that their statuses are transformed in the course of an act. It is, so to speak, the motor of the circus discursive dynamics.

7

Circus Animals as Symbols, Actors, and Persons

In the company of animals

The previous three chapters have shown how domestic animals are construed as actors in circus performances. Using examples taken from the contemporary traditional circus as well as spectacles of the past, we have discussed the symbolic and ritualistic values with which horses and dogs are endowed in the multimodal discourse unfolding in the circus ring. In Chapter 8 we will focus on performing wild animals, mindful of the moral issues which this long-established practice raises among some segments of the world population. The present chapter proposes to reflect upon the moral and legal status of animals in contemporary society and on the impact of various ideological attitudes on the ancestral art of the circus which has carved some resilient icons in popular imagination.

Through its use of trained animals, the circus embodies indeed the presence of wild nature within our urban fabric by periodically imbedding into it a bubble of visual, acoustic, and olfactory impressions which affect deep layers of the human psyche. At the same time, the circus blurs the ontological and cultural distinctions by ritualistically humanizing other mammals, including large predators. This is achieved not only through the performances themselves but also by publicizing in the media events involving animals in terms similar to those which are used for humans.

A telling example is the health report concerning a leopard called Rany which was published in the online daily French circus news bulletin, www.aucirque.com, on October 11, 2011. We learn that Rany, a 12-year-old female underwent surgery to remove a cancerous breast tumor. Nine photographs show the successive stages of the operation by a veterinarian surgeon, from the anesthesia to the recovery under the attentive watch of her trainer while a nurse dresses the site of the cut before the leopard wakes up. The scene took place in central France where Circus Arlette Gruss has its permanent quarters. This is where, in a countryside estate, Rany had been retired with her old trainer after a decade of performing in the traveling show. It is indeed common practice in the circus that animals which do not perform any longer because of age or sickness are not dispatched but are kept in the human environment in which they were born. Strong bonds develop to the point of giving a cross-species meaning to the notion of extended family. A 2010 documentary on the American Big Apple Circus showed how the whole circus mourned the passing of one of their oldest stars, the pony George, which had died of a heart attack at the end of the season. Such anecdotes are essential parts of the multimodal, multimedia discourse of the circus as they contribute to building the context within which circus performances make sense to their audiences.

It will be suggested in this chapter that the circus may play a significant role in the defense of species which are seriously threatened with extinction not only because it promotes sustainable breeding programs but also, and more importantly, because it sensitizes new generations to the concrete, existential presence of these animals through actual interactions with humans. By demonstrating the possibility of communication at close range and displaying the performance of tasks which require obvious forms of intelligence and social integration, the circus construes animals as persons, albeit nonhuman ones. I evoked in the first chapter of this book the gray dancing mare Roxane which as a child I was looking forward to seeing every year when Cirque Bureau was visiting our hometown. Roxane was for us as much a person as her rider Mrs Glassner. When, years later, I ran my own show in Canada, we were introducing to the public our six trained lions by their names. I was told once, almost a decade after we had gone out of business and retired the lions in Florida, that some people asked the folks of another traveling show if they knew what had happened to Cesar, Malika, Huli, Leonardo, Hoggar, and Zizi. I vividly remember the faces and personality of these animals, their particularities, and their life stories which are still a part of mine: Sweet and massive Queen Malika; shy, cross-eyed Leonardo; aloof Huli which looked like a tiger in a lion skin; young Hoggar which was growing a black mane; scruffy Zizi which was all noise and no harm; and honest and direct Cesar whose macho character matched so perfectly his trainer's character. The circus restores and develops a sense of vital continuum between us and species which share a common biological and behavioral heritage with us, and it replaces with forceful images and narratives the abstract and impersonal statistics which are mostly ineffective in motivating environmental protection. The human capacity for empathy needs to be primed through personal experience of the kind the circus offers in a safe, institutional context, even if it is only by proxy for most spectators. Providing that acceptable standards are respected in dealing with the keeping and training of animals, the circus tradition in its contemporary, updated forms remains an essential ecological resource. Through the high degree of personalization of animals which run the risk of being otherwise treated as mere commodities or quantities, trainers give them a human face, so to speak, by the narrative they stage in the ring. Their choreographed behavior is richer in genuine information than animation films like the popular *Lion King*, for instance, which owes more to Shakespeare and Kipling than feline biology and behavior. Heavily edited nature documentaries usually adulterate to such a point the ongoing existence of the wild animals they portray that they tend to misinform rather than enlighten. As to zoological gardens, they display mostly overfed and bored wild felines who sleep their days off in the grass of their enclosures or their sterile dens. Only the occasional presence of their keepers seems to motivate them to rise and seek social interactions. The circus fosters a culture of lifelong daily involvement of bounded existences in which the formal distinctions that set species apart tend to lose their relevance. This is a stark contrast with the abstract classifications which determine the intellectual representations of zoological categories. This latter aspect will be examined in more detail in the next section. It is indeed in opposition to these mutually exclusive definitions that the circus reinstates through its rituals the conscience of a common heritage and destiny shared by animals and humans alike.

The representation of animals in cultures

The categorization of animals and their differential integration in, or exclusion from human social structures has been the object of intense anthropological research. Each culture evolved its own way of distinguishing various statuses among species and of assigning them to particular places in its cosmology. Those animals which share an ecological niche with humans are expectedly the objects of more refined categorical and semantic distinctions in the particular languages of the populations concerned than those which are lumped in the less precise category of "exotic" animals. Distinctions among the latter are driven by a different logic which often mimics the classification of alien human populations with respect to their geographic locations. Modern descriptions and explanations of the ways in which animals are cognitively and symbolically treated in cultures are found in the works of mostly armchair anthropologists such as Claude Lévi-Strauss (1966), Edmund Leach (1964), and Stanley Tambiah (1969), to name only a few, who have elaborated comparative systems of animal classifications and scrutinized their pragmatic consequences for human behavior with respect to hunting, consumption, use, and ritual. Ingold (1988), Shanklin (1985), and Willis (1974) have summarized and further discussed the issues involved in animal categorizations. Animal species can be endowed by religions and philosophies with a vast range of meanings and values as preys or predators, evil or holy, edible or nonedible, useful or dangerous, pets or pests, reincarnated humans or mere instinctual machines, among other oppositional values. These distinctions are not purely abstract but have definite practical and institutional consequences in the cultures which foster them and which are, to a great extent, defined by them.

Naturally, the idea of a homogeneous and coherent system of classification attached to a particular culture is, to some extent, a fiction of the anthropological imagination. Many attitudes and values usually coexist within human populations and the cognitive mappings of animal species are not as clear-cut as it might appear from reading the literature. Systems vary across social groups, cultural grids overlap and intersect, and the validity of mutually exclusive categories can be trumped by transversal groupings and practical considerations. There are nevertheless more or less coherent semiotic universes which impact the social behavior of people toward animals. It should be kept in mind, though, that a system of values which is held by intellectual or religious elites is not necessarily fostered by other segments of the population. Quite often, contradictory attitudes and behaviors with respect to animals coexist in the same individual. It is symptomatic that, at a time when campaigns to prevent the extinction of the tiger are globally endorsed, Asia continues to maintain traditional beliefs in the therapeutic value of tiger bones, thus generating a lucrative market which is responsible for intensive poaching in India. Many other wild species are similarly jeopardized by the resilience of folk medicine and magical cures.

Descartes's philosophical theory regarding the ontological status of animals, for instance, influenced the European thought of the Enlightenment which coexisted with many other traditional beliefs and practices. The advent of Cartesianism imposed on Western modernity a model of the animal as a mere machine deprived of consciousness and feelings. Animal suffering was considered to be nonexistent. We know, for instance, from the record of complaints which neighbors lodged with the police at the end of the nineteenth century, that horses were skinned alive at the veterinary school in Paris in order to vividly demonstrate their muscular anatomy to the students. The complainants, though, were not concerned with the cruelty of the process but with the disturbance caused by the noise. Darwinism contributed to bridging in theory this ontological gap between animals and humans but provided at the same time a strong rationale for the distinction between the two, at least from the point of view of its popular interpretation which comforted the perception of their differences conceived as incommensurable degrees of evolution.

By contrast, there is ample evidence that in classical antiquity and medieval Europe, animals were conceptualized in complex semiotic webs rife with ambiguities as vehicles or messengers of the god(s), embodiments of witchcraft power, objects of worship, or carriers of curses and blessings. For example, the number of birds which appeared at a given time in the sky and the direction of their flights were interpreted by the Roman priests as providing divine answers to questions concerning future events. During the reign of the Inquisition, witches were identified among other signs by their familiarizing with particular animals. But there were also cases of elevating some animals to quasi sainthood such as the greyhound Guignefort who had saved a child from a snake but was unjustly killed by the boy's father who, upon seeing the blood of the snake, thought that it was coming from his child and speared the dog to death in anger. This martyr dog became the object of a popular cult sanctioned by the Catholic Church. There were shrines and pilgrimages dedicated to Saint Guignefort, a word whose etymology means "strong dog" (Gaignebet 1986; White 1991). Still nowadays, in the European countryside, owls are feared as harbingers of death whereas swallows nesting in a human dwelling are considered to be a blessing for its inhabitants. These customs and the attitudes they reveal have persisted in spite of the strength of Cartesianism among the European intellectual and scientific elites inspired by the Enlightenment. Many of these values have been carried over by circus folks and their performances which many saw with a mixture of suspicion and awe. For long, wild-animal trainers and tamers were credited with possessing a sixth sense which allowed them to communicate with, and be understood by, their lions, bears, and tigers. Fantastic stories circulated in the press and popular literature. The circus fed beliefs in the extranatural power of some humans who could control animals in a manner akin to the one which was attributed to African sorcerers or Indian magicians, whose legends were spread during the Colonial era. Still in the 1950s, circuses in Europe featured Damoo Dothre, a turbaned and bejeweled trainer from India, and Marfa the Corsican, a woman of exotic beauty, who were both advertised as presenting their tigers without using whips or sticks, assumedly through the mere strength of their glance. Still nowadays, the latest generation of the Kara Kawak family displays in European circus rings crocodiles and alligators which they claim to hypnotize. At the climax of the act, the presenter thrusts his head between the wide-open toothed jaws of the largest animal in his troupe. The poster advertising this act uses Indian imagery to convey a sense of mysterious power over the wildest, most uncanny forces of nature. The staging is all the more important as the "training" is necessarily limited to various manipulations of these slow-moving animals. The act nevertheless bridges extremes on the spectrum of life and opposites on the cultural grid.

The examples which were selectively marshaled in the above section are meant to characterize the resilient tradition of the circus as a cultural gray area in which humans and animals enter in actual and symbolic partnerships. As we have seen, these processes are not limited to the circus but pertain to a broader phenomenon which tends both to anthropomorphize animals and reintegrate humans into the continuum of animal life. In circus performances, biology is processed into art and forbidden channels of communication are opened to create common grounds between the wild and the tame. Entrenched discontinuities are questioned and animals emerge from the circus crucible not only as symbols but also as actors and persons.

Animal agencies: Legal and moral issues

In cultural contexts in which animals are construed as agencies living within human social groups or at the interface between human settlements and outside wilderness, their actions have necessarily some impacts on the populations and these actions tend to be interpreted in view of the current legal rules and moral norms. Their occasional abnormal or destructive behaviors marked individual domestic animals as responsible agencies whose actions were subject to categorizations in terms of transgressions. These actions could be assessed on grounds similar to some extents to those applying to the population at large. The normal behavior of cattle, for example, is a set of behavioral expectations not necessarily identical to those which apply to humans, but which must be at least compatible with the safety of their keepers. Bernard S. Jackson (2011) has documented through his early historical research and his more recent semiotic interpretations, the legal status of animal in the ancient near East and the Bible, in rabbinic law, Roman law, English law, and other European legal systems. As perpetrators of wrongs, animals were held responsible in various degrees, with or without intent, and punished accordingly. The historical record shows that trials of animals were a rather common occurrence in Western countries (Girgen 2003). Juridical procedures against animals are well documented both in medieval and modern times (e.g. Finkelstein 1973: 229–30; Jackson 1975: 108–52; Fensham 1988: 85–6). Even in more recent history, trials of animals took place in the United States during the nineteenth century (Finkelstein 1981: 48–85).

The assumed influence of supernatural powers could endow destructive animal actions with a meaning which required a different redress involving religious norms and rituals. In medieval times, the Catholic Church was prone to prosecuting animals which were accused of being manifestations or instruments of diabolic power. As dreaded manifestations of magic, they were treated like the witches with whom they were usually associated. We have encountered in Chapter 4 the story of a Scottish trainer named Banks and his educated horse Marocco. Both have been amply chronicled by contemporary writers who reported that they were repeatedly tried by the Inquisition and exonerated only after they could produce some proof of innocence either by having the horse kneel down in front of a cross or by the trainer disclosing the technical secrets of his trade. Some claimed that, eventually, the man and the horse were condemned for witchcraft in Rome where they were burnt alive in the early seventeenth century.

The notion of guilt presupposes the capability of making choices. If animals are construed as responsible agents who may be punished for their crimes or sins, they must also be endowed with the possibility of choosing good rather than evil, respect for the norm over its transgression. Although animal behavior has been stigmatized in Western cultures and languages in opposition to civilized and moral conduct, as is obvious from the numerous terms of abuse and common metaphors which set animals as abject creatures and mark humanity as nonanimal, there are celebrated exceptions which show that animals were also considered capable of reaching an exemplary moral status in some circumstances. There are indeed individual animals which have been construed as "symbolic types" in the sense proposed by Richard Grathoff (1970), that is, embodiments of values which transcend the relativism and inconsistencies of common social norms and behaviors. These animals survived their physical deaths by being "immortalized" through literature or art, in particular by having their commemorative statues set in prominent locations in town squares, temples, and shrines. The case of the greyhound Guignefort of medieval fame was mentioned above. But a more recent example is the Japanese Akita dog Hachiko whose statue stands in Tokyo in front of Shibuya train station. An indigenous pure breed, a detail which is not without relevance, this animal was born on November 10, 1923, and soon became the pet dog of a professor who was teaching at the University of Tokyo. Every day, this man was walking with his dog to Shibuya station to catch his train to work, and the dog had developed the habit of waiting for him to come back every evening in front of the station. After two years, the professor suddenly died of a heart attack while he was at the university. For the next ten years, Hachiko faithfully came back to the station each day, waiting for his master until he himself died in 1935. His loyalty had by then become famous and a campaign was organized to raise money for immortalizing this icon of national virtue. There are several statues of Hachiko in Japan and his story has been publicized in various literary forms including children's books in which this dog is celebrated as a moral example of friendship and loyalty. When in Tokyo, I personally make it a point to set appointments with my closest friends at Shibuya station in front of the statue of Hachiko which stands there. There are always fresh flowers and sweets which have been deposited on the small platform at the feet of the dog. Across the square, a monumental ceramic mural displays a series of relief icons of Hachiko.

In addition to exceptional anecdotes concerning pets, the semiotic foundation of the social construction of animals as responsible and liable agents rests in part on the traditional performances of trained animals which were framed by interpretive narratives as we saw above in the case of Banks's educated horse. The story of

Androcles's lion provides another good example. The Roman chroniclers reported the story of a slave being thrown to the lions in the amphitheater and being saved by one of the animals which came to his defense and protected him. The audience was then told that this man who was from North Africa had once removed a crippling thorn from the lion's paw. Both were captured separately later on and sent to Rome for the entertainment of the crowd. The story goes that the lion recognized his savior and reciprocated the favor by saving him. Any contemporary lion trainer can replicate the staging of this performance with a properly trained young animal. Androcles's lion has become a literary icon which embodies virtuous gratitude in most trying circumstances even though there is ample evidence that the story was fabricated in order to frame an instance of skilled wild-animal training. This interpretation might come as a surprise for those who mistakenly believe than the Roman amphitheaters were featuring only gory displays of fighting gladiators and animal slaughters. True enough men were often set against wild animals in ultimate combats. But there were also well-documented performances of trained felines essentially similar to the ones which are featured in modern circuses. The authors who reported the story of Androcles on the basis of eyewitnesses declare that as soon as the lion was seen to spare the slave, tablets were circulated among the audience to explain why the lion had not attacked the man. It should be obvious to anybody familiar with the circus trade that this extraordinary event was a cleverly staged stunt. It illustrates the point made in this chapter that circus training and staging contribute to construe wild animals as moral agencies. We will see in the next chapter how the trainer Alexander Lacey stages a heated "argument" with one of his lionesses with which he eventually works out a reconciliation.

Folktales and fables have also contributed to the attribution of a sense of moral norms to animals, a quality which justifies the accusation of a deliberate intent to transgress these norms. Bremen's celebrated four animals (the donkey, dog, cat, and rooster) whose statue adorns one of the main squares of this German city, exemplify the virtue of cooperation and innovativeness as opposed to the wickedness of the criminal humans these animals are credited to have overcome. Let us recall that the four had taken shelter in an abandoned house when they realized that burglars were trying to break in. To face the situation, they created a composite monster with the donkey as the base, the dog and the cat standing on each other, and the rooster at the top. When they all uttered their cries at the same time, the intruders ran away in panic to flee such a vociferous giant.

The emergence of a global culture has exposed the West to Asian attitudes toward animals that blur the ontological distinction grounded in Judeo-Christian theological thought. As we have seen in Chapter 1, when elephants in an Indian circus ring are trained to perform a Hindu ritual in the presence of a Shiva Lingam, the audience accompanies them with religious songs. There is no hint of sacrilegious behavior because these animals are endowed with a divine status. So are the mischievous monkeys which often harass people in Indian cities. They are not eliminated as pests but are captured by specialists who release them with all due regards in distant parts of the countryside. They are often causing fatal accidents but their agency as proxy of the divine Hanuman is considered sacred and righting their wrongs too radically would constitute a still bigger wrong in the context of Hindu cosmology. There has been in human history and probably prehistory a consistent semiotic drive to endow animals with ontological status and intentionality as subjects, helpers, or opponents of humans rather than being mere passive objects of a hunter's quest. This semiotic status was a prerequisite for their legal status as punishable perpetrators of wrongs. But, more importantly, it construed them as moral agencies confronted by the universal choice between good and evil. Although elephants are considered holy animals by Hinduism, their husbandry exposes their keepers to many unfortunate accidents. An obedient and fully cooperative elephant is very rare. This is why we can find in a temple near Trichur in the State of Kerala the life-size statue of an animal which had shown perfect consistency of friendliness and cooperation during all his long life. Like the Japanese dog Hachiko, this elephant's moral status is immortalized as an icon to be worshipped.

A cultural paradigm shift: Animals as nonhuman persons

The moral status of animals in Europe and the Middle East provided for a long time the legal grounds for their prosecutions and eventual punishments. But a semiotic sea change has occurred during the twentieth century to the point that an animal trial would be unthinkable today in any part of the global civil society. A regular monitoring of human deaths caused by tigers in India during the past decade, notably but not exclusively in the Sundarban mangroves in Bengal, show that elimination is considered a last resort even for confirmed man-eaters. The official doctrine is that rehabilitation should be the first line of defense. The same reasoning can be observed with respect to urban dogs which behave aggressively toward people. In all the cases involving tigers and other wild animals or pets, the animals are not blamed but the responsibility is ascribed to deforestation or encroachment on their natural habitat for the former or lack of proper attitudes for the latter. The guilt ultimately falls on the victims of these attacks because they are often illegal fishermen, hunters, poachers, or simply foresters who happened to be in the wrong place at the wrong time. Owners of problem pets are considered to be guilty of abuse or neglect and their victims are assumed to have indulged in provocative behavior. More generally, in contemporary global civil and democratic society, the legal status of animals has switched from perpetrators to victims of wrongs. And a corresponding legislation has emerged. It is interesting to identify the conditions of possibility for such a cognitive and moral change of attitude.

The discourses which sustain a legal semiotic landscape—let us call "landscape" the set of laws and court cases which define a norm with respect to a certain cultural area at a certain period of time—can be metaphorically conceived as tectonic plates in geology. All discourses are not necessarily logically coherent but their particular semiotic consistencies compete with each other. The Darwinian discourse has normalized the notion that the ultimate cause of animal behavior is Nature in the form of natural selection. This discourse still competes with the notion of the ladder of beings that had been previously elaborated by Natural Philosophy. Another underlying discourse is the Rousseauist argument for the fundamental goodness of nature and its perversion by society. All these discourses collide at many points of their semiotic interfaces but they concur to exonerate animals from deliberate wrongdoings and to put the blame on those who interfere with nature whenever animals cause harm to humans or their properties. In addition, being at the top of the great chain of beings, whether in a creationist or evolutionist perspective, should imply a moral grandstand that should not stoop to litigating with lower beings toward which we have responsibilities.

Modernity has developed a kind of pervasive anxiety of anthropomorphism conceived as an epistemological sin and, from this point of view, construing animals as victims even when they are the perpetrators of wrongs, allows human subjects to transcend their own animality. The fear of anthropomorphism is a consequence of the discourse of denial and resistance to the naturalization of humans confronted to evolutionary biology and evolutionary psychology, two discourses which tend to blur the distinction between humans and animals. In contemporary society, the legal status of animals rests at the nexus of several semiotic regimes which exercise contradictory pressures for the definition of norms and their translation into legal rules. It is not the purpose of this chapter to analyze the legislative texts bearing on animals, nor to scrutinize the court proceedings in which animals were the subjects of litigations.

Some animal rights advocates endeavor to make it illegal for circuses and even zoos to keep elephants with the assumption that these animals belong in the wild and should be released in Africa or India. Their opponents bring forth the arguments that elephants both in the Eurasian subcontinent and in Northern Africa before they became extinct have been domesticated for millennia. Nobody can ignore the fact that wild elephants are fast disappearing from their natural habitats because their range is curtailed by human demographic expansion and they are victims of illegal ivory trade. It is cost-effective to slaughter them in order to harvest their tusks. It has been reported by TRAFFIC, the main monitoring agency, that the year 2011 has been the worst since ivory trade was banned in 1989. Judging from the volume of illegal ivory seizures in 2011, at least 3,000 animals were killed by poachers, the largest number in 23 years. This number is, of course, only the tip of the iceberg. It raises the issue of whether the radical prohibition of captive elephants in circuses and zoos, where they now commonly reproduce, will not have the perverse effect of accelerating their extinction.

The goal of this chapter is to document the much broader semiotic net of relations which sustains the public consensus regarding the moral and civil status of animals in our society, and which grounds any new legislations on a virtual public will for which references are not rooted in mere anecdotes but in the contemporary scientific culture and its diffusion in the media.

There have indeed been several high profile publications during the past few decades, which spilled from the scientific literature over to the mass media and molded the public perception of animals. Primates, especially chimpanzees and gorillas, have been the focus of passionate reports and documentaries on their cognitive capacities, intense social lives, and meaningful interactions with dedicated humans.

But the scope of awareness of animals' commonalities with humans has extended beyond primates. Extreme cases of empathy have taken center stage with unlikely subjects such as the love story between psychologist Irene Peperberg and Alex, an

African gray parrot with which she claimed to have developed by an appropriate educational training, a code through which verbal communication could occur between the two. Whether the parrot was actually understanding the questions she asked him in English or was simply engaging in mimicking duets with variations as many birds do was debated in the scientific community. But the media coverage foregrounded the news value of the claim irrespective of the serious debates it had triggered. When it was reported that Alex had said "I love you" before dying, tears were shed and obituaries were published.

This general attitude is reinforced by credible scientific investigations of the emotions of animals (e.g. Bekoff 2007) and the transformation of data gathered by empirical inquiries into the rationale for a political agenda. Mark Bekoff, for instance, published an *Animal Manifesto* (2010) advocating the recognition of animals as beings endowed with personal feelings and values, as did John Sorenson in a publication squarely titled *Animal Rights* (2010). We are witnessing the cultural emergence of a moral and legal definition of animal rights which raises the issue of how to set the boundary between humans and animals in a civil society. Even in the animal advocacy literature, arbitrary distinctions are made between rabbits and mice when it comes to medical experiments (e.g. Bekoff 2010: 8). The extermination of bed bugs, flies, or mosquitoes does not raise any legal or moral objections in Western countries as it does in some Asian religions. The Jains of India, for instance, wear gauze masks over their mouths lest they would inadvertently kill a gnat when they breathe. But the defense of animals in Europe sometimes goes beyond the advocacy and implementation of lawful protection such as extreme cases in which circus animals were poisoned on the grounds that they were bound to be happier dead than alive in a circus. In 2010, the primatologist and media celebrity Jane Goodall has pleaded for the recognition of the rights of chimpanzees (Goodall and Pintea 2010) and, in the same year, during a special session at the American Association for the Advancement of Science's annual meeting, researchers have proposed to redefine dolphins (and some other animals endowed with humanlike cognitive and emotional competencies) as "nonhuman persons" (Grimm 2010). This new state of mind accounts for the facts that in 2010 a political party whose main agenda is the protection of animals has some elected members in the Dutch Parliament and that, in Switzerland, citizens were asked to vote in a referendum proposing to officially assign in each canton a lawyer in charge of litigating on the behalf of animals (who lack language for doing so themselves). Had the referendum been won, all regions in the Swiss Confederation would have been forced to assign lawyers to abused animals. Interestingly, the goal was to defend their rights as victims and, assumedly, argue for the punishment of their abusers, and the nature and levels of compensation rather than represent them as defendants.

These high profile moves are symptoms of a deep shift of attitude toward animal life which ultimately tends to integrate animals into the democratic process of the civil, and, probably, specifically urban society which projects its views and values toward the rest of the world in the name of globalization. Thus animal legislations have emerged in many countries as a result of the actantial transformation of animals in the public discourse of the media and the moral credit their behavior enjoys among a global society which mostly experiences animals as pets or protagonists of narratives displayed in virtual reality. However, it should not be forgotten that pets are tailored to the needs of their owners, and that even scientific documentaries are heavily edited with a view not to transgress what is considered to be community standards as far violence and sexuality are concerned. The legal and moral status of animals in the current century and the corresponding legislations which attempt to regulate human behaviors toward them are semiotic phenomena which selectively involve a limited range of species and situations. The categorical constructions of animals as *dramatis personae* within actantial structures and the psychological and legal consequences this entails are fascinating domains of inquiry. They are at the core of the circus discourse as we saw in the previous chapters with respect to horses and dogs, and as we are going to further consider in the next chapter when we discuss wild-animal cage acts.

8

Dancing with Tigers, Lying with Lions: Translating Biology into Art

Tigers in the wild

The closest I came to a tiger was in Bandipur, a part of a vast wildlife sanctuary which straddles the states of Karnataka, Kerala, and Tamil Nadu in Southern India. My friend Chandrabhanu Pattanayak had secured a bungalow for the weekend in a wardens' settlement a few miles within the forest. At dusk, a guard took us in his jeep and drove through paths which had been traced through the jungle over the past centuries, perhaps more, by elephant herds. As we were passing thick bamboo groves, the warden stood at attention and pointed to two nilgais which were trotting some 50 meters behind the jeep. The two forest antelopes were emitting a kind of whistling sound. "Alarm," said the man. "There must be a tiger hunting nearby, very near probably. They follow us to seek protection. They would never do that otherwise." He drove faster back to the camp. "The tiger has to eat tonight." Later, as we sip a sweet tea with our driver in the cantina, we learn that after twenty years in this job he has not yet seen a tiger. "Plenty of pug marks, yes, around the water holes or in sandy patches. But tigers, never. They are like ghosts." Censuses which point to a decline of the tiger population are indeed mostly based on the tracks they leave on the ground. They are as good as finger prints for the experts' eyes.

A book I had read a decade earlier comes back to my mind: *The Face of the Tiger*, by Charles McDougal (1977). This is the book I most often recommended to students who wanted to learn what semiotics was about. McDougal reports the results of years of research on tiger behavior in the Chitawan Valley in Nepal. Direct observations were conducted from well-hidden posts built in trees close to clearings where live baits were tied. Individual tigers were identified by cameras which were placed on the usual paths of the animals with a wire that triggered the flash as most of their hunting and patrolling occurred during the night. This work offers a wealth of information about the signaling repertory of a species which is not social and for which avoiding contacts with congeners is a survival imperative. Males defend vast swaths of land which include the territories of several females with which they mate. But after a few days of courting and copulation, the male is ferociously sent away and has better not to show up until the female is again ready to conceive once the cubs have grown up. When the latter become adults, they have to fend for themselves, emigrate, and stake out their own territories whose dimensions depend on the availability of prey and the presence of competitors. Tigers have to kill and eat every three to five days. Another invaluable source of information for tiger behavior is the classic by George Schaller (1969), *The Deer and the Tiger: A Study of Wildlife in India*.

A snapshot of the map of a land populated by tigers would show fixed boundaries marked by the many multimodal signs they keep creating and renewing: scratches on tree trunks, urine sprayings, feces deposited on elevated grounds. They also broadcast vocal signals. They recognize each other at a distance through the individual patterns of their striped faces combining symmetry above the eyes and dissymmetry below. To indicate that the intruder is not welcome to get too close, they twitch their ears which sport a tuff of white hair. This bright white warning cannot be missed by a tiger's eyes, even in low luminosity. But these boundaries are only as good as their residents can enforce them. Over a period of time, mortality takes its toll. Aging or diseased males are eliminated by younger, stronger ones. The same goes for females. Only a few cubs reach adulthood but enough do so for the territorial map to be under constant pressure and undergo semiotic redrawing as the density of the tiger population and their prey fluctuate. In addition, tigers have always competed with humans both for space and food, a fight that modernity symbolized by the great tiger hunts of the British Raj in India. On the verge of extinction, tigers are now protected by laws. They are glorified on national stamps and countless books. However, on the ground, the rapport between tigers and humans remain conflictual. When Indian farmers uncover cubs in a den, they destroy them as we do for rodent pests, that is, if no government officials are in sight.

The Times of India, September 25, 2011: VILLAGE MOB KILLS TIGRESS. As I read the online daily version of this national newspaper, I do not fail to catch this title. There are frequent reports in the Indian press of people being attacked or killed by tigers and the ensuing retaliation by the survivors. Often, the wardens who happen to be nearby tranquillize the aggressive animal and delocalize it. In that case they were absent. A mob of villagers stoned to death a tigress which they caught prowling around their houses. She had preyed on their cattle for some time and had recently killed an old woman. Forest officials claimed that a team of specialists trained to capture and relocate such animals had remained in the area for several days but were forced to leave because of the danger posed by the presence of Naxalites in this region. These political insurgents, who camp in the forest, tend to capture or even kill any government officials who come across their path. They also derive income from poaching elephants and tigers. The latter's bones are highly valued by antiquated Chinese medical beliefs and command a good price. In South East Asia, parts of Siberia, and Sumatra, tigers are feared by local populations, mainly villagers and foresters who often wear a mask on the back of their head as a protection against these powerful predators. Tigers indeed do not attack their preys frontally but ambush and surprise them from behind. Their approach is silent and their vertical stripes provide them by day and night with the most efficient camouflage among the reeds, bamboos, and long grass of their native environment.

The fifth dimension of space

Animals like humans live in the three-dimensional space which is abstractly described by geometry and topology. In addition, the consubstantial presence of this spatial environment cannot be dissociated from the sense of time because its experience is closely related to movements, interactions, explorations, and transformations. But in real life the experience of space is never purely quantitative and cognitive: space has an emotional, affective quality, a kind of ever-present fifth dimension which endows places with meanings. Lions, tigers, and humans share in common a sense of home, territory, and curiosity or anxiety toward novel surroundings.

Tiger cubs are born blind like the kittens of our housecats. Once they have gained an early limited mobility, the den in which their mother nursed them will be the place to rush to when they encounter something unfamiliar and potentially threatening. As soon as they start exploring the space beyond the den, the proximity to the tigress remains the safest place to be. They progressively take their cues from her as to what to do and where to go. They often learn the hard way, that is, the tiger-way, that they have transgressed some limits. Their eventual survival, something that cannot be taken for granted in the wild, depends on how well they learn their mother's lessons. It also depends to a great extent on how experienced this mother is. The rate of survival for a first litter is indeed very low.

Lions may appear to come to life in a more favorable context. As their species is more social than the tigers, the newborns are taken care of by the mother and the related females of the pride, and their learning experience is collective. Later, they will hunt as part of a team. The odds of reaching that stage is nevertheless not very high, mainly if the resident male who fathered them is killed by rivals, a common occurrence in the world of lions. It has been estimated that only 2 percent of lion cubs reach adulthood because of the combined effect of infanticide, predation, parasites, and diseases. Lion cubs have, of course, better chances if they are born in a successful pride, that is, a pride which can control and defend a rich hunting territory with a resident male in his prime (Schaller 1972).

None of the tigers and lions seen in contemporary circuses has been captured in the wild. They all were bred and nurtured close to human caretakers. Some have even been bottle fed when their mother rejected them at birth. This is not infrequent as maternal care depends on a hormone whose level remains sometimes below the critical threshold, notably in young females. But even when the cubs are brought up by their natural mothers, interactions with humans are an intimate part of their early life and they are soon attracted to them as potential playmates. Like most young animals they can be irresistible but a wise trainer will nevertheless abstain from letting them discover through playing that they are stronger than him or her. It is indeed their way of testing their mettle with their siblings and thus establishing an early ground for the ranking which will emerge as they grow up. Each animal has a character of its own. There are bullies and wimps, loud mouths and gentle souls. They show various degrees of self-confidence and shyness. They may bond selectively with each other and with their human caretakers. Between one and two years, they can undergo their primary circus education: learning their place in the arena space. This place is a stool assigned by the trainer along the circular cage. It is the spot they will reach later whenever they enter the ring and to which they will return after each trick is completed.

Training is not alien to the nature of the big cats. In the wild, cubs grow up paying close attention to the mother and they model their behavior on hers. She also actively growls or paws them into what a tiger or a lion must learn not to do if it is to survive, for instance, jumping on a porcupine or ignoring the pecking order. While hunting for preys is instinctive, this drive needs to be fine-tuned to particular environments in which all that moves is not necessarily safe to hunt and eat. Predatory strategies that are adapted to various species have better to be learned by proxy than by direct experience because most failures preclude the possibility of having a second chance.

Heidelberg, July 11, 2010. Alexander Lacey, the British resident trainer of Zirkus Charles Knie, is training five young lions, a male and four females. The 1-hour session, which takes place on a Sunday morning in the regular performing steel arena under the big top, is open to the public for a small fee. Equipped with a wireless microphone, Alex explains in broken German the meaning of his moves and the functions of the two thin rods, a long one and a short one, which he uses to guide the animals along the paths he wants them to follow. Seated on the first row, I scribble notes on my pad as this open training session is an important part of the ethnography of performance I have endeavored to document as precisely as possible. At the same time, I cannot fail to note the intense attention of the large audience which has been attracted by this opportunity to learn how circus animal are actually trained. From my personal, insider experience, I know that the demonstration is absolutely genuine and not a mere public relations stunt. It is an early stage in a process which will last months.

Through the tunnel which connects the arena to their outside pen, the young animals rush to the ring in which stools have been placed where they will always be when the act is performed. At first, they pay scant attention to these pedestals and start playing, that is, stalking each other, wrestling, mounting mock attacks, rolling over, rising on their hind legs to gain an advantage on their playmates. Some explore the stools, sniff them, and at times jump on them. Alex enters the ring and captures their attention by calling their names and driving them toward the stools. He knows who is meant to stand where once the act is ready for public performances. Along the steel arena, there are nine stools, four more than necessary. Those four will be occupied by tigers in the final act. The young lions must learn their place.

The male lion's stool is the one in the center of the arc. Whenever Masai, who does not yet sport its full mane, happens to have climbed on its stool, Alex tries to prevent it from climbing down immediately by catching its attention, encouraging it by voice, and preventing it from leaving the stool by barring the way with the rods which are extensions of his arms. When the lion has held its place for a few seconds, Alex gets a small piece of meat from the pouch attached to his belt, fixes it at the tip of the short rod, and gives it to the lion. Progressively, Masai will learn that this stool is its own safe place in the ring. It will also learn that it can claim the higher pedestal in the very center of the ring whenever Alex prompts it to reach for that spot. In the meantime, the trainer has monitored the movements of the young lionesses and done his best to make them stay on their own stools. Such multitasking requires a distributed attention and constant interactions with all the animals, directing encouraging "Good boy!" or "Good girl!" to whoever complies with the desired behavior, and occasional stronger "No! No!" whenever an animal yields to the temptation of straying out of the planned course of action.

All along, Alex is providing the audience with explanations, switching from addressing them to scolding or rewarding the lions. From time to time, he establishes a close contact with Masai and one of the lionesses: a caress on the back or a kiss on the nose. He also invites the public to clap their hands for the lions when they do well. They have to be used to that strange noise which Alex hopes they will often hear. After a full hour, the animals are sent back to their den and Alex, drenched with perspiration, answers the questions from the public.

From biology to art

The learning process we just attended is the basics of circus training. Each animal familiarizes itself with the spatial structure of the ring and learns its own place in it. This structure is supported by the layout of the stools and other pedestals which provides a private space for each individual and preserves the minimal distance between the animals which otherwise would feel crowded and would be permanently on the defensive as a territorial reflex. An invisible bubble surrounds each stool whose dimension varies with the animal which occupies it. Some lions or tigers are placed at a longer distance from their neighbors. This may depend on their age and character. Young siblings usually tolerate better some degrees of proximity. But, in general, whenever a feline's invisible bubble is invaded this causes an immediate warning signal: the opening of the mouth and the displaying of the teeth accompanied by a roar of variable intensity, and the swiping of a paw toward the animal or human invader. Any owner of a pet cat is familiar with this reaction. The trainer knows how to control this behavior and plays on it in the staging of the act as if it were the line of a score which is part of the orchestration of this multimodal symphony. During the performance he or she moves along some preset paths which respect the animals' sense of their personal space in the ring. There are usually a few lions and tigers in the group which accept close contacts with their trainer. These can be approached, touched, petted, and even kissed. Trainers skillfully alternate moments of tension whenever they bring their whip or rod, which are perceived by the animals as extensions of their arms, within the distance which triggers roars and swiping, and instants of harmony when they embrace those which are used to, and enjoy their hand contacts. The performance of the special tricks which compose an act is similarly based on the management of personal space along paths which progressively become essential parts of the routines. Some animals respond to being called and prompted to move toward their trainer. Some others react according to the flight or attack reflex, and rush toward the trainer when they are provoked since they cannot flee in the opposite direction. Once again, these forward movements become routines with time and are ritualized mock attacks rather than attempted real aggressions. They unfold in the fuzzy borderline between play and reality, and can be truly considered as biology-based behavioral performance. They emerge from the more advanced training which we are going to witness now.

Ulm, September10, 2011. During the last few months, I have communicated through email with Alexander Lacey. We have agreed that I could have some photos of his act made while the circus would perform in this beautiful Bavarian city about 1 hour from Munich. A day before our visit, Alex informed me that he will have to take one of his tigresses to the vet for a check up in the early morning but will be back on time to conduct a public training session from 11 to 12. As we enter the big top, Alex is already busy placing the stools and pedestals in the cage, making sure that they are correctly arranged. My friend Zbigniew will take the pictures from the space between the ring curb and the steel arena under the guidance of Alex's wife, Ellen, who assists her husband from outside the cage during the training and performances. At first, Zbigniew is a bit nervous. He is well known for his underwater filming of sharks in tropical oceans but he has never been so close to lions and tigers. He will soon gain self-confidence and take more than 2,000 daring shots during his weekend at the circus.

I sit down in the front row with my notebook. Four young tigers and a lioness are released in the steel arena. They start playing, stalking, and chasing each other, jumping on the pedestals, tussling and wrestling in mock fights. As Alex enters the ring, they direct their attention to him. He orders them: "Platz, platz" and guides them through combining voice intonations and gestures. Since last year, each one has learnt its place among the 11 stools which form an arc along the cage in front of the trainer. From the center of the ring, he will be able to monitor all their moves as well as their occasional changes of mood. As subadults, these animals are always ready to pick a fight for fun or to express their liking for their preferred buddy by rubbing cheeks with it. Alex must keep their attention focused on him alone as much as possible. Obviously, this is not an easy task. The tigers Max, Kashmir, Susi, and Bella, and the lioness Amba are prompted to climb on their stools ("Up, up, up Kashmir! Good boy") and stay there ("No, Max, no, no! Good boy"). At the same time, he addresses the audience and explains how he uses the long and short rods both to keep them at a safe distance and to guide their movements backward and forward, touching their backside or their chest (hence the difference in length of the rods) until they have memorized their routines and will then need mere promptings. The rods are also used to entice the animals with appetizing small pieces of red meat fixed at their tip. They come handy now that Alex is training Susi and Bella to jump from one low pedestal to another in the center of the ring. The distance is quite short but it requires jumping rather than climbing down and up. The immediate tasty reward does the trick. Alex dispenses a few chunks of beef. Then, I notice that suddenly he has hidden the meat on the tip of the rod he holds in his hand. The tip he shows to the tiger has no reward but the tiger jumps any way as it has done several times so far and, as it lands on the pedestal, Alex swiftly reveals the reward by swirling the rod. Thus, progressively, the jump will be disconnected from the view of the reward which motivated it at first.

Figure 8.1 Sitting on her stool, young tigress Bella intently looks at her trainer while the audience is captivated by another tiger which is approaching. (Photo Credit: Zbigniew Roguszka.)

Figure 8.2 Young lioness Amba stands to attention as she observes the trainer interacting with another animal. Note the relaxed but focused postures and facial expressions of both Bella and Amba. (Photo Credit: Zbigniew Roguszka)

Figure 8.3 Young tigress Suzi is trained to sit down on command. Note the functions of the long and short rods whose light touch convey to the animal the trainer's intentions. (Photo Credit: Zbigniew Roguszka)

Figure 8.4 After complying with the trainer's instruction, Suzi is rewarded by a pleasurable scratch under the chin. (Photo Credit: Zbigniew Roguszka)

Kashmir will now be trained to rise on its stool and hold this position with its front paws up. Alex fixes a tall metal rod shaped like a T in front of the tiger. To reach the piece of meat which hangs from the tip of the long rod, Kashmir raises its body and takes support by putting its paws on top of the T. Once in this position, Alex causes the tiger to use one of its paws to catch the tip of the rod. Then, he makes it switch to the other paw several times by swaying the rod from one side to the other. Once the tiger has learnt to keep its balance without the presence of the support, it will raise on command without effort.

Figure 8.5 Young tiger Kashmir is being trained to hold the upright position by taking support on the T stand alternately with its left and right paw. Briefly taking this position is natural but holding it requires the development of muscle strength combined with balance. (Photo Credit: Zbigniew Roguszka)

After some last roll-over exercises by the tigers, the 30-minute training session for this group has come to a close. The animals must learn how to leave the ring in good order, one after the other as Alex gives them their cues.

It is now the turn of the lions. A male and three females rush through the tunnel and cavort in the ring. The young animals I saw a year before have grown to their adult size. Masai sports a splendid dark mane but his behavior still tends to be playful. They have learnt their places on the stools but Alex needs to correct some mistakes as they appear sometimes confused by the number of empty stools and the absence of the other animals. They have to use the stools which were not used by the five animals which just left the ring. Once Mali, Princess, and Goldie are seated, Alex

Figure 8.6 The trainer prompts a tiger to rise on its hindlegs in preparation for the next trick. (Photo Credit: Zbigniew Roguszka)

Figure 8.7 Adult male tiger Max rehearses its upright walk across the ring toward the trainer who proceeds backward in front of it. (Photo Credit: Zbigniew Roguszka)

deposits his whip and stick on a stool, and approaches Masai to kiss him on the nose. Then, he drives all of them to the pyramid of pedestals which is built along the back of the cage. Masai sits down at the top and two lionesses take position on each side while the third one, Goldie, stands on a pedestal in front of the pyramid. The empty spots in the structure will be filled by the other animals to form a complete symmetrical tableau when the act is ready for public performances. Compared to last year, the four animals are more focused. They obviously know what is expected from them. The action progresses smoothly. The three lionesses repeatedly make long jumps over an obstacle from one pedestal to another. Goldie tends to react more aggressively when Alex reduces his distance to her. She swipes her clawed paws toward him, showing her already impressive canines and shouting at him in anger, so to speak. Eventually, this will be a part of the routine and will spice up the action in the final act. Some house cats display the same behavior when their own space bubble is invaded by the hand of a stranger. But they hiss rather than roar as a warning signal not to get closer.

Figure 8.8 The young lioness has now mastered the long leap from stool to stool. The training has consisted of obtaining this natural behavior on command. (Photo Credit: Zbigniew Roguszka.)

The lions have now been driven back to their assigned places. A big male tiger enters the ring and quickly reaches the first stool on its right, at the extreme end of the arc. The young lions have to be used to this older performer which, on the other hand, also has to tolerate their juvenile presence. But the two must be kept at a safe distance from each other. Alex prompts Prince to rise on its hind legs and walks across the ring following him who runs backward in front of it. At the end Alex exchanges a friendly "Pfrrr" with the tiger, a sound that signals an affiliative feeling in this species. It is commonly observed between a tigress and her cubs, as well as during the courtship progress, and it constitutes the most reliable sign of bonding between tigers and humans.

A last exercise will bring the five animals side by side. They will be prompted to sit down, then, raise their body straight up with their paws extended above their heads before leaving the ring, one after the other in good order, except Masai who remains in the ring to rehearse its last trick which will conclude the act. A revolving globe topped by a small platform is pulled down from above the cage. The lion first rushes toward the globe but gets confused and jumps on the wrong pedestal. Alex sends it back to its place and prompts it to start the routine again. Now, Masai can ascend the pedestals that form steps to reach the platform which tops the shiny sphere. He is followed by Alex who stands next to the animal, puts his arms around its neck, pets it, and, as he steps down, kisses it several times on the nose. After the lion's exit, Alex answers questions from the audience. He provides information about each animal, their age, their character, how much they eat, how often they work. He also gives some detail about what the people have seen and explains how they learn their tricks. These jumps and other movements are good for their health because they do not have to hunt for food and their muscles need these exercises so that they stay fit and can live longer. Why is Masai so friendly with him? Because he has taken care of this lion since it was a very little cub. Alex is beaming: "Masai is my best buddy!"

The poetics and rhetoric of the cage act

A public training session like the ones Alexander Lacey routinely offers to the public is a new phenomenon in the production of the multimodal circus discourse. For millennia, probably even more, controlling large predators was considered akin to magic, a power that was feared. In hunters' societies overcoming wild felines required exceptional stamina, skill, and courage. Before guns were invented, close confrontations were inevitable when pastoralists had to protect their cattle or their own life. We have seen in a previous section of this chapter that still nowadays in India these confrontations are not infrequent and deep ancestral means of fighting tigers such as mobbing and stoning remain efficient. Beyond self-defense, facing large predators was construed as a symbol of manhood and a triumph of civilization as witnessed by the iconography of many ancient empires. This has remained the case in countries where tigers and lions are not yet extinct. In Africa, for instance, the pastoralist Masai had instituted the bow killing of a wild lion as a rite of passage to adulthood for men. It is obviously this ethnic group which provided the inspiration for naming Alex's lion. The circus discourse is rife with such intertextuality and cultural irony. In Europe, the colonial era spawned countless popular tales of man-eating tigers and stories of attacks by lions. First fairgrounds, then circuses featured credible representations of such confrontations

Dancing with Tigers, Lying with Lions 127

Figure 8.9 Alex joins his lion on top of the platform and scratches its neck while uttering sweet words. (Photo Credit: Zbigniew Roguszka)

Figure 8.10 When the training is completed, young lion Masai will conclude the act by climbing to the top of the globe with Alex. This routine will be repeated at each training session. The conditioning reward is not a piece of meat but a pleasurable physical contact with the trainer. (Photo Credit: Zbigniew Roguszka)

until the last quarter of the previous century. Men, and some women, staged risky mock fights within cages of various dimensions. Iconic references were made to the gory spectacles of the Roman Empire through their gladiator outfits and, ironically, the names they traditionally gave to their lions such as Nero, Brutus, and Cesar. Evocations of the British Empire were found in Indian decorations and tigers called Raja or Kali. Quite a few trainers lost their life during the violent conditioning of their animals and even during performances which did not unfold as planned.

Anthropologist Yoram Carmeli (2003) has shown how these displays embodied the struggle between nature and culture, and, more politically, between the civilized and "primitive" worlds. At the same time, the aura of powerful magic which is attached to the nonviolent human domination over large predators persisted in circus acts in which tigers and lions appeared to obey mere verbal commands or gestures. Some trainers were supposed to have a sixth sense, or to have been blessed with a supernormal power of the gaze. Such deceptive discourses were sustained by folk biology and psychology. Over the past 50 years, a wealth of scientific knowledge has accrued concerning the ecology of the planet Earth and the biology and natural behavior of many animals. Books and films have popularized this knowledge and, as a consequence, the perception of predators has shifted. Simultaneously, the emergence of the postcolonial consciousness reframed the public attitude toward the traditional displays of conflictual rapport between ethnocentric culture and antagonistic nature. We have addressed this issue in the previous chapter when we examined the new moral and legal status of animals which is leading some countries to prohibit cage acts in circuses. The possible cultural extinction of such highly ritualized performances is an important motivation for providing detailed ethnographic accounts of these acts as they can still be observed in some contemporary circuses.

Like for any form of the performing arts, the circus cage act follows some canons. These esthetic norms have changed with time and have been implemented with variations in the style and contents of the acts. A few typical genres have emerged over the past two centuries. As we noted in the previous paragraph, a circus act is context-sensitive in as much as it refers symbolically to the history and the politics of the culture within which it produces meaning for its audience. There are also degrees of perfection within each genre. Lion and tiger acts follow a general pattern according to which the successive actions suggest a progression from simple to increasingly complex tricks. In this context an "action" can be defined as the implementation of a plan involving at least two agents, one making the other perform some task. As shown in Chapter 6, such actions can be conceived in abstract terms. They can be realized with variations in the degree of apparent cooperation between the two actors ranging from willful compliance to stubborn resistance. Thus, the action in a cage act can be performed in the antagonistic or conciliatory modes. This depends on choices made by the trainer when he or she constructs the narrative of the act toward which he or she is training the animals. This also depends to some extent on the characters of the individual lions and tigers involved. Some will indeed tend to behave more defensively than others. In some cases, the life story of an animal has created a special bond with the trainer who thus can usually manipulate its behavior without any form of coercion.

The observation of cage acts shows that some segments of the narrative involve all the animals present in the steel arena or a subgroup of these. In the former case, the rapport is one agent (the trainer) versus all the other agents. In the latter case, the action implies two simultaneous relations: the trainer interacting with one or more animals while keeping all the others in place so that they do not interfere with those performing a particular trick. A third relation must be included in this dynamic structure: the trainer has to establish and maintain a constant flow of signs toward the audience through directed facial expression and gestures. To use an orchestral metaphor, the trainer plays indeed two scores at the same time. The degree of perfection in the performance of a cage act can be assessed on this ground: how well the two behavioral scores are seamlessly implemented.

Two styles of cage acts will now be described and discussed in detail to show both the genre evolution which occurred over the past century and the compositional nature of the multimodal discourse of circus performances. We will focus on the choices available to the trainer as an artist in the schooling of his or her charges and the dramaturgy of the act. It involves, as a first decision, either foregrounding the differences between the two main species of felines, *Panthera leo* and *Panthera tigris*, by developing two types of contrasting staging, or achieving a kind of harmonious fusion through performances which, at times, have been dubbed: "Peace in the jungle." These two strategies remain a productive contrast in the contemporary circus but some acts achieve a most interesting balance between the two, with a tinge of irony in the currently most perfect of them as we will see in the concluding section of this chapter.

The lion's anger

Male lions assert their territorial claims, which cover both hunting grounds and a pride of females, through powerful roaring and sawing. The latter is a succession of noisy expirations which bear some acoustic resemblance with the sounds made by a saw. These vocal signals are characterized by low frequencies that can reach a radius of 7 kilometers. Because humans resort to shouting or simply raising their voice to signal aggressive dominance, the effect of a lion's roar at close range is very upsetting. The world of male lions is extremely competitive but before they get their opportunity to conquer a pride and a territory, they form all-male nomadic small groups whose members exhibit affiliative behavior with each other. As lions have evolved as Savannah animals, vision is a prominent means of interacting at a distance. John Eisenberg (1983) has tabulated the repertoire of the multimodal communicative behavior of *Panthera leo* which includes 25 visual patterns (facial expressions, tail movements, and body postures), 8 distinct vocalizations, and 7 modes of tactile interactions. Schaller (1972) had identified 17 visual patterns, 13 different vocalizations, 7 modes of contact, and 5 olfactory signals. A significant number of these means of communication, variously indicating dominance or submission, overlaps with interactive human behavior and can form the basis not only of actual cross-specific bonding but also of performance displays which are meaningful for an audience. We have witnessed above the friendly contacts between Alex and Masai in the context of an act which foregrounds harmony rather than antagonism. But in old-fashioned lion cage acts the confrontational repertory was played out: strutting, high-head posture, increased volume of the mane, fierce vocalization, and mock charges. The latter is a cost-effective way of impressing a rival without running the risk of being maimed in an actual fight. These displays can be manipulated by trainers who are able to distinguish a mock charge from an actual attack. The roaring which accompanies this behavior is nevertheless nerve-racking for an audience which is not privy to such patterns of behavior, as it must also be to a great extent for other lions when they are charged by their conspecifics. It nevertheless takes a great deal of courage on the part of the trainer who responds to a charge by a counter-charge. Roaring is hard to match with a human voice. In fighting with other males, lions use this vocal means as an index of their size and strength in attempts to impress and bluff their adversaries, and prompt them to give up the fight. For some psychologists, the same strategy is at work when humans raise their voice.

But common sense has constructed a range of expressive emotions and accordingly labels this behavior: anger. It is assumed that anger is based on frustration and often leads to violence. It fosters situations which can easily get out of hand. Not all lions are equally prone to roar but those which do react so to the slightest provocation have often been chosen by trainers who wanted to use their behavior in the staging of their cage acts. This section will document a style of performance that was characteristic of the lion cage acts in the nineteenth- and early twentieth-century fairgrounds and circuses but which is now used mostly as an intertextual allusion to a past genre as we will see in the following sections when we examine in detail Alexander Lacey's mixed act which includes tigers and lions.

An icon of the fighting lion act was the American Clyde Beatty who was still performing when visual recording became possible. It will suffice to analyze the first 30 seconds of this act as it was performed in 1950. A number of adult male lions were released in the steel arena and they started tussling and growling. As Clyde Beatty is announced with emphatic phrases by the ringmaster, a short man dressed in a "colonial" outfit, with the typical tropical hat which symbolizes this era, rushes to the door of the cage well in view of the public. A revolver is hanging from his belt. A lion dashes to the door while roaring and swiping its paws preventing him from entering the arena. The lion makes several such charges. Clyde Beatty throws his hat unto the ground to signal his own anger and readiness to meet the challenge, a behavior frequently seen in films of the Western genre when men put on a fight. He grabs a chair which was standing nearby as if it were an improvised response to an unexpected emergency. He forces his way into the cage, confronts the lion while cracking his whip and protecting himself with the legs of the chair he thrusts toward the animal. At the same time he drives the other lions to their stools and occasionally fires some blanks from his pistol. The roaring chaos has been brought to a temporary order but quickly the next episode still starts in the confrontational style at a hectic pace with much whip cracking, gun firing, shouting, and thrusting of the chair. This old style celebrated violence and domination over the staged resistance of the wild. In the last decade of his career, as a different circus ethos was emerging, some other trainers were making fun of Clyde Beatty. One told me once: "This is not a circus act; it is the Korean War!"

October 1956. As a student in Paris, I cannot resist going to the Cirque Bouglione which is performing at Porte d'Orléans, near the school where I am boarding. I cannot afford a front row seat but from the bleachers the visibility is good. The program starts with a lion act presented by a charismatic young man, Henri Dantès. It is for me an epiphany. Cage acts had always bored me so far. This one is totally different. It blends war and peace in the most effective manner. The response of the audience is overwhelming. At the intermission, I rush to visit the traveling zoo in the backstage. The trainer is there, perfunctorily cleaning the cages of his five lions and stuffing straw through the bars for the night. I cannot refrain from expressing my enthusiasm: "Congratulation! What a performance! Never saw anything like that before!" My compliment is acknowledged by a condescending smile.

Unforeseeable circumstance, three years later, led to my hiring by Firmin Bouglione, one of the owners of the circus and its head trainer. I was assigned to the zoo and became within a few weeks a cage attendant to Henri Dantès whom I could soon count among my best friends. He was only two years older than me. A native of Datteln in the North Rhine Westphalia region of West Germany, Heinz Honvelhmann (1932–97) was known as Hans among the circus folks. They all loved and admired him and nobody would miss his act at the beginning of each show. Whenever I was not given other chores to complete, my task was to monitor his act with a chronometer: "Not more than 17 minutes! You understand! You know each trick. If it slows down, make me a sign. Not more than 17 minutes!" The act included some pauses between fast action episodes but all had to be paced within a consistent rhythmic structure. It usually lasted a bit longer as lions can be unpredictable and Hans had to adapt to their moods when they were not cooperating.

Henri Dantès had a variety of ring costumes provided by the circus where he worked. Some were somewhat formal with a hint of military uniform but most often it was his signature outfit, sporting black boots and white riding pants with a short-sleeve white shirt. In earlier photos he wears a colonial hat similar to Clyde Beatty's. The act included five lions, four of them with imposing dark manes. Between the tricks they were not sitting on stools but on narrow platforms fixed on the sides of the steel arena at approximately 1.5 meter from the ground. There were four pedestals of two different heights in the ring.

There is a unique atmosphere in this Gypsy circus, a kind of creative informality combined with signs of exotic affluence. The tent is saturated with an animal-scented air, a blend of horse manure and carnivorous effluvia. The lighting is subdued and cozy. The band in red and gold uniforms is warming up with muffled circus tunes. At times a roar is heard in the backstage. The public fills the bleachers and the loges. The big top is packed. Expectations are high in the audience. All their senses are stimulated at the same time in ways they do not experience anywhere else. The ritual can start.

A strident whistle is blown. A brief, emphatic announcement is made. The ring is flooded with light. The band blasts a heroic march. Dantès rushes in the steel arena and chases the first lion which enters from the tunnel to its high hanging stool. A slap from behind on its lower back triggers a fierce roar and swiping of the paw. The next three lions are pursued in the same manner without pausing but the last one is accompanied to its place in a more relaxed manner. Four lions are now quickly battled to the pedestals which are lined up across the ring with the higher ones in the middle and the two lower ones on each side. This minimal version of the pyramid facilitates the rapidity with which the four animals are now made to raise their body and extend their front paws upwards. Much roaring is going on. As soon as they have been driven back to their stools, Dantès grabs the lower pedestals and throws them to the side. The two higher ones remain in place for the next tricks. Dantès prompts a lion to jump on one and, at the same time, he takes position in the space between the two platforms. He cracks his whip toward the lion's side and, as the lion gathers its energy to clear the gap, he quickly forms a triangle above his head holding both ends of his whip in his hands. The lion clears the gap through this narrow space very close to the trainer's face. Another lion is driven toward the centre as a circle of metal covered with burning fuel is handed to Dantès from outside. Holding this ring of flames high in his left hand he tries to make the lion jump on the pedestal. The animal resists and roars, attacks and withdraws, and finally clears the gap through the fire.

Suddenly a peaceful configuration of the actors succeeds these bouts of noisy fighting. Dantès has spectacularly removed the high pedestals by displaying his muscular strength and has dragged back to the center a lower one. He sits down on it and calls three lions which come in turn to take places at his feet. The fourth one sits next to him. The fifth one approaches him from behind and puts its front paws on the pedestal so that it stands very close with its head next to the trainer's. This "tableau vivant" embodies for a moment a powerful symbol of peace and reconciliation. But this harmony is quickly broken as all the animals are sent back to their respective stools. The ring is cleared of all obstacles for the next trick which is the apex of this act, a combination of what is called in trainers' jargon "the back shoulder stand" and "the cover."

Dantès lies down in the sawdust and, taking support on his left shoulder, cracks his whip toward two lions which come and lie down on top of him across his abdomen. The trainer must regain the back shoulder position by sliding up a bit under the heavy weight of the lions. He prompts a third one to join them but the fourth one makes several dramatic charges toward his face until it eventually rests close to his feet. The fifth lion slowly approaches Dantès and lies down on his chest. During all the process the music has switched from the heroic mode to the American romantic melody "Only you."

A shout and a brisk movement of the trainer send the lions back to their stools. Now the exit can start. Each lion has a special way of leaving the ring. One opens the door to the tunnel with its paw. One is made to walk backward. One is provoked to attack and rushes toward the exit while Dantès is standing in front of it. At the last second, Dantès jumps up to let the lion go between his legs. Then he walks around the ring with a lion on his shoulders. Finally he rides the last one across the ring to the tunnel's door. When he bows to the audience, the response is ecstatic. The boldness of this young and charismatic trainer, the fast pace of the performance, and the increasing suspense that was built into the action have brought them to their knees.

The staging of this cage act was extraordinarily effective because in its first part the lions' ferocious anger was foregrounded by prompting roars and mock charges, and the second part displayed episodes in which the trainer was putting himself at the mercy of the lions. The interpretation of the "cover" by Dantès is what established his fame during his lifetime as it was admired by the general public and the professionals alike. He was considered by circus historians as the last romantic hero of the fighting cage act, an act he had brought to esthetic and dramatic perfection. The "cover" part of the act was preserved in some visual recordings and in John Wayne's movie, *Circus World*, in which Henri Dantès played his own part.

A master at work

A circus performance is an ephemeral event. Its traces may be recorded in the press in the form of journalistic allusions and a few photographic snapshots. Historians of the circus are mostly concerned with genealogies, itineraries of tenting shows and urban implantations of permanent premises, and occasional accidents which have been documented. But precise accounts of what the normal performance of a particular act consisted of are to be found nowhere. We mentioned in Chapter 2 the unique attempt to counter the failings of human memory and the destructive power of time by two visual artists, Juliette and Marthe Vesque, who, during the previous century, devoted their lives to graphically hold the temporal flow, so to speak, in order to preserve circus acts in the archaeological record of their present.

The purpose of this section is to offer a verbal copy of Alex Lacey's lion and tiger act as it was presented on September 10, 2011, in Ulm (Germany) as a part of the program of Zirkus Charles Knie. This account is based on three successive viewings of the act.

As the intermission is drawing to a close, the spectators walk back to their seats. The show was almost sold out. Only a few rows in the cheapest section are left unoccupied. The audience has appreciated the first part and has honored with standing ovations the young equilibrist René Sperlich and the Columbian flying trapeze troupe which concluded their act with a perfectly executed triple somersault. During the intermission, the steel arena was constructed and as the public trickles in they can see a man adjusting the distance and testing the stability of the stools which now furnish the ring. This is Alex Lacey, the trainer we have met earlier in this chapter, who makes sure that everything is safely in place. His costume is hidden under a circus worker's overall. In the dimmed light, a woman, his wife, walks along the circular path along which he will move during the act and picks up pebbles and small pieces of wood in the sawdust, which could cause him to trip or could distract the animals. The audience is now seated and becomes silent in anticipation of the act. As a lion and five lionesses enter the cage and start playing, Alex rushes from the wing, quickly crosses himself in the penumbra, and makes his entrance as the spotlights flood the ring. With a charismatic smile and welcoming gesture toward the public, he prompts the lions to climb on their stools. Then, three tigers join the group and reach their own stools among the lions. Finally, a fourth tiger arrives and slowly takes its place at a distance from the others.

The pace accelerates. Alex walks briskly as he drives the male lion toward the top of the pyramid of pedestals which is constructed opposite to the line of stools across the ring. Two tigers take places on each side of the lion, then two lionesses, thus forming a symmetrical pattern in which lions and tiger alternate. This is a compositional principle we will observe several times as the act unfolds. Now Alex calls the other animals to the five pedestals which are aligned in front of the pyramid. Three lionesses occupy the central ones and two tigers climb on the lateral ones. They all raise their bodies and put their paws up. By voice and gesture, Alex holds all of them in this position, thus forming a complex tableau using the contrasts in the appearance of the two species to introduce a chromatic order within the symmetry itself. For a brief while, the tumultuous chaos of play has been transformed into a stable architectural design until the trainer signals to the animals that they can return to their respective stools.

As the music changes its rhythm, Alex piles up some central pedestals on the side of the ring and quickly builds a new configuration of stools across its diameter. It is clear that the lower and taller pedestals, on each side of a gap in the middle of which stands a higher obstacle, are intended for a display of jumps. Soon four lionesses twice clear the distance in turn with impressive "flights" while holding their tails up.

In no time, the pedestals are removed and the arena becomes an open space. Alex takes off his jacket which is caught by an attendant outside the cage. The four tigers are lined up side by side and using his long rod as a conductor's baton the trainer makes them roll over several times in each direction. Then, they rise up and stay like that with their paws up until he sends them back to their seats. He moves toward the fourth one which stands on the last stool on his left and prompts it to rise and cross the ring on its hind legs as he runs backward in front of it at a close distance. Alex gestures to the audience encouraging them to clap their hands for the tiger thus giving credit to the animal for having perfectly performed this difficult trick.

With a small piece of meat, Alex entices the lion (Masai) to come and stand still, facing him, in front of the pyramid. He then calls a tiger which jumps back and forth above the lion ten times. This tiger eventually stops jumping and stands parallel to the left side of the lion at a distance. Another tiger is called from its stool and clears the standing tiger and lion with an impressive jump. Now, with energetic vocal and gesture prompting, Alex makes the two tigers face each other and put their front paws on the back of the lion. Again, a stable pyramid emerges from a fast succession of moves as the three animals are frozen in this position while the audience expresses their appreciation for the complexity of this trick and the apparent ease with which it was achieved. After the tigers have returned to their stools, Alex pets and kisses the lion and sends it back to its place.

Before the act started, nine flat metal squares were lined up across the ring. They are regularly spaced. They now have the function of place markers for the animals

Dancing with Tigers, Lying with Lions 135

Figure 8.11 With the male lion at the center, and tigers and lionesses alternating on each side, Alex makes an elegant gesture toward the audience to direct their applause to the performing animals. (Photo Credit: Zbigniew Roguszka)

Figure 8.12 At the end of this synchronized display Alex thanks his lion with a kiss. (Photo Credit: Zbigniew Roguszka)

which Alex brings one at a time in front of them first by making them lie down through dragging his whip and rod in front of them, then by making them sit on the squares. The process causes much roaring and growling with swiping of the paws as he gets closer to them to prompt them to advance toward him. They also come somewhat too close to each other for feline comfort. Once again, the male lion, Masai, is at the center and on both of its sides tigers and lionesses alternate forming a symmetrically organized, albeit noisy line. It is the stage in the act when the tension between the natural biological behavior of the animals and the esthetic constraints imposed by the trainer as an artist comes to the fore. There is no obvious coercion, though, as Alex takes risks by prompting the felines to advance toward him: he actually acts as a decoy by offering himself as a prey easy to catch and quickly withdrawing as soon as they have moved forward to the spot where he wants them to be for the line to be perfect. He now endeavors to make them rise up, standing on their backsides and raising their paws above their heads. They all hold this position which exposes their white- or light-colored bellies. Then Alex runs around the line up, causing them to turn toward him, and prompts them to rise again facing the other direction. Finally, running around the line a second time, they are now oriented anew toward the back of the cage. The animals are sent to their den one after the other. Suddenly, the last lioness on the row rushes toward him as if she was spontaneously attacking. He has actually provoked her by getting too close but now he has to run backward and fight back. The music stops. A tense situation develops as he lets her drive him right against the bars of the cage. He shouts her name to call her to order but she attacks again: *Stella! Stella! Platz!* (Stella, go to your place!) The trainer then takes a microphone and asks the audience: "Are you scared?" Most reply "Yes"! But some voices are overheard saying "No!" "Ah! You are not scared? Then, come here!" Alex retorts. A big laugh ripples through the public. After another bout of fighting, Stella eventually withdraws as the trainer advances toward her waging his finger as if he were reprimanding an unruly child. She stops in front of her place holder and, as she shows signs of needing to rest, Alex utters: *Sitzen* (sit down), an order which nicely coincides with her sitting down. Then, Stella leaves the cage through the tunnel without further ado.

Another lioness moves calmly ahead and lies down on her back, offering her belly to be scratched. Alex kneels down next to her and pets her before letting her go.

Three tigers remain in the ring which has now been cleared of all the lions. Two of them are called and made to sit at equal distance from each other and from the trainer. Alex makes a brief pause, obviously concentrating and gathering his energy. He suddenly directs a vigorous impulsion with his two arms toward them. They rise on their hind legs and walk fast or hop in synchrony with Alex, making a circle as if the three were dancing.

After their exit, a globe topped with a platform is hauled down from above. The last tiger ascends the pedestals and takes an upright position on the high platform as the apparatus revolves under the spotlights casting around a flow of multiple reflections from the mirror-studded sphere, an apotheosis which concludes the cage act. The tiger leaves the ring and Alex makes his bow to the audience.

Dancing with Tigers, Lying with Lions 137

Figure 8.13 As the act is winding down, lioness Bella stops on her way out of the ring and lies in front of Alex who kneels down to pet her. (Photo Credit: Zbigniew Roguszka)

Figure 8.14 As Alex scratches her back, Bella raises her head in expectation of a kiss. (Photo Credit: Zbigniew Roguszka)

Figure 8.15 Dancing with the tigers. (Photo Credit: Zbigniew Roguszka)

Figure 8.16 Having prompted two tigers to rise on their hind legs, Alex joins them in a round as the three keep hopping along a full circle. (Photo Credit: Zbigniew Roguszka)

A work of art

The verbal rendering of Alexander Lacey's cage act provides us with a ground to reflect upon the artistic construction and implementation of this work aimed at creating an esthetic impression on the public whenever it is performed. Because of the emotional path which drives the attention of the audience from one event to the other, it is difficult to be fully cognizant of all the subtleties of this act while it is experienced in real time. However, the spectators process this structured flow of multimodal information and their mass response, which can be comparatively evaluated from the volume and duration of their applauses, indicates that the performance of this act achieves its purpose. But beyond the immediate reactions of a particular audience in a particular city, there are objective measures of the success of a circus act: the degree with which it is highlighted in the advertisement of the show; the length of time during which it remains a part of the program offered by the circus company which has contracted it; its regular presence in festivals; and the status of the circuses which can afford the price it commands. From these various points of view, Alexander Lacey's act ranks among the highest. We will see in this section that there are good reasons for this.

Keeping in mind that the successive actions which compose this act are based on the natural behavior of the two species involved (*Panthera leo* and *Panthera tigris*), we can see that in each segment the trainer creates a situation which elicits one or several of these biological patterns of interaction. As we mentioned earlier, when we were witnessing the training sessions, these natural elements include affiliative behavior (e.g. mutual contacts through rubbing cheeks, nose to nose touching, scratching, and playing); multiple spatial modalities of the fight or flee reflex (e.g. moving forward and backward, displacing and being displaced, holding one's ground, and defending territorial space); exploring and patrolling (e.g. climbing on elevated places, jumping from one to the other, raising one's body to reach a prey or an object of interest); social interactions within the species (e.g. flashing the white tuffs of one's ears as a warning signal, rolling over as a sign of submission, and rising on one's hind legs to defy or bluff a rival by making oneself to appear bigger or to reveal one's full size); all these tactile and visual moves are complemented by acoustic signals which vary from affiliative softness (e.g. "pfrrr" among related tigers) to the high decibels of the male lions' roaring and sawing. Some of these patterns of behavior have been highly ritualized as a natural evolutionary process but some combinations of them can be further ritualized as a result of training which creates routines based on habits. In this sense, it can be claimed that a cage act represents the emergence of an elementary microculture between humans and animals. They have mutual knowledge of each other's individuality and they communicate through signs whose values have been forged by social experience. They can symbolically express their mutual liking or disliking and they have learned the limits they cannot transgress during their interactions.

With all this in mind, let us take a second look at the cage act which was described in the preceding section of this chapter. The spectators' attention is captured and entrained in a constant dynamic flow as the successive tricks are performed at a quick tempo with only brief pauses which are timed so that they do not break the overall rhythm of this complex cage act. The verbal copy in the preceding section attempted to convey this sense of continuous development by not numbering the successive parts. But from the point of view of the trainer and, to a certain extent, of the animals, there are twelve distinct episodes, each one being supported by a plan involving two or more agents. This forms the score which Alex follows with precision because anything that would not be anticipated by his charges could cause a dangerous disruption. Whenever something unexpected happens such as a tiger leaving its stool out of turn, or a lioness jumping on the wrong pedestal, the "discourse" is repaired: Alex brings back the animals to their point of departure and again starts the cueing from the beginning of the particular routine.

Two preliminary remarks are in order. First, let us notice that the trainer is a young man in his early thirties, slim and athletic, endowed with an engaging personality and beaming charismatic smiles when he is not intensely focusing on his animals with an expression which never shows anger or repression. His gestures toward them are elegant and his steps in the cage are quick and proportionate to the narrow space available and to the movements of the wild cats. He adjusts his pace depending on the species with which he is dealing from moment to moment, faster with the light lionesses than with the heavier male lion. Tigers generally command a slower approach. As from a distance there is no obvious sexual dimorphism in *Panthera tigris* except of course in the expert's eye, we can refer to the tigers collectively but it is relevant to distinguish the maleness in *Panthera leo* which is marked by an abundant blackish mane. We thus take the spectators' point of view.

Secondly, Alex's ring costume is monochrome and functional, closer to a dancer's tight outfit than the gaudily decorated garment which some wild-animal trainers often prefer. The range of colors he uses—circus performers always have several costumes they alternate—harmonizes well with his animals' and enhances their natural beauty. The music contributes to blending the actions without distracting the audience with popular melodies.

Let us now review the 12 episodes which can be identified while commenting on their relevance to the construction of the meaning which the multimodal discourse of the act as a whole conveys to the audience.

1. The trainer asserts his control by bringing order to the initial chaos of the playing lions, then bringing the tigers to their respective stools.
2. This order is broken to create another stable but more complex configuration: the pyramid, a symmetrical design in which lions and tigers alternate or are embedded within each other's group. This concludes with a return of all the animals to their initial places.
3. Four lionesses now come to center stage by performing several long jumps from pedestal to pedestal above an obstacle.
4. Once the central area has been cleared of the pedestals, four tigers perform simultaneous rollovers in one direction, then in the other, several times. We notice that while (1) and (2) involved all the animals, (3) and (4) apply each to a subgroup of the two species comprising the same number of animals.
5. A tiger is singled out to walk on its hind legs across the whole diameter of the cage.

6. The male lion now becomes the focus of attention with the first instance of physical contact with the trainer, including a kiss, and it is driven to the spot, in front of the pyramid, where the next trick is going to take place.
7. Both species are involved in this trick which demonstrates an advanced and unusual degree of training: a tiger jumps ten times back and forth over the lion which stands still in front of Alex. This tiger takes his place beside the lion at a distance and a second tiger comes over and makes a long single jump over the two animals. Then both tigers walk toward the lion and put their front paws on the back of the lion, thus forming a new pyramid, a close, tactile symmetry involving the two species. They hold the pause quite a while, facing the trainer, before he sends them to their respective stools.
8. Nine animals are aligned side by side across the ring with the lion in the center and tigers alternating with lionesses on both sides. Three times in succession they are all made to raise their body, then come down and change direction to repeat this exercise.
9. One of the lionesses mounts an attack and forces Alex to run backward. She is then pushed back to her initial place, and is verbally ordered to sit down, and it complies. It is interesting to note that this episode is embedded in the act as a quotation of the old style of cage act. It is construed both as a personal tiff between the two as Alex clearly calls her by her name, Stella. He uses social gestures during the interaction which mean something like: "What is the matter with you?," and eventually solves the issue by a simple verbal command. Furthermore, this episode is dedramatized by a bout of comedy when the trainer addresses the audience and asks them if they are scared with the punch line inviting those who claimed they were not to join him in the steel arena.
10. The tension generated by the fight with Stella is completely defused in the following episode when a lioness on its way to the exit lies down in front of Alex who kneels down and scratches her belly before kissing her.
11. All the animals have left the ring except three tigers. Two of them are called and take position at equal distance from each other and in front of the trainer. Once they are settled in the upright posture, Alex prompts them to rise on their hind legs and walk with him in a circle as if the three of them were dancing around. This figure achieves a high degree of humanization of the animal irrespective of the fact that the raised position among tigers is an aggressive behavior as we noted earlier but which is also observed in play among young animals. This episode is the apex of the act not only because of the sophistication of the training which made it possible but also, and not contradictorily, because of the symbol of harmony it embodies since dancing together is a universal way of expressing sociality. It is also obvious, upon reflection, that no amount of brutal coercion could have obtained such a ritualized result.
12. The last move is the construction of an apotheosis for a single animal, here a tiger in the act which was observed in Ulm. But ultimately it will be the lion Masai which is still being trained as we witnessed in the training session we observed and which was described in detail earlier. An animal standing upright on a revolving platform is spectacular, mainly with the visual effect produced by

the mirror-studded globe. However, this trick requires competent rather than exceptional training. We can perceive the rhetoric which constrains the form of this conclusion: on the one hand, the lion will have seen his preeminence continuously constructed by the intimate behavior of the trainer toward him and by the central position he occupies in all the configurations. In the final version of the act, his triumphal place at the very top of the globe will correspond to his standing at the summit of the pyramid at the beginning of the act but with an amplification of the height and decorum. The use of the personal masculine pronoun in this case is justified by the fact that Masai has been redundantly personalized through the display of his personal relationship with Alex. In addition, lions are more expressive than tigers as we noted in "The poetics and rhetoric of the cage act" section in this chapter. This young lion responds to Alex's tactile contacts with facial and gestural behavior which the audience can relate to because they are better visible than the enigmatic face of tigers, and are somewhat similar to the behavior of dogs interacting with humans. The triumph of Masai is (or rather will be) a consistent conclusion to this cage act which features this splendid lion as the star.

The poetics at work in the conception and implementation of this cage act is now obvious. Great care is brought to the visual compositions of the collective configurations in which tigers and lions alternate like in segments (1) and (8) or achieve more complex symmetry like in segment (2) with two tigers inserted among three lions on the pyramid and three lions framed by two tigers on the pedestals which are placed in front of the pyramid. The odd number of animals allows a special central position for Masai in all cases as it always has an equal number of animals on each side. Another esthetic feature is the alternation between collective episodes and segments involving subsets from the animals: first, four lionesses (3); then, four tigers (4); and eventually a mixed group of two tigers and a lion, the latter being again in the central position (7). We also observe a progressive reduction of the number of animals leading to solo performances such as the upright walk of a tiger (5), the kissing of Masai (6), the argument with Stella (9), and the petting of another lioness (10). Finally, the dance with the tigers (11) and the triumph of the lion Masai (or the tiger) on the revolving globe which mimics the cosmic depth of a starry night (12) brings the act to its conclusion with two powerful visual metaphors conveying a sense of the accession of these animals to human culture through peaceful fusion rather than domination. The rhetoric of this multimodal discourse has followed a progression toward more information with respect to the circus tradition of cage acts from the expected initial pyramid, a visual metaphor which asserts with more or less brio the capacity of the trainer to control natural chaos by imposing an architectural order, to the "dance with the tigers," an outstanding achievement by the trainer, probably never done before, which dynamically translates a biological behavior into a cultural metaphor of sociality. In this clockwise movement of three equidistant actors, any apparent hierarchy dissolves although this ritualized behavior involves the fight or flee reflexes since one of the tigers advances forward while the other one withdraws as the man runs toward it. But there is more: the civilizing process which this act symbolizes succeeds in peacefully integrating two different species into an orderly narrative, once again evoking through this metaphor the goal of forging a global civil order from the fragmentation of ethnic and cultural diversity. This cage act progressed from the geometry of straight lines and angles which generated the pyramids, the alignments, and the diametric crossing of the ring to the legendary perfection of the circle and the sphere which inspired its conclusion.

9

Clowns at Work: A Sociocritical Discourse

Clowns unmasked

Clowns are a major component of circus spectacles. Their function is to make the audience laugh. They engage in multimodal dialogues through words, gestures, music, and noises of various kinds. A superficial approach to their antics is that they mostly rely on slapstick comedy and provocative transgressions of the social norms which prevail in the population. This chapter will offer a different perspective on the nature of their art. We will see that their language—in the sense in which we used the expression "language of the horse" in Chapter 5—articulates social and cultural contents and addresses sensitive political and ideological issues under the guise of jokes.

Traditional circus clowns wear masks in the form of heavy makeup, artificial noses, wigs, and other transformative props which hide their civil identities behind their circus personae and make them unrecognizable. Their costumes are equally designed to set them apart from the clothing norms of their time. In the traditional stereotypes which have emerged in Europe during the nineteenth century, circus clowns come in pairs: an elegant whiteface character dressed in a glittering, precious looking garment and a scruffy tramplike, ill-mannered partner with a gaudy garb which is either too large or too tight, and oversized shoes. In previous works, I have shown that they embody the opposition between the lowest commoners who are close to a state of nature and the upper social elites who epitomize highbrow culture (Bouissac 1976a: 151–75; 2010: 103–19). The short comedies which they perform generally enact conflicts and their resolutions. The apparently trivial nature of their bickering hides but does not defuse the seriousness of their antics which, most of the time, touch sensitive ideological nerves, so to speak, of the society in which they perform and where they live. Like the typical hat of the medieval fool, their mask and disguise make their transgressive behavior immune to prosecution and retaliation because their appearance positions them outside the social grid. They are in a way already symbolically excluded or ostracized. Their stage names exhaust all that they are. Clowns exist only in the ring. Whenever they appear outside, they insert a fragment of circus space within the fabric of everyday life. They are not like theater and movie actors who interpret various dramatic characters over a period of time and preserve a civil and public identity, often as celebrities. The mode of social existence of clowns as performers can be explained by the fact that the nineteenth-century clowns who emerged from the circus and Commedia dell' Arte traditions were under the constraints of strict censorship. Popular entertainments were closely watched in Europe by governments wary of potential subversion. The well-documented history of Cirque Fernando, a popular place in the margins of Paris during the second half of the nineteenth century, shows that spoken and sung sketches had to be vouched by the authorities (Remy 1979). This situation has changed only to a certain extent nowadays, an aspect of circus performances we will examine later in Chapter 11 when we consider the use of the circus as a tool for political and cultural activism.

The contemporary circus preserves the nineteenth-century tradition of contrasted pairs of clowns, sometimes as a nostalgic gesture. Some of these clowns have renewed their repertory of short comedies, called "entrees" in the trade's jargon, but most keep recycling the classics of the genre with more or less original twists in their interpretations. In this chapter, we will probe other forms of circus clowning. With the lessening of moral and political censorship and the bright lighting of the performance space, heavy makeup is much less necessary than it was. Today's circuses feature in the ring some comedians who do away with the paraphernalia of the tradition. However, the more subtle makeup they use, the facial expressions they display, and the common outfits they don perpetuate the same fundamental social opposition which was redundantly embodied in the traditional pairs.

September 2007. The Swiss National Circus Knie has pitched its tent for three days not far from Zurich. I arrive in time to catch the evening show as the performance was just starting. In what seems to be the preparation for an act to come, a tall man dressed in a formal dark suit brings what appears to be a large wooden plank, throws it on the ground in the center of the ring, utters an order, and makes an imperative gesture toward a smaller, meek character who wears a workman-outfit. I cannot understand what is said—they speak in the local German dialect—but it is obvious that the tall man is a director of sort and the other an employee. The "plank" is actually a bench with collapsible metal legs which are folded and the order obviously is to make the bench stand for whatever purpose this may be. The worker looks puzzled, hesitates, and makes an interrogative gesture while asking how to proceed. The boss shows impatience, gives further explanations, and bends down to demonstratively touch the metallic frame which has to be pulled. But exactly what to pull and in which direction is not clear to the employee who increasingly looks helpless. The director has no choice but to demonstrate how to do this and very easily makes the legs stick out on one of the sides. The employee scrutinizes intently the legs with an expression of wonderment, approximately repeating the gesture of pulling up in the air. Now the other side has to be done but how to approach it and pull up the other legs in the reverse direction is problematic. Without stopping to give angry explanations as time is short and the job has to be completed fast, the boss again demonstrates how to do it. Now that the collapsible legs are sticking up, the bench must be put in place so that someone can sit on it. The same process continues for this new task and the director, obviously exasperated but eager to see the work done, shows how to place the bench on its legs under the gaze of the puzzled employee who is impassibly standing in front of him. The work is done. The act is over. The audience gives a hearty laugh.

Why some people order other people to do what they could very well do themselves is a question which raises the issue of social inequality. The difference between the two characters that perform in this act is not a difference of technical competence but one of socioeconomic status. The task was so simple that anybody could do it in no time. This was not something that required the complementary competences of the members of a team. The portrayed situation reveals under the magnifying glass of a brief clown intermezzo the crude abuse of power based on status rather than merit. The social prestige of a directorial function carries the privilege of exploiting the muscular energy of the "little people" who are by necessity put in their service. The comedian who plays the director bears all the attributes which the audience can recognize, at least in part, in their employers at work or in the office: physical stature and self-confidence, expensive clothes, well-groomed appearance, poise and facility of elocution. His partner embodies the opposite of these properties: lower stature and resigned look, worker's uniform, restricted means of expression. Of course, these are caricatures and may conform more to the visual representations of these roles in cartoons than in actual individuals. But they express a truth which does not escape the attention of the popular audience of the circus. Reflecting upon the action which unfolds in this clown act brings to the fore that the underdog, through his passive resistance, has succeeded in reversing the initial situation since the bench has been set up, not by him but by the director himself who, in addition, carries his partner away at the end of this act.

In the same program, the Duo Lapsus—the circus name of these two comedians, also known on stage and on television as (Viktor) Giacobbo and (Mike) Muller—further develops the sociosemiotic transformation which was presented in a minimal format in their opening sketch. Following a horse act, Muller, behaving like an authoritarian director, enters the rings shouting orders and brandishing a long equestrian whip. He wears the same formal suit as earlier. The curtain opens to let in a motorized yellow excavator manned by his sidekick who sports at the top of his construction-worker helmet a colorful plume like the ones which traditionally decorate liberty horses. The shape of the excavator vaguely evokes the silhouette of a horse with the shovel representing the head and the telescopic extension resembling a long neck. Although Giacobbo as the driver of the excavator is in the position of a jockey, his identity is merged at first with the mechanical horse since he wears the feathers on his head and lifts a leg when Muller orders him to do so as if he were a trained horse. Indeed, Muller rewards him with a sweet which he places in his mouth every time Giacobbo performs what is supposed to be a horse trick. Quickly, though, the "horse" starts asking for a reward more often by opening his mouth toward his trainer until he demands rewards even before performing tricks. The pace accelerates and the driver suddenly shifts to the position and behavior of a jockey. He now takes command and leads the action. When Muller confronts him back in an attempt to regain control, Giacobbo lifts him in the shovel, and exits carrying him this way.

Once again the initial situation posits the dissymmetry between an employer and an employee. This relation is expressed through the visual metaphor of a trainer and his horse. The use of a modern excavator makes explicit the industrial theme which invites the audience to generalize the comedy beyond the ring to real-life situations. The overlapping is constructed by the brutal symbolic assimilation of a construction worker to a circus horse who works for a few titbits of food. This is achieved visually not only by creating the hybrid sign of the helmet from which the plume sticks out, but also by the gestures of Muller who, dressed as a chief executive officer, mimics the behavior of a master equestrian. It is obvious, though, that the driver of the excavator actually holds the real power since he commands the machine. When he ignores orders and takes control, that is, switches from the position of the horse to the position of the jockey, the master is powerless. In fact, the latter is treated like dirt since he is carried away in the shovel. His power was illusory.

Circus acts unfold fast in the ring. Audiences have no time to reflect and analyze, let alone verbalize what they see. But information is nevertheless processed cognitively and emotionally. The signs are not ambiguous. Laughter does not signal the perception of just someone tripping on the ground or being carried away by an excavator but of who is falling or who is taken away in a shovel. This short comic act achieves through the symbolic discourse of the circus the same effect as those which happen in cultural and political revolutions, at least when violence remains on the semiotic level. During the May 1968 student uprising in France, as a prominent university professor was trying to reason with the students who had occupied a lecture hall, one of the students forced an empty wastepaper basket on his head. There was laughter in the assembly. Like Muller in the mechanical shovel, the words of the official academic were symbolically reduced to garbage. More examples could be adduced to show how tenuous the line is between clowning and sociocultural subversion. In the next section of this chapter we will follow in detail the complex ideological subtext of a full-fledged traditional clown act in modern garb.

Clowns at work

Charlie Cairoli (1910–80) was a clown who had been trained by his father in the European tradition. The father, Jean-Marie Cairoli, was a prominent whiteface clown who used his son as the sidekick, the "Auguste" of the pair. Shortly before World War II, they were hired by the Tower Circus. After his father died, Charlie remained in Blackpool where he became the resident clown of this prestigious circus which is built inside the four-leg base of this diminutive Eiffel Tower. Until 1979, Charlie Cairoli produced new acts every year. Year after year, the audiences were mostly made up of regular visitors from industrial North-West England who came to this popular seashore resort for their brief summer holidays. The circus program, including the clown acts, had to be changed annually. Charlie Cairoli became a celebrity who was loved by his working-class public and beyond. For an ethnographer of the circus, this situation offered a unique opportunity to observe the creativity of a clown who, over a long period of time, remained relevant to socially consistent audience by constantly innovating within the tradition.

The clown act in the 1978 program started with an apparent accident: a circus attendant who was carrying props spilled a pail of paint on the table which was being hastily placed in the ring for the next act. Norman, the Ring Master, is upset as this is going to delay the beginning of the act. He looks for help when Charlie and two other men informally walk in from the secondary entrance opposite the main one through which the artists usually enter and leave the ring. One of the men pushes a wheelbarrow full of plaster (actually foam) with some plasterers' tools affixed to it. He is followed by another worker. They have just completed a job and they are going to enjoy their tea break. This sets the initial situation: a manager meets a team of workers at a moment of crisis.

We will now follow in detail the successive episodes which will bring this act to its conclusion. Besides Norman, the Ring Master, and Charlie Cairoli (Charlie), the cast includes two sidekicks, Jimmy and Charlie Cairoli, Junior. Two anonymous circus hands also play minor but significant parts. My early description of this act was elaborated in French from the cursory notes I took during two visits to Blackpool in 1978. I had been struck, and at first puzzled, by the overwhelming response that this act received from the audience. I eventually submitted my tentative description to Charlie Cairoli, himself a native French speaker, who kindly returned it to me with corrections and additions. In the text below which I translated into English, the italics signal Charlie Cairoli's insertions.

Under the direction of Norman, the attendants carry in the circus arena a table upon which a chair is standing. A pail of white paint has been left on the chair and when one of the attendants seizes the chair carelessly to put it on the floor the pail is overturned and the paint runs across the table and drips on the floor. *Supposedly someone has left by mistake a can on the chair. The can will prove later to be full of yellowish paint. When the boy seizes the chair to place it on the ground he let it tilt at a 45 degree angle and the paint spills on the table and drips to the floor. The public believes that it is an unexpected accident.*

Norman scolds the boy for his awkwardness and acts as if he were actually panicking at the sight of the situation which delays the clown act. *Actually only very few in the audience have bought a program and read it in advance. Most do not know that the next act is the clowns'. A table and a chair could make them anticipate that it is for an acrobatic act.* Norman looks for someone to clean the table and the floor in preparation for the act to come. The musicians, indeed, keep the suspense by playing softly the tune which indicates the transition time between acts.

Charlie, Junior, and Jimmy enter the ring. Their costumes and accessories show that they are a team of workers doing plastering and painting. Charlie wears a red helmet typical of construction workers, a light blue shirt, and gray trousers. He carries a pail in one hand and a tray full of foam /*supposed to be plaster*/ in the other. Junior and Jimmie have no helmet but are dressed in blue overalls. Junior carries three pails and Jimmy pushes a wheelbarrow full of white foam /*plaster*/ and several implements of the trade: brooms, sponges, shovels, and still another pail hanging from the side.

Norman rushes toward them and the following dialog takes place: "Charlie, have you finished your job?—Yes and I also fixed the wall with plaster.—Can you do me a *favor?—Sorry, I have no money.—No!* I mean clean up this mess.—No, you are too late. We are going for a drink. We are finished." Norman insists with an imploring tone of voice: "Please, Charlie, for old time's sake, do that for me!" Charlie is reluctant but eventually decides to ask the shop steward (Jimmie) if he can grant them permission to work a bit longer than the legal hours. They hesitate. *Then Norman states that the payment for this job will not be declared but will be made under the table. Under such conditions they immediately agree to help him.*

The three men walk toward the table and Charlie asks Norman: "How long do we have to get the job done?—About two minutes!" Norman, looking relieved, walks away. As the three men are close to the table, Charlie stops and says: "Shall we have a cup of tea?" But they decide to get to work first.

Charlie is now *standing with his back at about 2 meters from the table. He appears to be making some complex calculations with his fingers. He notices that Jimmie is staying motionless like a zombie watching the paint which is dripping from the table to the ground. "Stop looking at the paint! Clean up!" Jimmy suddenly starts sweeping the paint away with his hand but with such force that some paint reaches Charlie's pants. Charlie retaliates by hitting Jimmy on the head with the bottom of the plaster tray he holds in his hand. Charlie shouts: "Idiot! Get some water and a broom to do some good work!" Jimmy grabs a pail and without paying attention throws the water on the backside of Charlie. He then quickly takes the mop ready for action. Furious, Charlie seizes the mop and starts soaking up the foam which is on the floor. There is a very brief pause during which Charlie winks to the public which now anticipates why Charlie is so intently saturating the mop with that stuff.* Jimmy has stopped moving and stupidly looks at Charlie mopping the foam when suddenly Charlie slaps Jimmy's cheeks one after the other with the mop and plunges it within his pants from the front. *This latter gag is done only at certain performances depending on the reaction of the public.*

Junior who was holding Charlie's tray while the latter was busy mopping the water, gives it back, and catches the mop, indicating that he is going to do the same trick to Jimmy. Charlie takes a few steps with the tray of foam in his hand. Jimmy anticipates the blow from Junior and stoops in time to avoid being hit. The mop reaches Charlie instead and splashes his butt. This destabilizes Charlie who plunges his nose into the tray of foam he was holding in his hand.

This makes Jimmy laugh so much that he sits down on the chair which is at the end of the table. Charlie fetches a pail of water and places it at the other end. While Jimmy keeps laughing, Charlie slowly lifts a hinged plank from the table top (*as if it were a lose part because the public does not realize that this table has been engineered for this trick*) and the pail slides toward him, overturns, and soaks him in water.

Jimmy goes to the wheelbarrow and picks up the trowel which he garnishes with foam. He comes back toward Charlie, pulls the front of his pants and stuffs the foam inside.

This makes Junior laugh. He leans on the side of the table but the part upon which he tries to sit gives way as it is another hinged plank and he falls on the floor.

As Junior jumps to his feet, the plank suddenly springs up and pinches Charlie's fingers. Charlie shows pain and anger, fetches a pail and fills it up with foam. He chases Junior to throw the foam at him but Junior seeks refuge among the audience. Jimmy follows and encourages Charlie to go ahead. (*The pail has two compartments, one for* the real foam, the other filled with fluffy white cotton.) When Charlie eventually throws the contents of the pail toward Junior who is among the spectators, it is the cotton, not the foam, which falls on them.

The three men return to the center of the ring with the busy look of people who, at last, are getting serious about completing their job. Charlie takes his tray, puts some foam on it, and mixes it with the trowel as if it were plaster while Jimmy stares at it, fascinated by the movement which he follows with his head. Suddenly, Charlie wants to stick the tray of foam on Jimmy's face but the latter bends over and the foam lands on Junior's face.

Jimmy laughs and sits down on the chair which is now at the center of the arena. Junior fills a pail with foam and walks toward Jimmy from behind. He overturns the pail on Jimmy's head, pushes it down full length, and makes it rotate before taking it out slowly as if he were unmolding a cake.

Jimmy leaves the chair. Junior sits down on it and keeps laughing at Jimmy's foam-wrapped face. In the meantime, Charlie sneaks behind Junior and forcefully put on his head a black bowler hat full of foam. As there is a small hole in the top of the hat, the foam shoots up through the hole while the rest runs along his face.

Junior walks away from the chair and, as Charlie moves toward it to sit down, Jimmy takes the tray which is full of foam and sneakily places it on the chair. But the children in the audience shout warnings to Charlie in spite of Jimmy gesturing to them to keep quiet. When Charlie starts turning toward Jimmy, the latter quickly removes the tray and hides it behind his back but returns it to the same position as soon as Charlie does not look in that direction. As the children shout more loudly, Charlie walks toward the audience and lets a child whisper something in his ear. Charlie then watches Jimmy suspiciously and rushes toward him to check what he is hiding behind his back. Junior quickly catches the tray and Jimmy can demonstrate his innocence by showing that his hands are empty. As Charlie prepares to confidently sit down, Junior puts the tray back on the chair and Charlie heavily sits down in the mound of foam.

At this precise moment, the Ring Master Norman returns to the ring and is appalled at the situation he finds. He asks angrily: "But what is going on here?" He then summons a ring boy and orders him to clean up this mess fast. In no time the floor is mopped and the table dried to the obvious satisfaction of Norman who congratulates the boy and scolds Charlie and his colleagues: "Look! You see. This was simple! Five seconds. Everything is clean, even the boy! Look at yourselves!"

Charlie, Jimmy, and Junior rush toward the boy, lift him, and throw him in the wheelbarrow which is still full of foam. As he surges up all smeared in foam, they empty several pails of water on him. They all exit the ring covered with foam and dripping with water. Charlie is the last to leave and acknowledges with smiles and friendly gestures to the applause of the audience.

Syntax and semantics of chaos: Herbert Marcuse at the circus

Charlie Cairoli's act, which was performed toward the end of the 1978 program of the Blackpool Tower Circus, was particularly well received by the audience. There were many bursts of laughter coming from all members of the public, not from the children alone. The applause at the end was vigorous and sustained. The spectators were obviously engaged by this act and were making sense of the narrative which framed its numerous gags. However, when the same act was performed at the International Circus Festival of Monte Carlo, in January 1979, it was politely applauded and Charlie Cairoli who was expected to receive the first prize in view of his age and reputation, was granted the Silver Clown instead. The commentaries published in the press emphasized his reliance on slapstick comedy, thus implying that he somewhat lacked the profundity usually found in great clowns. In this section, we will analyze in detail the construction and performance of this act and we will show that its contents and staging were more attuned to the socioeconomic situation of Northern England than to the affluent audience of circus fans which flock to Monaco to attend this festival each year in January. This will provide us with an opportunity to discuss the relevance of the context for the production of meaning in performance.

Charlie Cairoli was not wearing a heavy, disfiguring makeup. When he enters the ring, the public recognizes immediately his familiar look and gait. His small, rounded red nose lends him an air of mischievous innocence. His eyebrows and mustache are blackened. His eyes and lips are circled by fine dark lines to enhance his smiles which he projects far, up to the last rows of spectators. In this act, he has traded his iconic bowler hat for a working man's helmet and his semiformal suit for a plasterer's outfit. But his latest avatar as a local proletarian lets his personality radiate. Likewise, his partners are dressed in clothes with which everybody in the audience is familiar. They have no makeup except for the touch of color which the glare of the spotlights makes necessary. Jimmy is phlegmatic, rather expressionless, like a dumb stooge should be. Junior is taller, younger, and ebullient. His face shows surprise, anger, pleasure at a rate as fast as the action requires. For the public, the three men embody characters who could be their neighbors or fellow workers. Toiling for a boss is a familiar situation for most of the audience. The work context evokes in England, particularly in the 1970s when the act was created, the advantages and constraints of the trade unions which regulate the relationship between employers and employees, a theme which comes quickly to the fore and remains the subtext of the narrative.

Indeed, the act starts with a professional mistake (the careless spilling of the paint), followed by a violation of the specialty of the workers (plasterers are required to do a cleaner's job) and the breaking of a law (undeclared payment made under the table). The power of the unions is played out at the outset of the act when Charlie asks the permission of the shop-steward (Jimmy) before agreeing to transgress the union's rules: working outside the legal hours; not respecting the workers' right to a tea break; doing the job of another specialty than theirs; and accepting bribe money. Once this dramatic step has been taken, everything gets out of hand.

However, the chaos which is ushered in is scripted with great precision. It is in this sense that we can describe its syntax, that is, the formal organization through which meaning is expressed. Two effects will now be examined in turn: first, the team is transformed into its inverse since instead of engaging in complementary tasks the individuals act against each other; secondly, instead of cleaning they produce dirt and increase the problem they were supposed to solve.

This act is structured in three parts: (1) an introduction which defines the situation and introduces the actors; (2) a succession of mutual aggressions among the team; (3) a conclusion. If we take an abstract look at the gags which form the main part, we notice that they all belong to the same paradigm: an agent aggresses intentionally a victim who does not expect it. Furthermore, the aggressions come in the form of a liquid or semiliquid which is thrown at, or applied to a part of the victim's body. Various props mediate the actions (pails, tray, mop, table, wheelbarrow) but this does not alter the basic formula. The whole sequence could be expressed in algebraic form with the actors A, B, and C who are in turn agent and patient, the variables being either foam or water, and whether the upper part of the body (the face) or its lower part (front or back) are soiled. Thus the main part of the act can be expressed as a series of antagonistic relations among the actors. It is noteworthy that two episodes of this central part of the act involve the audience: first as a potential victim when Charlie, who is chasing Junior, throws a pail of foam, which is actually a decoy, toward them; secondly, when he makes alliance with the children who warn him of a forthcoming attack as Jimmy conspires with Junior to place the tray on the chair. Thus, before the MC returns to restore law and order, the chaos threatens to spill over in the public.

If we scrutinize the development of the action, using a simple system of notation as a heuristic device, we uncover a progressive complexity in the syntax: the first segments are made up of straightforward aggressions: Jimmy splashing involuntarily Charlie's pants with paint triggers the deliberate retaliation of the victim, and so on. Progressively, the attacks are mediated and involve cascades of unpredictable moves. Finally, alliances form between two agents against a third one. However, we discover that there is a perfect circularity or reciprocity if we compute the number of times each actor is the object of, or initiates an aggression. Charlie remains the focus of the act since he is involved as many times, as aggressor or aggressed, as his two partners together. The chaos is well distributed and patterned.

Engaging in such an analysis is in fact a kind of semiotic reversed engineering because it essentially consists of reconstructing the very script which the actors follow and which has been crafted by its creator, namely Charlie Cairoli. Before being presented in the ring, this act, as all clown acts, had been rehearsed, tested, adjusted, and timed so that it would fit the program and meet with the director's approval. Clown acts are scribbled like musical scores either on paper or recorded in the actors' memory. In this act, there was a definite concern for a rhetorical progression toward an increased integration of all the actors who moved from a one-to-one game of retaliation to more complex configurations of alliance and conspiracy. All the moves and the magnitude of the attacks, though, were logically justified by what preceded them until the three clowns join force against the "good worker," a thought-provoking action which we will discuss now.

The second aspect of the clowns' actions which commands attention is the fact that they mess up the ring and themselves instead of cleaning up the small amount of paint which had been spilled. They produce dirt instead of making it disappear. But it is not any kind of dirt. They use liquid and semiliquid material. It is also noteworthy that they do not smear any part of the body indiscriminately. The targets are the face—that is, the region where food and drink are ingested—and either the bottom or the lower abdomen—that is, the areas where excretions take place. The latter's relevance is indeed so much the focus of attention and the explicit butt of the prank that, in his written comments on the text of my first tentative description, Charlie Cairoli indicated that the wetting of Jimmy's pants from the front with the mop was omitted when he felt that the audience might consider this to be too crude and in bad taste. Obviously water and foam are metaphors both for drink and food, and for urine and feces. The collapse of social order which is staged in this clown act through the transformation of a team into its inverse is consistent with a represented regression to a state of nature in which, like children before they become integrated into society, feeding and excreting is messy and undisciplined.

Let us turn now to the conclusion of the act. The "good worker" is congratulated by his employer but the three clowns seize him and immerse him into the foam. Then, they soak him with water. This action can be perceived as an instinctive retaliation although it is not clear what he is guilty of. Can we assume that he did not belong to any trade union? But the three plasterers were the first to break the union rules. He accomplished exactly what he was ordered to do and he did that in time. He complied with the desire of his employer who congratulated him. However, the audience reacted positively with approving laughter when the young man was plunged in the wheelbarrow, then splashed with several pails of water. He ended up in a much worse condition than the "bad workers" who had subverted the system to the point of putting it upside down or inside out. Is there a lesson to be read into this unexpected conclusion? The least we can say is that, to put it mildly, the work ethic is questioned in a narrative which staged a crisis set in the context of an industrial region of England. To my knowledge, Charlie Cairoli was not familiar with the writings of the Frankfurt School. The name of Herbert Marcuse was unknown to him. He was, though, exquisitely attuned to his working-class audience. His clown acts were not created lightly as a great deal of thinking was involved in devising ways of making classical gags relevant to the public of the Blackpool Tower Circus. The objective result of the drama which unfolded in 1978 in the ring was remarkably similar to one of the radical theses of Marcuse who claimed that the workers are always the big losers, whether or not they accomplish their work conscientiously. The work ethic in the service of consumerism (working better and more in order to earn more in order to buy more goods) is an illusion which contributes to further enslaving the workers to the capitalists (1964). Whatever the inspiration, the logic which was driving the orchestrated chaos in the circus arena was to make a mockery of the system which ruled the socioeconomic context. Its cathartic value should be obvious. Its subversive power was not negligible.

Power of the mask

Mister Charlie Cairoli in the street had the look of an ordinary citizen, a kind of typical Mediterranean man, with a prominent nose, a serious expression, and a rounded belly. He was always leading the way with decisive authority. At home, dinner was served to him first as the head of the family. In conversation with his guests, he was affable, even charming. He must have been, though, a tough negotiator when the terms of a contract were discussed with the entertainment companies which hired him. As a movie actor, he could have impersonated police inspectors or Sicilian godfathers, harsh fathers or heroic cavalry officers. When Charlie Cairoli the clown entered the ring he radiated benevolence and childish happiness. Although his makeup was comparatively very light, his persona was transformed to embody a mischievous avuncular figure which could get away with murder. Let us try to retrace the steps through which every day before the show he was achieving this metamorphosis with a few touch of white, red, and black which he carefully added on his face.

The photograph which he used as a logo on his stationery offers a clear view of the results of his transformative craft. In human interactions, eyes are the prime focus of attention. We can contract the muscles which circle our orbits to reduce the opening of the lids, frown, or, on the contrary, retract our lids and protrude our eyeballs. We do the latter when we express surprise or claim innocence. In this facial pattern, the pupil forms a strong contrast with the sclera, the white background of the eyes, and the direction of the glance can be accurately assessed. Charlie drew a fine black line around his eyes to enhance this contrast. In this picture, he produces a submissive and seductive expression with the pupils drawn to the upper region of the sclera while the head is tilted down and sideway. The red ball which he has added to his natural nose defuses all sign of authority and aggression usually carried forth by a prominent nasal appendix. The bowler hat contributes to foreground the roundness as opposed to angularity of his head, morphology typical of a baby's facial features which are also found in very young animals. If we draw a line from the tip of his chin to the top of his hat and mark the exact middle of the line, we will notice that this midpoint corresponds to the level of his eyes. This is a constant characteristic of the face of infants, kittens, puppies, and other neonate mammals. It has sometimes been claimed that these particular facial proportions trigger protective feelings on the part of adults. In grown-up humans, the forehead generally becomes less prominent and recedes while the eye line tends to move up in the upper area of the face.

The mouth is the object of great attention because it is the source of smiles which project far around the circus ring a nonaggressive attitude and a feeling of happiness. These kinds of smiles are characterized by the half-circular white pattern of the upper teeth which is revealed when the corners of the lips are symmetrically drawn up and the lower teeth are hidden by the lower lip. We can notice that Charlie's lower lip has been whitened and that this enlarged smiling white pattern has been circled with a black line with the result of freezing on his face a quasipermanent expression of pleasure and joy. We have to remember that circus makeup is by necessity cruder than other kinds of cosmetic grooming. The face of a clown and the emotions it expresses must be identified from a distance. It cannot be too subtle but it must be effective. The two strokes forming the mustache further underline the chromatic contrast which make the smiles very visible from various angles, an important consideration given that the audience encircles the performer.

Finally, let us take a look at the eyebrows. Extensive research, notably by Paul Ekman and by Irenaus Eibl-Eibesfeldt, has shown that a very fast rising and lowering of the eyebrows—a facial gesture which lasts only a fraction of a second—is a spontaneous signal of positive feeling toward someone, an affinitive sign which

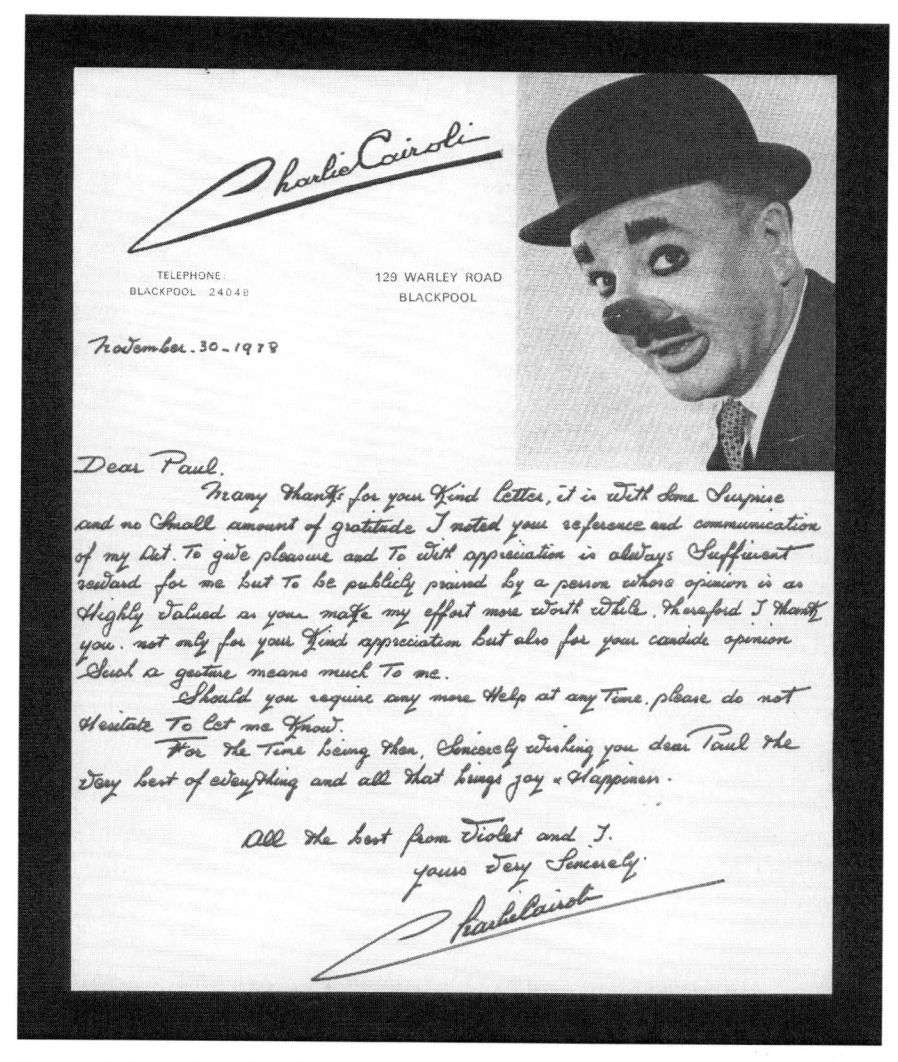

Figure 9.1 Letter from Charlie Cairoli to the author (November 30, 1978).

betrays our true attitude as it is produced as a reflex rather than a deliberate muscular contraction. Since it is the natural eyebrows of Charlie which are enlarged and enhanced, nobody in the public can miss his friendly flashes.

Reviewing item by item the modifications brought to the natural face by the makeup should not make us forget that what is relevant is not the individual changes made here and there but the whole pattern which is thus created and its dynamic use during the interactions between the clown and the spectators. When performing, Charlie Cairoli was constantly addressing the audience with glances, winks, smiles, and gestures while he was conducting whatever dialogues and actions with his partners in the ring as the script of the act unfolded.

The difference between makeup and mask is only a matter of degree. Charlie Cairoli belonged to a generation who started to emancipate itself from the constraints of a tradition which had established the whiteface clown as the center of attention and the main protagonist of the comedy while his partner was the butt of the jokes. A second partner was sometimes added to the team. Charlie's father was such a powerful whiteface clown who long used Charlie, under the name of Carletto, as his second sidekick. When Charlie inherited the mantle, he quickly reduced the role of the whiteface clown and soon became the main protagonist of the act he created. His persona emerged as a loveable clown who did not frighten children but made both them and their parent laugh, although at times for quite different reasons. His outfit was not exotic any longer as he adopted the bowler hat and jacket of a British gentleman with a dose of an expectable eccentricity. As we have seen in the act which was described earlier, he could also don the garb of a local proletarian and remain at the same time the Charlie Cairoli who had entertained several generations of Blackpool vacationers as well as visitors from afar. His mask of innocence was lending him the immunity he needed to break taboos and mock the rules while straddling the fine line that runs between order and chaos. This general program, though, is not the explicit purpose of clowns who create or interpret dramatic narrative, and invent or imitate gags. Gags are indeed the tools of transgression, so to speak. Clowns vary in the degree of creativity of the acts they produce and in the originality of the slapstick they integrate into these frames. The relationship of narratives to gags is a challenging issue for understanding the multimodal discourse of circus clowns in their traditional as well as contemporary forms because gags rather than narratives is what makes people laugh. In informal interviews I conducted with several professional clowns during the past three decades, the topic of gags was always central to the discussions. We will now further explore this problem through a summary of recorded conversations I had with Charlie Cairoli between 1974 and 1978.

What is a gag and how it works: A conversation

The kernel of a gag is an idea which grows like a kind of seed. Charlie Cairoli is always in search of new ideas. It is something unexpected like bringing two objects together or using an artifact for a function which is alien to its usual purpose. For instance, it might consist of a guitar which has been modified so that it contains a fire extinguisher which at some point will spew out a huge quantity of foam. This gag was a part of the act the year when we had this conversation. I then remind him of an object he had invented a few years earlier. It was a toilet seat to which he had added strings as if it were a lyre. The idea can also be a gesture or a cascade of moves in a certain order. However, Charlie insisted, these ideas will not make people laugh if one just comes in the ring and shows the modified toilet seat or pulls the trigger of the extinguisher which is hidden in the guitar. These actions must be motivated and prepared by the context. They must happen in a particular situation. Constructing the contexts which will transform the ideas into gags is the real work of the clown. Expressed more abstractly, we can say that a gag is an effect of discourse. We can describe objectively the meaning of a toilet seat which is used as the frame of a lyre in the same way as we can provide the semantic definition of a word, but this hybrid artifact *signifies*, that is, brings out laughter in the audience, only when someone uses it in a particular manner in a particular situation which has been developed through the narrative.

Charlie gently mocks some of his clown colleagues from other circuses who come to him sometimes asking if he would rent out one of his artifacts to them. He claims that he always liberally lends these objects to them because he knows that it is not the objects by themselves which are comical but his own personal use of them, something, in his opinion, these colleagues do not fully appreciate. A pie in the face is in itself an act of mild aggression which can convey either mere surprise or bring the house down in laughter depending on the actors and the sequence of events this assault concludes. Then Charlie mentioned with excitement that he recently invented a way to make the pie come back to the thrower's face like a boomerang. But, once again, he insists that the situation will have to be precisely crafted for this gag to work. He spends hours in his workshop building contraptions which look as simple as any usual kitchen utensil but create surprises when they are used as musical instruments or plumbers tools.

> *July 1976. It is not quite dark in July when the evening show is over. I spent time interviewing Charlie Cairoli after his first act and during the intermission. This is my second visit to Blackpool this year. The light rain which sprinkled the town all day has stopped. Charlie invites me to join him after the show for a drink and pizza in the neighborhood with his wife Violette and his son Charlie. The internet era has not arrived yet and news are welcome when travelers have recently met friends who are currently performing in faraway circuses. As we drive along Queen's Promenade, Charlie remarks that I should come back later in the summer when the famous illuminations are on. Relaxing and having dinner after the show is the best time of the day for circus artists.*
>
> *After some small talk, Charlie questions me about the kind of interest I find in his acts. He is certainly flattered to be the topic of scholarly papers in academic meetings but our discussions are not a mere public relations stint for him. He is engaged by ideas with which he is not familiar and once the jargon is dropped he quickly catches the argument. My point concerning the toilet seat stringed as a lyre was that the association itself was breaking a powerful taboo in Western cultures according to which excretory noises such as the breaking of a wind is unacceptable in most social settings. On the axis of acoustic values flatulence is as far as can be imagined from music. Bringing signs of the two opposites in a single image creates an extremely shocking association which transgresses a powerful taboo. Charlie remarks that he had not thought about that when he got the idea. He did it by instinct. But he quickly adds that, indeed, many vulgar clowns produce farting sounds when they pretend to play wind instrument and these gags always trigger loud laughter in the audience, mainly among children who are on constant constraints to control this kind of bodily noise.*

> *Suddenly, as he sees clearly the implications of my interpretation, Charlie leans toward me and half-jokingly says: "Well then if you could tell me what all these rules are, it would help me to invent new gags!" Unfortunately, I have to confess that it is only when he breaks these tacit rules in his gags that I become aware of their existence. Otherwise we take them so much for granted that we are not conscious of the fact that these unwritten scripts control our normal social behavior. We share a good laugh and raise our glasses. Instinct wins.*

Gags in theory could be generated by some algorithms since we can identify, through reversed semiotic engineering, the norms they break or simply reframe by transposing them to new contexts. However, this process would require that we first make these rules explicit. Cultural normality, though, rules our behavior because we cannot imagine that it could be otherwise. Questioning the social and moral norms entails serious risks of being ostracized, jailed, or entrusted to mental institutions. Clowns can do this within some limits because their status already classifies them in the margin of society. They tinker with ideas by recombining objects, behavior, and situations. Then, they put these new cultural constructions or collages to the test: does it make people laugh? Sometimes it does; some other times it is considered outrageous or too far-fetched. Inventing gags is a sensitive enterprise. Charlie Cairoli reported to me two cases of censorship. One year, he was leaving the ring hopping on a hobby horse. He had imagined a visual punch line, so to speak, which consisted of releasing some potatoes from the back of the horse just before he disappeared behind the curtain. The circus management objected on the grounds that this was a scatological joke not appropriate for children who are precisely all too prone to such transgressions. Discreet flatulence would have been the only allowable limit. Another year, he had conceived the main act as a hospital scene in which clown nurses were dropping heavy tools on patients with broken limbs and were playing with the pulleys holding their plaster casts at an angle. This was also vetoed as lacking compassion for the sick. Obviously, gags remain within the constraints of tacit thresholds lest they really corrupt the consistency of the culture norms they transgress. The genius of an artist like Charlie Cairoli was to sense how far he could go while fiddling with propriety.

10

The Imaginary Circus

Romancing the circus

Toward the end of the eighteenth century, the nomadic and immemorial arts of the tumblers, jugglers, and other mountebanks, which had been thriving for centuries in the seasonal fairs, as we saw in Chapter 4 with the case of Bank's educated horse, formed the basis for a new, developing kind of entertainment which was to become an important popular focus of nineteenth-century urban life. This new institution took, in most European languages, somewhat inappropriately, the prestigious Roman name of "circus" after having toyed with the still fancier Greek word "hippodrome." The historical Roman circus was actually an oval track where chariot races were held. As the etymology of the Greek word indicates, the antique hippodrome was literally "where the horses ran." In Rome and its provinces, spectacles similar to today's circus shows were presented in amphitheaters. On a smaller scale, nomadic performers who roamed the Roman Empire were called *circulatores*, that is, "those who move around" or, perhaps, "those who perform in a circle." Thus, when the circus entered the Western cultural landscape in the form which we experience today, it was not the continuation of a historical institution but a new type of organization. The acts themselves, though, were based on very ancient skills. The merging of scores of performers under traveling tents or in permanent buildings was made possible by the convergence of modern technologies, rising demography, urban concentration, and secularism.

During the nineteenth century, a time of intensive industrial, political, and cultural expansion which exalted individual heroism and the conquest of exotic frontiers, the circus provided a rich "crucible" in which both the anxiety of change and otherness, and the exhilaration of novelty and liberty combined to form a sort of magnet for artistic imagination. The dynamic which was created then still operates today, and has reached international dimensions after having merged with other similar traditions during the contemporary process of cultural globalization. Circus has become nowadays a truly cross-cultural language of the creative imagination, accommodating various ideologies as well as socioeconomic systems. It remains the object of a more or less tacit cult both in popular and elitist contexts. But it also continues to carry the stigma of its nomadic origins as bear witness the current attempts to criminalize its traditions with regard to the treatment of wild animals, which are kept captive, and children, who are trained at a young age at the expense of a normal, mainstream education.

The circus's haunting presence in the nineteenth and twentieth century's European art and literature cannot be taken for granted, and poses a challenging question: why a way of life and its corresponding performing techniques, which had been ignored as if they were "untouchable" for so long, almost suddenly became a major cultural theme reaching the highest forms of artistic expression. This chapter will address this issue through examining some significant literary reports of "sublime" aesthetic experiences nested in the circus as a sacred space of ritualistic transformations. Circus icons have permeated poetry, fiction, art, drama, and film. But these aesthetic and philosophical appropriations have transformed actual performances into representations which soon became driven by their own dynamic and contributed to the emergence of what can rightly be considered to be an imaginary circus, an artistic and philosophical multimodal discourse which runs parallel to the performances themselves and amplifies their meaning like an orchestrated echo.

A telling example is a text by French Symbolist poet Stéphane Mallarmé which was first published in 1875 in a Parisian literary magazine, then appeared in 1891 as a part of his collection titled *Poëmes en prose* [Prose poems]. The title of this prose poem, *Un spectacle interrompu* [An interrupted spectacle], refers to a personal experience of the poet as a spectator. The text recounts an accident which occurred during a performance of *La bête et le génie* [The beast and the genie] which the poet attended. The place was a popular theater; the play was a *féerie* [a pantomime], a genre of performance on stage which straddled two popular genres, the melodrama and the circus. One of the actors was a real bear, that is, a circus-trained bear. The hero was a clown magnificently dressed in a silvery garb who at some point in the drama interacted with the bear.

That evening, the tricks performed with the animal triggered loud outbursts of applause among the popular audience when suddenly a tense silence takes hold of the theater. The bear has grabbed the man. The potential tragedy which is always lurking behind a wild-animal act like a threatening hidden agenda—the ancestral confrontation and its bloody consummation—brutally comes to the fore. Mallarmé recalls the sublime vision he then experienced, distancing himself from what he assumes to be the vulgar reactions of the crowd excited by the novelty of the accident. The bear's attack, which will remain suspended in the poet's visionary imagination, is however stopped when someone, presumably a helper or the trainer himself who was monitoring the action from the backstage, throws a piece of meat from the wing in order to capture the attention of the animal and distract it from its potentially deadly attack. The strategy succeeds, but the spectacle is interrupted and the fire safety curtain falls, separating the stage situation which went awry from the relieved audience which is asked to leave the theater.

The interest of this short but dense text is manifold. The trivial circus anecdote is construed as a cosmic vision, played in the mode, so to speak, of Mallarméan "Ideal," a transcendent, absolute beauty which only poetry can approach. In almost evolutionary terms, the poet describes the bear as "a human of lower status, stocky, good-natured, standing straight on its two furry legs, forming a sublime couple with its luminous and supernatural brother, its refined elder, both being united by a secret, essential proximity." The performer is not perceived as a mediocre clown in spangled silvery garb, but Man-the-Dreamer, the cultural hero, the metaphysical being obsessed by Ideal.

The bear is not viewed as a dangerous predator which can be manipulated by training but is conceived as a mythical beast, so close to and so different from us at the same time. In his interpretation the poet evokes the bear which haunts our fairy tales, both ancient and modern, and our arctic nocturnal sky in the form of the pivotal polar star. Indeed, the etymology of "arctic" is the Greek word for "bear." The French call "Great Mother Bear" the constellation named the "Great Chariot" in English. On the earth, "Martin" the bear is the furry character of countless folktales. Its symbolic resilience is acknowledged by the poet who alludes to Heinrich Heine's *Atta Troll* (1843) in the first paragraph of his report. The title of Heine's satirical poem refers indeed to the name of a dancing bear which escaped its trainer and whose capture and eventual death provide the narrative thread which is the pretext for this mock epic.

The almost deadly hug which was witnessed by the poet was experienced as "a drama of cosmic dimensions which had chosen to enact itself in this modest, popular theater" (Mallarmé 1945: 277; translation mine). Mallarmé asserts in the last sentence of the text that what he has *seen* in this spectacle and in its essential accident is a *true vision*, in other words, a cosmic epiphany. This poem is symptomatic of the emergence of the circus as the locus of mythical, transcendental experiences. It complements the better known fascination of Mallarmé for the clown (*le pître*) and the acrobat by providing clear evidence that the third archetypal hero of the circus, the wild-animal trainer, was also a focus of this aesthetic imagination.

The fascination for the circus and its three archetypal heroes goes back much earlier in the nineteenth century and continues today. Three quotations spanning 100 hundred years will give a measure of the extent to which the romancing of the circus goes far beyond an interest in the unusual and the exotic but takes on a mystical dimension. In 1853, the Parnassian poet Théodore de Banville wrote about a troupe of mountebanks: "I will never forget these faces made beautiful by poetry and pain.... Is not a mountebank an independent and free artist who makes miracles to earn his daily bread, who sings in the sun, and dances under the stars for the sake of his art without any hope of being accepted in any academy?" (1–13). Aesthetic considerations gloss over the usually miserable conditions in which nomadic families eked out a living in European societies which feared and persecuted them. Social insensibility was indeed compatible with the poetic theme of the wanderers who performed contortions and somersaults, or showed trained dogs, dancing bears and monkeys on streets and city squares.

Almost half a century later the Symbolist poet Gustave Kahn has the hero of his novel, *Le cirque solaire* [The solar circus], a literary antecedent of Cirque du Soleil, proclaim: "Circus, circus, all is circus, all is round. All events can be found in any conjuncture in the circular microcosm of a circus ring" (66). Then a full century after De Banville, Jean Genet writes in *Le funambule* [The wirewalker]:

> This leads me to proclaim that the circus must be loved and the world must be despised. A huge beast emerges from the deep past and lands, heavy, on the cities: you enter and discover that this monster is full of mechanical and cruel wonders: equestrian girls, clowns, lions and their tamer, German acrobats, a horse which speaks and counts, and you [Abdallah, the wire walker whom the poet loves and

worships, and to whom the text is addressed]. You are the remnants of fabulous times. You cannot accommodate our world and its logic. You are forced to accept your miserable destiny: living during the nights the illusion of your deadly tricks; staying during the days at the door of the circus, fearful of our city life, firmly anchored as you are by the powers of the circus which are also the powers of death. Do not ever leave this enormous womb of canvas! (201–2; translation mine)

These three quotations, as well as Mallarmé's text, are very representative of the progressive elevation of the circus to the status of a transcendental object through the works of poets and painters from Romanticism to Surrealism and beyond, notably in the cinema from Charlie Chaplin to Federico Fellini and Ingmar Bergman. Within the French domain alone Théophile Gautier, Théodore de Banville, Charles Baudelaire, Paul Verlaine, Jules Laforgue, Guillaume Apollinaire, Max Jacob, Jean Cocteau, Andre Prévert; and, among the painters, Seurat, Degas, Renoir, Toulouse-Lautrec, Léger, Picasso, Chagall and many others convey the impression that the circus has progressively become a compulsory *topos*, even though they deal with its icons and symbols with obvious enthusiasm. Edmond de Goncourt's *Les frères Zemganno* (1879) and Alain-Fournier (*Le grand Meaulnes*, 1913) orchestrate this *topos* in works which have reached the status of classics. Eventually, circus figures were also appropriated by philosophical poetry, for instance, in Nietzsche's *Also Sprach Zarathustra* (1954 [1892]) and Rilke's *Duineser Elegien* (1943). Henry Miller's *The Smile at the Foot of the Ladder* (1953), which will be considered later in this chapter, represents a point of convergence of all the dimensions of the circus phantasm.

A powerful discourse has thus emerged in European culture, establishing the circus as a unique source of values at the interface of the technique—perceived as an ascetic exercise leading to a profane sainthood—and a sort of metaphysics in which mystification, mystery, and mysticism become one and the same thing. Volumes have been written on this theme, among which the most exhaustive and insightful undoubtedly are Naomi Ritter's *Art as Spectacle: Images of the Entertainer since Romanticism* (1989) and Helen Stoddart's *Rings of Desire* (2000).

The circus as a phantasm

The close examination of the texts mentioned above as well as texts from other European literatures shows that at least four aspects combine to form this complex imaginary representation: (1) the spatial and social uprooting of the performers; (2) the decontextualizing of their bodies and their framing within the idiosyncratic *apparatus* of the circus; (3) the romantic idealization of risk and death framed by a cosmological metaphor which creates the oxymoronic trivial representation of the sublime; (4) the paradoxical status of the clown as an outcast and a saint.

The first aspect is determined by a particular modality of the production of social space, namely the nomadic mode of life and its existential implications. The romantic imagination and its twentieth-century continuation in Surrealism and Existentialism advocated a radical emancipation from the constraints of real estate. Land and building ownership, which establishes the social definition and stability of individual identities, is experienced as a "curse" rather than a "blessing." By contrast, nomadic existence is glamorized and envied from a distance as a mere negative value of the constraints implied by sedentary life. Ceaselessly moving through the landscape is dreamed as a constant erasure of the past and the guilt it carries. For the urban or landed outsider it also usually means emancipation from family strictures ever haunted by the power of inheritance. This is, of course, pure phantasm because most circus families maintain equally strong bonds and constraints upon their members as Yoram Carmeli has demonstrated through his ethnography of a circus family in his unpublished doctoral thesis and in a host of articles (e.g. 1991: 257–89). It is also the case that many circus families own valuable real estate, or at least a house or an apartment. They nevertheless tend to project through the media the image of a people always on the move, thus feeding the phantasms of their public. They often deliberately play out, for the enjoyment of their audience, their assumed nomadic existence. The wealthy owner of Cirque Romanes, a Gypsy circus which has been performing in Paris's popular districts since the beginning of the twenty-first century, makes sure that the tent and its surroundings look like a somewhat ragged travelers' camp and he always stays in front of a small battered house trailer when he is interviewed by television journalists. This is an essential part of the performance which, incidentally, is a spectacle worthy of attention as it features basic circus acts in the warm atmosphere created by the informality of the presentation and the exhilarating music of a Romanian Gypsy band. These images are sustained by a long literary tradition in Europe. The romantic vision of the circus wanderers was, and still is, to a certain extent grounded on the actual living conditions of a nomadic minority but, as we saw earlier in the brief quotation from Théodore de Banville, these performers were perceived as the embodiment of an ideal of beauty and freedom which transcended the relatively uneventful experience of sedentary everyday life. The powers of literary narratives and imagery color the contemporary reception of the circus. The public imagination is haunted by novels which were and still are read at a young age such as Hector Malot's *Sans famille* (1878) or Alain-Fournier's *Le grand Meaulnes* (1913), appropriately translated into English respectively as *Nobody's Boy* and *The Wanderer*. The former, which was retranslated in 2007 under the title *Alone in the World*, inspired several television series and a Japanese anime feature film, *Chibikko Remi to Meiken Capi* (Toei Animation 1970). Malot's narrative recounts the tribulations of a young boy who was sold by his adoptive parents to the mountebank Vitaly who trains him in various circus skills together with a monkey and three dogs among which the most gifted, Capi, becomes his sole companion when adversity strikes the group (hard weather, wolf attacks, persecutions, police harassment, jailing of the mentor, and other hazards of a life on the road). There is a happy ending, though, but the nomadic wanderings of the troupe, the heroic confronting of hard luck, and the resourcefulness of the characters made countless children dream of a life on the loose, including the author of this volume whose passion for the circus might have originated from the pages of this novel. *The Great Meaulnes* [literal translation of the French title] addresses adolescents' yearning for escaping into a world of magic and fantasy under the inspired guidance of the mysterious traveler who bursts into the sedate life of a village in Central France.

The multimodal discourse of the circus carries with it a powerful subtext, a literary memory which forms a background that is consubstantial with its appreciation. Symbolism permeates the circus's own space which takes over and cancels for a very brief, precarious time the civil space of functionality and legality. It sets up arbitrary fences and controls thresholds; it transcends distances, differences, and borders. Circus metamorphoses space, seems to ignore its partitioning and alienating forces because *The Circus Has No Home* (1941), as, for instance, Rupert Croft-Cooke claims in the title of his passionate account of a British circus family.

The second aspect of the circus phantasm concerns its focus on the body. In everyday life, bodies are usually hidden under layers of clothing and enclosed within a network of physical, social, and moral constraints. Even on beaches and nudist camps, bodies are regulated by minimal dress codes or etiquette. They are imprisoned by their social context. Taboos and prejudices render them almost invisible under their cloak of conventional functions. The way they are revealed in the circus ring dissocializes them and, at the same time, recontextualizes them by the apparatuses which have been built exclusively for them so that they can exteriorize their dynamic presence within a space which has been disencumbered of the clutter of things which, in our everyday life, control our movements. They are framed as totally visible corporeal epiphanies by the wires upon which they walk, the trapeze they catch, and the bars and poles they grasp. Their minimal decorations enhance their shapes and contours. As we will point out in the next chapter, natural curvatures and bulges are underlined. They are introduced by stage names. They are creatures of the circus which displays them in the glare of the spotlights. The skills they deploy make them spin and fly, stand straight and bend, rise and lay down as pure bodies reduced to their vital potential and glorified as icons of exceptional humanities, as demigods and demigoddesses made to be watched, admired, and loved. In *Circus Bodies*, Peta Tait (2005) has retraced the historical emergence of this spectacular visual celebration, in particular the female body which displays in the ring its strength and skills with self-confidence and dignity in the whole range of aerial specialties. This idealization, though, which is inspired by the feminist agenda, pertains to a great extent to the same kind of phantasm we find in poetry and art. Those who have approached the female condition in the circus through ethnography rather than historical iconography have provided a more nuanced picture. For instance, Donnalee Frega's *Women of Illusion* (2001) and Nell Stroud's *Josser: The Secret Life of a Circus Girl* (2000) have demystified the decontextualized images found in circus posters and artistic imagination. Stroud's account of her experience of running away to the circus dramatically illustrates the collision of the phantasm with the reality of a show on the road.

The existential vision which interprets circus acrobatic display is indeed largely a social phantasm, but it is necessary for construing archetypal circus heroes as embodiments of "pure" bodies, as "symbolic types" as Don Handelman contends (1991: 205–25). It is because they are not defined by the civil coordinates of all those who are forming the social tissue of everyday life that they appear as pure beings of desire so close to the power of death that they acquire a sort of immunity from the trivial morality and legality of the common herd. They walk in the inebriating atmosphere of Nietzschean anomy, a rigorous and demanding freedom which sanctions by instant death the mistakes which they seem to be tragically bound to make, rather than administering petty retaliations for the mediocre faults and sins of those who do not dare. They liberally reveal their flesh and show off their seductive resources and the power of their violence, but always in the constantly evoked presence of death. This, of course, is a matter of staging which is part of the trade, since the risks involved are relatively low if they are compared to other professional activities. However, they came to replace the Catholic saints in the popular imagination of a secular era to the extent that those who died by accident during a performance were actually considered as "martyrs" at the peak of the Golden Age of the European and American circuses. At least one *Martyrologue du cirque* [Repertory of circus martyrs] was published in the first part of the twentieth century (Thétard 1978 [1947]: 611–15). The combined effects of spatial emancipation, and apparently deliberate exposure to death in the heroic mode, form the basis of the poetics of the glorious body and its reversed and necessary condition: the tortured body, on the one hand, which acquires its glorious metamorphosis through an ascetic training, or the ruined body, on the other hand, which disappears under the garb of the clown when time has taken its toll. Hence, the fourth aspect, the paradoxical figure of the clown fascinated poets and painters alike.

The ascent of the clown

The text which crystallizes, perhaps in the most efficient manner, the role of the clown in the circus phantasm is Henry Miller's *The Smile at the Foot of the Ladder* (1953). It encapsulates in a mere 60 pages all the ingredients of the literary theme and cultural icon which developed during the preceding century: the deep and paradoxical sadness under the makeup; the despair of the artist who realizes that he is nothing but this mask which exhausts all his existential status; the metaphysical vacuity of an identity which does not exceed the stage name by which he is known and appreciated by the public; the tragic freedom of the circus antihero who is not only deprived of the coordinates of a stable space but also of sexual and social identity; the unspeakable suffering of the grotesque, childlike being who straddles boundaries; messes up good manners, fashion, and proper language; and whose eternal lot seems to be the ultimate scapegoat or martyr.

As we saw in Chapter 9, clowns actually are skilled professionals whose business is to make people laugh and who address sensitive sociocultural issues through their slapstick comedies. They exhibit robust, sometimes even violent humor. But this archetypal character of the circus has been exploited and transformed by the Romantic imagination. If circus clowns conformed to the tragic figure celebrated by poets, novelists, and painters, no circus would ever have hired them to perform in their programs. The cultural clown is an elaboration based on precious little evidence. Its image, at times, feeds back to the circus itself and generates some actual characters who imitate their artistic representations with limited professional success. By and large, these derivative clowns are mostly found on stage in plays which orchestrate their pathos and transgressive behavior. Donald McManus has masterly retraced the ascent of the clown in modernist and contemporary theater, as well as in popular culture, in his book *No Kidding! Clown as Protagonist in Twentieth Century Theater* (2003). This discursive interpretation of the circus clown, which trickles down to design workshops influencing the production of marketing icons, may appear to the professionals and connoisseurs as a betrayal of the tradition but is nevertheless an important component of the reception of the circus among its popular audience.

Henry Miller writes in the first pages of *The Smile at the Foot of the Ladder*: "Within the radius of the spotlight lay the world in which he was born anew each evening. It comprised only those objects, creatures and beings which move in the circle of enchantment. A table, a chair, a rug; a horse, a bell, a paper hoop; the eternal ladder, the moon nailed to the roof, the bladder of a goat. With these, *Auguste* and his companions manage each night to reproduce the drama of initiation and martyrdom" (1953: 12). The text provides a definitive formulation of all the essential features of the clown according to his literary elaboration. For example: "To be a clown was to be fate's pawn. . . . It was his special privilege to re-enact the errors, the follies, the stupidities, all the misunderstandings which plague the human kind. . . . The master of ineptitude has all time as his domain. He surrenders only in the face of eternity" (1953: 80–2). In the "epilogue" to the story, Miller recounts the circumstances in which it was written. This was initially a commission to accompany a series of forty illustrations by Fernand Léger on clowns and circuses. Once Miller had accepted the offer things did not go smoothly. He documents what could be best described as a confrontation with the *topos*, typically alluding to the necessity he felt to meet the challenge and to the inhibition caused by the intimidating achievements of those who had so successfully tried their hand at it before him. Besides a passing reference to his own passion for the circus—but is this not an obligatory element of the *topos*?—it is quite remarkable that no substantial mention is made of the circus itself. Miró, Chagall, Rouault provide the points of referential anchorage, so to speak, to the extent that the very objects he depicts in his story do not refer to implements he might have observed in a real circus but to pictorial items: the ladder is Miró's, as is the moon; the horse is Léger's; and so on. As to the kernel of the tale, it obviously draws from Mallarmé's famous poem *Le pître châtié* [The punished clown] and its many derivations along the successive literary periods of the nineteenth and twentieth centuries. Like Jean Starobinski in his celebrated *Portrait de l'artiste en saltimbanque* [Portrait of the artist as a mountebank] (1970), Miller's moving and profound story implements the common theme rather than documents the popular institution, that is, the circus, to which it is assumed to refer while he actually remains within the confines of the phantasm.

Circus mystics: The juggler and the funambulist

Two circus specialties, juggling and funambulism—the art of walking on a stretched cable high above the ground—have been elevated by poets and philosophers to the status of mystic experiences. Both skills embody the opposite of what Nietzsche called despicably "Der Geist der Schwere," the "Spirit of Gravity" which holds humans down and prevents them from ascending toward their superhuman destiny. Although these techniques can be practiced by teams of men and women, they have been illustrated by individuals—male or female—who reached perfection in their solo acts and, in some cases, encountered a tragic death. Both specialties demand an exacting training which requires true self-abnegation, a total dedication to an ascetic art. They both involve triumph over gravity, a kind of aerial mastery. Both in their own way reach toward the sky and figure an existence which escapes from the common lot. They provide true embodiments for the metaphors through which poets and philosophers express the sublime and the transcendent. It is not by chance that Nietzsche's hymn to the advent of the superhuman, *Also Sprach Zarathustra* (1954 [1892]), starts with a celebration of a rope walker whom the prophet encounters on his path. This text, with *Die Geburt der Tragödie aus der Geiste der Musik* [The birth of Tragedy or the Spirit of Music] (Nietzsche 1872), inspired Jean Genet's *Le funambule* (1958), the lyrical poem mentioned earlier which elevates the funambulist Abdallah to the status of a saint dancing in "the sun of death." This prose poem is rich in allusions to the classics of Symbolist poetry. It unfolds as a series of injunctions, a kind of *Ars Poetica* (or perhaps *Ars Acrobatica*) which glorifies the acrobat's body and construes his skill as a sublime work of art. It is congruent with Romantic ideology in as much as the artist is perceived as a radical individualist contemptuous of the crowd, the common herd, and implements his destiny in total solitude.

> *I saw for the first time Chris Christiansen performing his early juggling act in a small circus which had set up its tent for the summer in a Paris square. I was struck by the intensity of the experience. The composition of the act, the economy of movements, the lack of submission to the audience through soliciting more applause than they were prepared to grant him, and the utter seriousness and dignity of his performance quickly convinced me that he was not a run-of-the-mill juggler. A few months later, circumstances brought me in professional contact with him. Until he totally vanished from my horizon in recent years, I treasured his friendship. I often met him in the circuses in which he performed or on the sidewalks where he occasionally was busking when times were tough. His life story is emblematic of youngsters from working-class or middle-class backgrounds who are irresistibly attracted to the circus as a mode of life. It is an existential project rife with risks and promises. A few succeed in accomplishing their destiny of choice. Some are propelled to fame by the media. Some reintegrate the common lot when their body or their will gives up. Most eventually disappear in solitary anonymity unless they have been adopted by a traditional circus family.*
>
>   *In the 1960s, Chris's family did not have a television at home. In his early teens, he used to peek through the window of neighbors who were watching regular programs in the evenings. This is how he saw for the first time La piste aux étoiles [The Ring of Stars], a weekly feature of the French official television channel showing circus acts. The juggler Paolo Bedini was a part of the program that evening. In a flash, Chris's life was changed: "This is what I want to be." In secret, he learnt how to throw balls in the air and catch them before they hit the ground. This was a long and painful process. There were no circus schools then. Even if this had been a possibility, where would the money have come from to pay for the tuition? Without a mentor, he had to reinvent this art and rediscover by himself the most elementary tricks of the trade. He did not quit.*

Over the years, I spent days listening to Chris who needed to resource his energy and will from the narrative of his life poured in sympathetic ears. There were times of despair such as the night when he went to the river which runs through his hometown and threw all his juggling equipment in the water in a gesture of artistic suicide. He would be after all like his parents, an ordinary guy who would work in a local factory and be trapped in this boring life until he dies. The next day, he bought new balls and new clubs. He won't quit. It was decided. It was a matter of life or death. Chris was good at school and knew that he would easily pass the final exam. He was 18. He was the only child of hard-working parents who dreamed to see their son become a white-collar employee. How could he escape the destiny he refused if not by running away the day of the exams? This he did in favor of a life on the road and on the edge, from contract to contract, from circuses to night clubs, always trying to perfect his art, never happy with the results. On his way he met great jugglers, names which belong to the history of the circus. In him, they recognized one of their own and they gave him advice and help. I saw him reach the apex of his art, performing his innovative act in great circuses. He was always dismissive of the applause and the occasional favorable comments in the media. How could they know what is good? He would be the sole judge. He had to meet his own standards of excellence. Never satisfied, though, by what he had achieved. Always worrying about what would happen if arthritis or other ailments would slow him down, or stop him on his way.

I do not know where Chris is. I have not heard from him for years. Chris lived in a van or a small house trailer on the road. There were books in the car: Jean Genet, Friedrich Nietzsche, and Heinrich von Kleist among others. He gave me once a used copy of the latter's essay on puppetry which, he claimed, summarized his own philosophy. He used to perform on sidewalks when he needed some cash. I saw people moved to tears while watching him and leave banknotes instead of coins in the plate that lay on the ground. He would not beg, passing it around. "I juggle for the sake of juggling" he told me once. The most perceptive account of Christian's life, art, and personality can be found in Stephen Riggins's The Pleasures of Time (2003: 140–5, and passim).

The imaginary circus is a symbolic force able to mold existences into chosen destinies. More than any other creative vocations, the circus implements the Nietzschean imperative which commands humans not to be artists but to become works of art themselves. Funambulist Philippe Petit is a contemporary icon of this process. His life story parallels Chris Christiansen's but, unlike him, he was born in the Parisian middle class. His budding drive toward an unconventional life was not discouraged by his family. A bright but rebellious student, he taught himself the hard way how to walk on a cable in his teens while getting involved in theatrical performances. He relishes in breaking rules which are not spelled out in the law. Nobody ever formally made it illegal to cross the distance between the two World Trade Center skyscrapers or the towers of Notre Dame on a cable. Philippe Petit has thus redefined unexplored limits of human transgressive power. He was not born in the circus. He stole the fire, so to speak. But his inspiration came from this cradle of human dreams.

Illustrated books have been published about him. Films have been made. He reached global fame through his daring crossing and climbing of stretched wires and cables at altitudes which only birds and planes can claim to be their own. But Philippe Petit is also a poet who has long been living in New York City. *The High Wire* (1985), also published in his native French as *Traite du funambulisme* (1997), is a set of short texts which can exemplify better than any other documents the depth and resilience of an art which immemorial shamans practiced when, in front of fearful tribes, they were performing their ritualistic ascension toward the heavens.

11

Ideology and Politics in the Circus Ring

Poetics and politics of the body

The circus is celebrated in modern art and literature as a humanistic tradition which displays beautiful bodies and exemplifies a demanding physical and mental discipline. In most circus programs, acrobatics in its many forms is indeed prominently represented. The men and women who engage in exacting feats of strength and balance usually are not encumbered by fabrics which hide their natural morphology. Although they perform sometimes in light versions of formal dresses or suits, their most frequent and more functional costumes minimally cover their bodies. As their training generally develops their muscles in a harmonious manner, their tightfitting leotards enhance their natural forms and their stage trunks and bras reveal their partial nudity. Their behavior, though, is usually constrained by the technical and aesthetic requirements of their acrobatic specialties, and they refrain from overtly indulging in gestures or facial expressions which could be construed as sexually provocative. Even if, in general, the spectators' attention is captured by the challenging tasks acrobats endeavor to achieve, the latter's attractiveness cannot nevertheless be ignored and certainly plays a role in securing inclusive audiences. There is a joke among circus directors who often promote circus as a family entertainment, which hints at this tacit dimension: "you need three things to make up a program: animals and clowns for the children, girls for the fathers, and acrobats for the mothers." This crude, cynical, and politically incorrect, albeit revealing guideline does not do full justice to the artistic merits of most acrobatic acts and to their genuine aesthetic appreciation by amateurs of the circus.

There are indeed many qualities which acrobats share in common with the highbrow arts such as ballet, sculpture, and opera: first, acrobats are similar to dancers both of the classical and avant-garde brands with respect to movements and rhythm; second, they are sometimes compared to live statues and quite often they explicitly imitate in their poses Greek, Renaissance, and modern marble icons; finally, their acts are constructed with a flair for dramatic suspense and lead to triumphal climaxes with appropriate musical accompaniments. There are differences, though, which bring forth the specificity of the circus: musical scores are adapted to the acrobats' movements rather than the reverse; the statues they compose have the color and dynamics of warm bodies; and their dramas are performed without words in a universal visual, even at times voyeuristic language. These are precisely the specific qualities which focus the attention of the spectators on the bodies which are displayed, if not exhibited, in the full light of the circus ring.

Eroticism, of course, is in the eyes of the beholders. There is nothing pornographic in the staging of regular circus acts. The costumes, even when they are functionally reduced to the minimum because the movements of acrobats cannot be impeded by extra weight or interfering decorations, are within the range of the circus dress code. Moreover, the intense perspiration caused by physical exertion must be allowed to evaporate as quickly as possible. The demeanor of the acrobats from their entrance to their exit is regulated by artistic conventions and etiquette. But the broad smiles they broadcast toward the public can be at times enticing and everybody in the audience may fancy herself or himself as the privileged addressee of these attractive strangers' eye contacts and inviting gestures.

Although there are usually some solo performers in circus programs, the majority of acrobatic acts involve two or more individuals who display close, if not intimate body contact as a part of their routine. This cannot fail to raise the issue of sexual politics even if mentions of their family relationships are often made in the printed program or in their introduction by the presenter. Such indications are assumed to be true by the audience but, in some cases, this results from staging decisions which betray a concern for respectability by the artists or the circus management. Framing these acts as family cooperative works defuses, to some extent, their erotic charge whether they involve members of both sexes or same-sex duos and groups. This semiotic move also makes more acceptable to conservative audiences the mixing of genders and ages which is very prominent in some acrobatics acts. However, it is not always as simple as adding a mere verbal labeling to an act. There are indeed cultural constraints which cannot be transgressed with respect to the norms prevailing in some countries. We will discuss two examples below, which show that sexual politics is ever present in the multimodal discourse of circus acrobatics.

The Indian circus is a huge industry which, during the last quarter of the previous century when I had many opportunities to observe it, presented only single-sex acts. Men and women were segregated in the ring. Most acrobatic acts on the ground or in the air were performed by troupes of unrelated females, including some very young girls. All major circuses could display as many as 50 to 100 of them in a great variety of acrobatic specialties: balancing, bicycle tricks, jumps, hanging by the teeth or the hair, climbing, trapeze, and so on. Featuring a man and a woman, both being lightly dressed, who interact in close contact on a single trapeze, as is often seen in American and European circuses, would have been unacceptable in the context of a culture which enforces norms incompatible with such exhibitions in public settings. Naturally, the status and destiny of these circus girls, who were displayed in relative nudity with respect to the common standards, could not fail to raise some serious concerns as documented in *Starkiss*, a courageous film by Chris Relleke and Yasha De Wilde. These two Dutch filmmakers provide evidence that, at least in some major circuses, the acrobat girls and young women were kept in quasi slavery. In these spectacles, there were also troupes of men only, particularly specializing in flying trapeze acts.

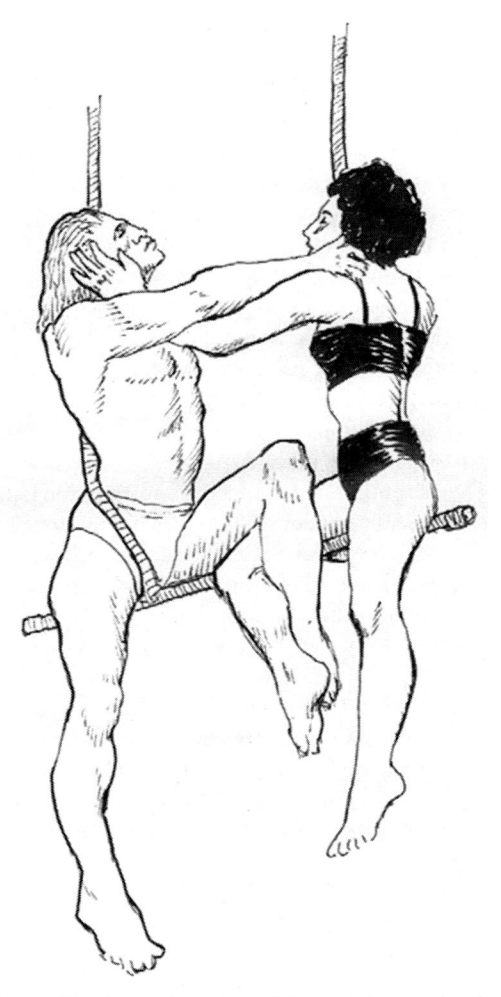

Figure 11.1 Duo a deux: The title and staging of this aerial act redundantly convey a sense of sexual harmony between the male and female acrobats. (Drawing by David Blostein.)

The second example deals with an age-old taboo in Western societies concerning homosexuality. Until the gay liberation movement brought about a relative change of mind in Europe and North America, two acrobats on a single trapeze, balancing and catching each other, and going through synchronized movements which necessarily involved close and continuous body contacts, could only feature a man and a woman. These acts form a rich paradigm which is often explicitly staged as a romantic display with appropriate music. Some of them play out very effectively the passionate dimension of the acrobats' interactions while some others keep the erotic potential at a lower level. Traditionally, featuring two women in such acts was acceptable as long as they were billed as sisters and the emphasis was on the gracefulness of their acrobatics rather than on the danger implied by these kinds of exercises. However, no circus would have dared to include two men performing such a single trapeze act which was strongly identified with the heterosexual stereotype of absolute romantic love, potentially involving death in a kind of "Romeo and Juliet" mode since the two aerialist acrobats survived life-threatening situations thanks not only to their skill but also to their mutual, unconditional trust. Indeed, these acts often include one of the two partners making an unsecured jump from a higher position to be caught at the last moment by the other who grasps his/her feet or hands. Fatal accidents have occurred in the past and this memory keeps haunting the vision of this trick when it is performed without a safety net or lunge.

Figure 11.2 Duo Sorellas: The aerialists reclaim the right of representing mutual commitment between two men by displaying death-defying acrobatics. (Drawing by David Blostein.)

When the new, innovative *Zirkus Roncalli* included in its programs such an act involving two men, it was perceived as a strong statement of sexual politics. Billed as "The Lindors," Martin Ender and Walter Joss, were featured, for instance, in the 1983 program. With their radiant smiles, theatrical gestures, and daring acrobatics they were coming out as partners in life as well as in the ring. There was no pretence that they were brothers and the romantic flavor of their act was unapologetically played out. Audiences in Germany and Holland responded very positively to this demonstration of inclusiveness in the circus's visual discourse but no circus director would have tried then to feature this act or similar acts in Southern Europe where homophobia was still the norm. It is around the same time that the French all-women circus, Cirque de Barbarie, performed in France and Northern Europe with an explicitly feminist if not lesbian inspiration. Nowadays, same-sex acrobatic couples can be observed in most circuses, such as the two-male aerial act which is unambiguously billed as the "Duo Sorellas" (the two sisters in Spanish). Like the Lindors in the 1980s, these two men display the dramatic performance of absolute mutual trust high above the ground. These acts, however, appear to remain context-sensitive in the sense that they can be perceived as too provocative by conservative audiences. The heterosexual stereotype remains, indeed, the dominant productive paradigm which generates inspiring acrobatics and staging. The following section will further demonstrate the capacity of the circus as a language to articulate a multimodal discourse by using all the resources of poetics and rhetoric in the service of both traditional and alternative sexual politics. While interpreting some acts in this light we should be mindful, though, of not confusing symbolic representations with real life situations as the two may differ.

Erotic circus: The tame and the wild

The image of the circus as an innocuous spectacle which is appropriate for entertaining and instructing children is historically relatively recent (Assael 2005). Circus has been progressively made morally aseptic through deliberate efforts to gain respectability. Its fairgrounds origins, with the ruthless enticing of male customers by means of displaying female acrobats and dancers mixed with other attractive feats of strength and balance in front of the show's enclosure, have never been totally eradicated from its ethos and its folklore. We will see in the next chapter how an assumed sexual license colored the abundant novels and films which have used the circus as a context for fiction and fantasy. But the image which has prevailed in the modern circuses of the twentieth century is a tame version of the potential eroticism of its displays. A focus on the family status of its performers has played an important role in this process (Carmeli 2007) at the expense of arousing desire through displaying exotic and seemingly emancipated bodies of either sex in suggestive postures and interactions. But even when the family theme is not foregrounded, most contemporary circuses remain within the conventional boundaries of a genre which steers clear of explicit sexual contents. This, of course, does not mean that eroticism is absent. We will probe now from this point of view one of the first programs of Cirque du Soleil and we will see how this erotic dimension was orchestrated in three successive acrobatic acts each involving a young woman and a young man. We will examine these three acts in the context of the program in which they appeared.

The Cirque du Soleil masterfully demonstrates that technique, poetics, and rhetoric are all required for the felicitous conception, composition, and performance of circus acts and programs. The 1988 spectacle provided a beautiful balance between teamwork at the beginning, middle, and end of the show (chair balancing, teeter board, trick cycling), and items performed by a couple (tightrope walkers, hand-to-hand balancing, and aerial acrobatics). The presentation of these three latter acts deserves special mention not only for their individual artistry and acrobatic merits but also because of their relative positions in the program. This reveals Cirque du Soleil's deep sense of the power of the art it has inherited and its capacity for unfolding a discourse which produces more meaning through its composition than what could be derived from mere technical, literal descriptions of the individual acts. This 1988 program incorporated the theme of the couple as an anaphora leading to a climax.

Three young couples were involved, each with their own acrobatic specialty. Their acts could be performed at any point of this program or separately in other, different circuses as they have done during the past few years. But having been contracted for that season by the Cirque du Soleil, their proximity and order of appearance brought forth dimensions which otherwise might not have been fully apparent.

The first couple, "Agathe et Antoine," displayed courtship behavior on the tightrope. The young man played oboe as he danced on the wire facing the girl who, in turn,

Figure 11.3 Agathe and Antoine: Multimodal metaphors of love 1. Agathe and Antoine: courtship on the wire. (Drawing by David Blostein.)

made her gracious steps while her suitor watched. An acrobatic dialogue was taking place with increasing intensity culminating with somersaults executed by the man and daring balancing by the girl. The act included extraordinary feats such as Antoine making a headstand on the tight cable and concluded by face-to-face synchronous splits. At no time, though, did the acrobats touch each other, except for a very brief moment when, walking one toward the other, they crossed on the wire—incidentally, a notable feat from a technical point of view. During the act, their acknowledgments of the public applause were discreet; their demeanor suggested mutual fascination and idealization rather than showmanship. This strategy evoked the first steps of love, adolescence more than maturity.

Figure 11.4 Erik and Amélie: Multimodal metaphors of love 2. Erik and Amélie: Tango, dance of seduction. (Drawing by David Blostein.)

In the second act, "Eric et Amélie" performed a hand-to-hand balancing routine beautifully blended into a tango. The printed program commented: "Theirs is a world of passion, of perfect yet unspoken communication, of two bodies and minds moving, feeling and thinking as one." Their acrobatic specialty implied a constant physical contact of the limbs and head rather than the whole body. The staging conveyed a sense of seduction, passion, foreplay, and reciprocal attraction. It also displayed signs of mutual respect as the woman was in turn the bearer, balancing the man on her hands—a meaningful "detail" which was instantly caught by the audience and usually triggered an intense response. In agreement with the sexual politics that was emerging at the time, the woman was not represented as the "object" being manipulated by the man but as an equal partner who could perform feats of strength as well as her companion.

The last act, an aerial act high above the ground, brought the image of the couple to its full realization. "The Andrews"—note that the two acrobats are now introduced

Figure 11.5 Consummation: Multimodal metaphors of love 3. The Andrews: high and close in the cradle of passion. (Drawing by David Blostein.)

by a patronymic stage name—were dressed in a nuptial white in contrast to the pastels of the first act and the deep colors of the tango; the music picked up the earlier theme of the oboe but in a rich orchestration. The introduction of the act unfolded as a ceremony, the two acrobats ascending toward their *cradle*—the technical term for the metal frame in which the catcher secures his/her hold—from the midst of a huge veil of white gauze. "With nothing but one another for support," as the program underlined, they displayed exercises which involved full body contact between the hand-catching and leg-grasping episodes. In brief, this act was staged as a metaphor of love both in the sense of absolute bond—literally a matter of life and death—and complementary labor including once again an occasional switching of roles. That is, showing the woman in the catcher's position. However, this apotheosis of the couple was not the conclusion of the spectacle. The three stages of love: courtship, seduction, and consummation, were bracketed by team acts—as were the solo items (juggler, contortionist, bicycle acrobatics).

The final display, which succeeded a bicycling collective act, foregrounded the communal dimension which characterized Cirque du Soleil at its beginnings: all artists appeared in a climactic charivari not as individual heroes, but as the group from which all talents had emerged and into which they now all returned. As we will see in the next section, the language of the circus can indeed express ideological and political values beyond the sexual politics we are probing here. An alternative, often witnessed in the traditional Western circus, consists in bringing back to the ring, for a last salute, the individual performers in increasing order of importance, expectedly concluding with the owner of the circus or his/her representative.

The resurgence of the circus as a major popular art during the last quarter of the twentieth century provided opportunities for innovative staging. We will examine some of the most significant ones in the last chapter in this book. Let us focus here on the ways in which the erotic relevance of circus performances was liberated, so to speak, and in some cases ran wild. Circus Archaos, which was founded by Frenchman Pierre Bidon in 1984, is a good example of how far the potential sexualization of circus acts can be spectacularly developed.

May 3, 1991. Stopover in Koeln to see Cirque Archaos. For the past two years, rave reviews have appeared in the cool media. The conservative press, though, has repeatedly asked: but is this circus? No parent would dream of taking their children there. Where are the elegant equestrians and the clowns? Whither the decorum and the pompous music? It is a huge success in Germany. The tent is set up in the industrial outskirts of the city, actually in a wasteland, among some remnants of an old factory which has been half dismantled. The show is to start when the night starts falling. There is already a crowd struggling to reach the ticket booth made of recycled corrugated metal sheets. We have to walk among car skeletons and barrels of burning oil, spewing acrid smells and eye-burning smoke, like a Dantesque descent to hell to see "The Last Show on Earth." It is almost sold out. I manage to get a portion of plank at the top of the scaffoldings which serve as rows of seats. It is dark and smoky inside. Heavy-metal type music saturates the inside of the tent which looks more like a messy warehouse with stuff spread around: containers, barrels, broken-down cars, and twisted bicycles. It soon becomes clear that this is planned chaos. Mayhem explodes at the set time; hordes of ragged musicians and horror clowns invade the ill-defined performing space. Suddenly some spotlights target a billiard pool. On the green felt, a very lightly clad couple, a man and a woman, engage in a hand-to-hand strength and balancing act. The two bodies slide against each other more slowly than it is usual in this type of acrobatics. The technique is superior. These are not sex workers on a teasing stint. This is a high-class circus act which is played without pretending to be purely muscular and comes through as a sublime homage to human sexuality, oscillating between dominance and submission, pleasure and pain, hate and love. Located in the space around the ring and in higher positions on the scaffoldings which surround the gate, I notice that the male circus hands, obviously as part of the staging, simulate masturbation under their overalls.

For two decades, *Archaos* has performed in the industrial outskirts of major European and North American cities. In the latter, though, the sexual contents were subdued and the circus boys kept their arms crossed on their chest during the hand-to-hand act. The staging of all acrobatic acts can indeed be modulated along a scale between the tame and the wild. But it should be clear that the latter is ever present even if it is performed in a restrained, modest manner. The successive programs of Cirque Archaos have expressed to a maximum the erotic spectrum of the circus while consistently featuring some of the best acrobatic acts available at the time.

Circus Charles Knie which we have encountered in earlier chapters in this book could not be reproached for such excesses. It is a typical traditional circus. It features regular items such as horses, seals, lions and tigers, balancing and juggling acts, a flying trapeze troupe, and the like. The MC is authoritative and eloquent. The equestrian is formally dressed in an embroidered costume. Only the twelve-dancer ballet, including ten girls and two males, which appear between the acts to provide a visual link and establish the themes, occasionally indulge in emphasizing body curvatures and undulating movements.

However, when the circus visits a major German city such as Frankfurt, Hamburg, Berlin, or Stuttgart, it schedules a "Gay Circus Night." For the time of a performance, all the sexual potential of the acts is unleashed without symbolic restraint: the show is introduced by a drag queen; the Master Equestrian dons a black-leather minimal outfit of the kinds which are found in sex shops, exposing his butt through a cutout bottom with a mere G-string in the middle; the pas-de-deux acrobatics executed by a man and a woman on their two horses is transformed by their substituting fetishistic uniforms for their usual romantic costumes; the boys of the flying trapeze act enter the ring in tight jeans and climb the rope ladder to their platforms where they undress suggestively before revealing their leather briefs in which they will go through their flying routines; the hula-hoop girl, the woman who trains the seals, the dancers, all reveal more skin and let their hair down. Technically, the acts are not changed with respect to the regular program except that their erotic potential is played out. These displays should not be interpreted as a coming out of the artists but as a representation which reflects the values and icons of a powerful subculture which is a very much alive in the population at large. On such nights, the circus is packed and the crowd is ecstatic. But this is not a pornographic show. It is sexual politics expressed through the language of the circus.

Ideology, politics, and propaganda

August 26, 1983. After a semiotic conference at the Technische Universitaet Berlin, my colleague Professor Roland Posner offers to drive me to Berlin East to visit the National Armenian Circus which is hosted by the official Zirkus Busch. Roland is curious to observe my heuristics. He obviously wants to examine firsthand how I conduct my fieldwork which was the topic of my paper at the conference. As the show starts I quickly scribble words and diagrams on a small notebook. I was then using a pen which had a battery-powered miniature bulb at the tip so that I could monitor my handwriting even during the dimming of the lights and the blackouts which often punctuate a performance to enhance the drama. Roland cannot believe that I can write down every single detail. The rate of information is too fast. However, as I explain to him, a familiarity with circus acts makes them very predictable. I know what horses do in a liberty act. I just need some keywords as shorthand symbols. I note only whatever is new information for me, for instance, any creative deviations from the norms. Suddenly, as the wild-cat act is starting after the intermission, I can hardly cope with the flow. This is not the run-of-the-mill tiger and lion act I am used to. This one has a political agenda. It is, at the same time, a beautifully staged cage act with lighting and music moving from a pastoral, bucolic mode to heroic and tragic accents.

The spotlights first reveal a rock shelter and a cave at the base of a ragged hill with a backdrop of mountain trees. Bare chest, with an animal skin wrapped around his hips, a man plays with wolves which join him as they enter the ring from the mouth of the cave. But an ominous, powerful orchestral music changes the atmosphere as the spotlights move toward the top of the hill. Tigers and lions appear and descend toward the ring following inclined passages which meander toward the ground. They form an impressive and menacing column walking slowly but irrepressibly. The ring is now illuminated by six massive burning torches spread along the periphery of the steel cage and a Roman imperial décor, all red and gilded, emerges from the shadow. With ritualistic countenance the man stands in the center of the ring as an ancient warrior outfit is hoisted down from above. Once he has donned it, the first lions and tigers reach the ground. He confronts them and drives them to their stools. These are long, decorated platforms on which the animals recline in the position of the Egyptian Sphinx. Obviously, the wolves had retired while the public's attention was focused on the newcomers. Now more lions and tigers arrive with two pumas and a black panther.

Regular routines in the fighting mode unfold in the ring. The ferocity of the animals is played out. But progressively, they calm down and act submissively. With his bare hands, he gives them big chunks of red meat which they come to eat at his feet. The man even feeds one lion with one of his hands kept behind his back. That is, the lion takes the meat from behind, an act of total trust in his power on the part of the man, *which is also a sign of total submission on the part of the animal since it implies that the trainer has gained absolute control over the wild beast. All the animals are placed around him while a sword slowly descends from the top of the tent. He seizes it and executes a saber dance in front of them. He then drives the wild cats out of the ring accompanied by a triumphal music with Wagnerian accents. After reading the comments printed in the program, Roland explains to me that this type of act is a specialty of the famous Yerevan Circus which commonly uses the rich Armenian folktale tradition. Special mention is made of S. Isahakyan who gave a new direction to the training and staging of wild-animal acts. The act we had seen was inspired by the story of Sasunti Davit, a 8th century hero of Armenian independence.*

This performance was taking place toward the end of the Cold War. This was the official circus of a Soviet Republic. The Roman Empire imagery distracted from the temptation of reading allusions to the current political situation. But the trainer was impersonating a folk hero of the Armenian past, a simple man who lived with wolves which were local animals when he took it upon himself to defend his homeland against ferocious invaders with the help of a magic sword. Obviously, a political agenda was hidden behind the mask of an anachronistic legend. Who were these invaders coming down from the mountain? What was the meaning of their association with an imperial setting? Were they not overcome by a simple man from the countryside with the help of heavenly powers? Was not his symbolic triumph against forces much stronger than he was, ominous for the party officials who were clapping their hands at the end of the show?

The language of the circus can be used metaphorically to convey political propaganda and ideologies. This results from spontaneous representations of the ethos of a culture. The American dream is an individualistic proposition. Thriving for excellence and efficacy brings rewards to those individuals who dare to take major risks. The American circus tradition glorifies the lone acrobat who surpasses everybody else by exemplifying self-reliance and courage. This, of course, involves a high degree of staging even if it is based on skills acquired through demanding training with the invisible help of others.

The Soviet Union circuses which were touring the world in the 1950s and 1960s with the goal of presenting a positive image of Communist culture were emphasizing human concern and artistry as opposed to the assumed recklessness and gaudiness of the American circus. Acrobats performing highly skilled but dangerous exercises were protected by a safety lunge on the grounds that letting a human being risk his or her life to entertain a crowd was inhuman and a symptom of the cruelty of the Capitalist system. After all, an acrobat in a private circus is a worker exploited by a wealthy owner. At the same time, great effort was brought to the artistic choreography and staging of the acts and classical music was often played with stunning aesthetic effects. Two examples will be offered to illustrate this point.

The first one is a high-wire act which was observed in August 1986 in Buenos Aires. The Moscow Circus was performing for several weeks with great success at Luna Park. This was the first act of the second part which included only two acts, the last one being the spectacular transformations and manipulations of a magician. The large printed program provided enough blank space for me to take extensive notes. The act includes five acrobats, two women and three men, led by Nikolai Nikolski. My diagram of the apparatus shows a straight cable between two poles with small platforms on each one which constitutes the first level. There is a second straight cable about 4 to 5 meters higher, parallel to the first one, which is the second level. An oblique wire joins the two across the space from the left platform of the first level to the right platform of the second level. From the latter another oblique cable reaches up to another platform which is located much higher, almost at the top of the building. Seven exercises are performed in succession involving first the crossing of the wire by one acrobat, then by an acrobat balancing two women on his shoulders. The first oblique cable is ascended by the acrobats and the second level cable is crossed with various acrobatic combinations. The eighth and final segment of the act is staged in a way which introduces a dramatic dimension in addition to the performance of technically demanding feats of balance. The goal is set among the three men on the platform: to reach the last platform at the very top. With the supportive attention of the other two, one man undertakes the ascension but, as he is almost at the end, he fails and slides back to the platform. Another one will try. His companions show concern and support. This one achieves the goal but the staging has construed this eventual victory as the result of a collective endeavor rather than the brash triumph of a lone hero.

The irony is that, a week later, the following news was broadcast by Reuter: "Two Soviet high-wire performers, who slipped away from the Moscow Circus while performing in Buenos Aires were granted asylum in the United States. 'We did not come here to buy blue jeans or clothes,' Bertalina Kazakova told reporters through an interpreter. 'We came here for freedom.'"

She and her husband, Nikolai Nokolski, both 35, were quickly cleared through customs at Miami International Airport and taken away for hours of interviews with immigration officials." The Nikolskis were soon recycled as dare devils in the American circus, starring in Circus USA's big top in South Florida as announced in the September 27, 1986, issue of *Amusement Business*.

The second example is a flying trapeze act which was a part of the Moscow Circus which visited Canada in 1988. It was titled "The cranes," an allusion to the Slavic belief that the souls of heroic warriors who have died for their homeland were embodied in the graceful white cranes who return each year to the countryside. It was a flying trapeze act with a more complex set of trapezes and platforms than the regular straight frame with a single bar swaying like a pendulum under the impulsion of the flyer until the latter releases his or her grip and is caught by the catcher after a somersault. In this eight-acrobat act, two different levels of trapeze and two diametrical axes crossing above the ring were combined. The choreography involved dramatic sequences during which, for instance, an acrobat simulated a fall in the net. As if he were a wounded soldier on a battlefield, two of his companions gracefully descended to rescue him and bring him back to the secure platform. Some bungee cords were making slower flying effects possible. The lighting and the music were lending an eerie atmosphere of poetic mystery and solemnity. The general theme was solidarity and self-sacrifice. It was an organic kind of team in which everybody was a hero. This contrasted with the typical narrative of the Western-style flying trapeze act in which the one who concludes the act with a triple somersault is treated as the triumphant hero irrespective of the fact that the catcher has an equal merit since he finely tuned his timing to be at the right place at the right time in the air, and grasped the hands of the flyer with an appropriate strength to prevent a hurtful shock and a fall.

But the ideological dimension of the Soviet Union circus acts was not always as subtle as the two examples above showed. Straightforward propaganda was often the order of the day, particularly in times of international crises. In the summer of 1983, NATO under the leadership of the United States was planning to deploy mid-range Pershing missiles in Western Europe, which could reach strategic targets in the Soviet Union. This plan was resisted by large segments of the population in Western Europe because they feared that this would put them on the frontline if there were retaliations in case of a NATO attack. This issue became a topic of interest in elections which were to be held that year in several countries. Influencing the European populations was obviously on Moscow's agenda. The language of the circus could be used to deliver subliminal messages aimed at making people think twice before they agree to host batteries of Pershing rockets. Some circus acts could indeed be staged toward this goal without compromising their acrobatic and aesthetic integrity. The Russian State Circus presented at least two such acts with a propaganda tinge in the program which toured Europe. Both acts were technically and artistically irreproachable. Eventually, though, the missiles were deployed in West Germany in November 1983.

The first one was a low-flying trapeze act. Two metallic towers were erected facing each other across the ring. Two acrobats were standing on platforms fixed on the top. The act consisted of swinging a flyer several times to gain speed and momentum, and to release him or her so that the flyer would shoot through space and be caught by the man standing across on the other platform. Various tricks were performed in succession. In the final trick, the two flyers were launched with such timing that they could pass each other in their flights to reach their respective catchers. However, before they implemented this last exercise, the launchers (who also were alternately the catchers) were giving the impression that they intended to propel the two flyers one against the other. At this moment the clown Nikulin, who was intervening from time to time during the show with gags and comments, stopped them, mimicked with his hands the two bodies which were going to crash into each other in the middle, and made a sign meaning "they are mad" by pointing repeatedly to his forehead with his index finger. Launching two projectiles at the same time on the same trajectory is indeed suicidal behavior. This episode in the act was executed with great clarity of gestural expression and carefully staged so that nobody in the audience could miss the message.

The second act displayed acrobatics on horseback. Five men impersonated American cowboys and a scantily clad woman evoked a character usually found in the saloons of the movies set in the Far West. The men wore cowboy hats and had typical belts with gun holsters. They performed their ground and horse tricks with mutually defiant attitudes, bullying each other, and firing blank shots at the first pretext. At the end, as they were all riding the horse one behind the other, they all pulled their guns and, in a gesture of mindless violence, shot each other. All tumbled to the ground and a sudden blackout provided a few seconds of darkness and silence so that the audience could ponder this "shot" at the American ethos and the reckless politics it was assumed to inspire. Portraying one's enemies through negative images is one of the staples of war propaganda. This latter act, though, was more subtle as it undermined the very icon of the American hero in Europe, the cowboy, which had permeated popular culture through its countless dramatic representations in films and in comics.

The body politic in performance

The idea of the body politic is a biological metaphor which construes the various parts of a society as organs serving complementary functions. It implies constraints according to which each group, class, or caste is assigned a place in the social structure. Ultimately it relates individual bodies to the political and cosmological order. It regulates the behavior and demeanor of each group whose identity and destiny are expressed by a pervasive discourse. Each one is held in place by powerful semiotic systems which determine the ways individual bodies conform to the rules of the dominant ideology. It is in this sense that the body politics we have discussed above can be understood in the wider context of particular cultures. These often tacit rules apply to clothes, food, speech, mating, working, and expectations. These constraints are taken for granted but they become manifest when they happen to be transgressed either by chance or by design. Any dysfunction or disruption of the body politic is perceived as pathological. Depending on the magnitude of this tinkering with the rules, the perpetrators are ridiculed by laughter or repressed through legal and physical violence.

In its self-presenting discourse and imagery, the circus projects itself as a perfectly functional body politic which reproduces on a smaller scale the orderly system within which it exists without totally coinciding with it. The circus is both inside and outside society. It is characterized as a city within the cities it visits. Its image is one of diversity, cooperation, and hierarchy with its own norms and values. The root metaphors which irrigate the discourse of and on the circus are the family tree, the pyramidal organization, and the body itself. Some circuses do not shy away from making bolder claims such as the Director of a traditional German circus who included in her introduction to the show: "Circus is a well-ordered microcosm that reflects a harmonious society in which everybody works at the place which God has assigned to them."

> *December 1985. Cannanore (India). Duccio Canestrini, a former doctoral student who has joined me to research the Indian circus, and I are working our way through the dense crowd which assaults the ticket booths of the Venus Circus. We feel lucky to be guided by Mahesh Mangalat, a student at the local university, who has agreed to assist us and shows us how to survive the inch by inch struggle to reach the wickets. The tent forms a huge space with a capacity of at least 4,000 if not more when everybody is squeezed together on the bleachers. The rainy season is over and the countless holes in the canvas create a kind of starry milky way all across the big top.*

Many people carry a book with them. Mahesh proudly tells us that the State of Kerala has reached 100 percent literacy—a detail whose relevance will appear below.

The show starts with a parade of some 50 girls and women in their acrobatic outfit, holding colorful flags representing imaginary countries. Then the program unfolds in a way which we feel could be a little more formal. We have already realized when we were in Mumbai, then Bombay, that the appreciation of the Indian circus must be an acquired taste. We understand now that this is true of all circuses anywhere in the world and we really enjoy the show. When the clown act comes, I immediately recognize an old staple of the European circus repertory: the crazy taxi. However, it soon becomes obvious that it is an idiosyncratic version of it. A woman dressed in a short skirt sits down on the ring's border with a dwarf who follows her. When a taxi enters, the dwarf tries to stop it so that the woman can board it. Unfortunately, there are already two men dressed in local garb occupying the taxi; one is next to the driver, the other in the back seat. Some argument and tussling ensue because the woman wants to take her place in the front seat. The first man moves to the back with the other passenger. As soon as everybody is situated and ready to go, something goes wrong with the car. This is repeated a number of times. A succession of mishaps (flat tire, falling wheel, motor breakdown, water tank explosion, abundant smoke) force the passengers to leave the taxi and wait for the problem to be fixed. Some gags are clear to us. Some others are puzzling. Eventually, the car leaves the ring with everybody on board but on its way out, it explodes, splits into two connected parts and the backseats tip over. The taxi exits with the 2 men upside down with their feet wagging in the air. It was truly difficult to account for the constant bursts of laughter which these antics were triggering. This is a question I would ask Mahesh while we eat our spicy chicken curry after the show.

In research as in life, a lot can be learnt from mistakes. The ethnographer cannot take anything for granted. Even what seems obvious may be deceivingly so. I found myself in such a pitfall when I asked Mahesh if he could clarify a few aspects of the taxi clown act we had just seen. I tried to list what I had understood, starting with the first character which had entered the ring, the woman in a short skirt. To me, it was a prostitute hitchhiking a lift from passing cars. This remark triggered in Mahesh a loud laugh. First, she was not a woman but a man in drag. It would be unacceptable to have a woman perform in a clown act. But, more to the point, she represented an Anglo-Indian lady, that is, the daughter of a mixed couple from the time of the Raj. This was clear from the European style of her clothes. She was very proper and was escorted by her servant who was played by the dwarf. The taxi driver and the dwarf were local folks. But one of the passengers in the taxi was impersonating a Hindu priest from Tamil Nadu, a state which shares its South-West borders with the State of Kerala where we were. The other one represented an intellectual Muslim from the North of India. How could Mahesh know this? The way they were dressed, of course. They were stereotypes of their respective social class. The fat "priest" was a Brahmin typical of conservative and religious Tamil Nadu, with his white loin cloth which partially draped his bare body. He was bearing signs of his sacred functions such as some yellow marking on his forehead, some small trinklets hanging from his neck, and, above all, his demeanor was unmistakable for the audience. As to the other man, his elegant suit fitting a slim body, his hat from the North, the way he was holding a book and kept reading in the taxi, all this was declaring visually his faith, culture, and geographical origin: an intellectual Muslim from Kashmir or Gujarat. The act was suddenly becoming much more complex and interesting than I had first thought. It was clear that the audience was engaged for good reasons. They were Kerala people, the first state which elected a Communist government after independence and had achieved total literacy. The three main characters in the act were like cartoons and their antics were loaded with meaning.

Let us return to the beginning: a taxi carries two unacquainted passengers, a common trait of the Indian way of life. However, the preferred place on the back seat is occupied by a Hindu and the secondary seat next to the driver by a Muslim. The driver is a common man. Everybody is at the right place according to their comparative status in the Indian body politic. There are no women. The car is functional.

By her own hybrid class, the woman represents a disruption of the system. Moreover, she wants to be transported in the taxi, thus mixing sexes and forcing a reconfiguration of the positions. How are the seats to be distributed so that she can be accommodated? This is what triggers a series of upsets which forms the substance of this comedy. The two men are made to get out and after trying several impossible combinations, it is decided that the woman will take the seat in front, next to the driver, and the two men be together in the back. As soon as this plan is implemented, the first breakdown occurs: a flat tire. Everybody has to get off the taxi and wait while the repair is completed. But how to make sure that they will stay apart and the woman will be safe? The driver makes them sit down on the ring's curb at a distance from each other. But both men try to get close to the woman with obvious intentions of seducing her. There are some scuffles which are staged as gags. One of them is particularly significant: in order to pull the priest away from the lady, the driver grasps the white piece of cotton which is coiled around his body. As he pulls on the fabric the priest starts whirling and the piece of cloth keeps unrolling endlessly until it reaches the other side of the ring. This is a version of a gag which has become routine in the Western circus: a clown pulls the shirt of another clown but it is an extralong shirt whose lower part was folded in his pants and keeps coming out as the shirt is pulled. However, there was a special twist to this gag as it was applied to the priest. It irresistibly evoked in the audience a well-known episode of the Mahabharata, the Hindu epic whose characters and narratives permeate Indian culture. To make a long story short: Draupadi, a woman, has been lost in a game of chance by her husbands (several brothers could indeed marry the same woman in ancient times). When the winner wants to enjoy his prize and starts unfolding her sari, the God Krishna miraculously transforms her sari into an endless piece of silk. Applying this trick to a fat Hindu priest, who starts spinning madly in the center of the ring, changes the miraculous into the ridiculous.

Four times, the car breaks down as soon as everybody has boarded it again. The pace goes faster. They get in. The motor explodes. They get out. They come in. A wheel runs loose. Eventually, the taxi seems ready to go and, as it takes the road to the exit, the back part of the car tips over and the two leave the ring with their legs up and their heads down.

Mahesh appreciates the sophistication of the comedy in spite of the crudeness of some gags. He shows pride in the fact that the population in the State of Kerala is free-minded enough to be able to accept these jokes. But he insists that such an act can be performed only in Kerala. In conservative Tamil Nadu, making fun of a high priest would not be taken kindly. In any case, this one does not look like a local one. As you move toward the North, a comedy like this one could easily trigger communal violence. The next day, when we meet the actors after the show, they confirm the risks that this comedy would imply, should they perform it outside Kerala. They are actually professional actors who enjoy the continuous success they meet in this circus, playing for large popular audiences.

Incidentally, 25 years later, this act was still being performed in the same circus as it was witnessed by Mahesh Mangalat, now a Professor of Malayalam Literature, and Dr James Skidmore who was then pursuing postdoctoral research on the Indian circus. It should be noted, though, that the crazy taxi act at the Venus Circus was not a unique creation but rather a skilled development and interpretation of a narrative kernel which can generate a variety of versions. During the same year, I recorded such an act in a small circus which was performing in a suburb of Kolkata, then Calcutta. It was reduced to three actors and the vehicle was a rickshaw. A Hindu priest was seated in it. An Anglo-Indian "woman" wanted to be transported. This disruption triggered a cascade of gags with all things ending upside down as the outcome of the process.

Over 200 years of Indian history must be kept in mind if one is to understand the sociopolitical relevance of this clown act: the British Empire, the fight for independence, the partition, and the ensuing delicate balance between the two main communities which make up modern India. It is symptomatic that in both versions of the narrative which these performances embody, the factor that triggers the crisis is a symbol of the Raj, a child of a union between the dominant conqueror and a local inhabitant. The Anglo-Indian woman symbolizes through her demeanor the outside intervention which generated imbalance and violence. Significantly, if one of the three main characters has to be eliminated from the cast for the sake of simplification, economy, or self-censorship as it might have been the case in the Kolkata version, it is the Muslim character who is dispensed with. Take out the woman and the very possibility of the act disappears.

Vehicles of all kinds—horse-drawn or motor-driven—traditionally have been used as metaphors of the State. Carrying people side by side over a distance is like guiding a political institution over time while maintaining peace among the population. The circus comedy we have described and pondered is loaded with political significance. It illustrates how the body politic becomes dysfunctional and eventually is turned upside down when an intruder compromises the balance which the centuries had worked out. Of course, this is not an objective, scientific account of the rich and variegated history of India. It concerns rather the ideal vision which is fostered at a given time in the public imagination. But it is with respect to this discourse that the language of the circus articulates its own multimodal text which produces a deep, albeit tacit meaning for its audience. This is why, in spite of its oddities, the circus makes so much sense.

12

The Postanimal Circus

A cultural revolution: The animal liberation movement

On November 25, 2011, the Bundesrat, the Senate of the German Government, voted to prevent circuses from keeping large mammals such as elephants, giraffes, and hippopotami for the purpose of displaying or training them as parts of their performances. Bears and monkeys were also prohibited. The grounds for this legislation included the claim that these animals are confined in narrow trucks during their transportation from city to city and suffer from the general conditions in which they are kept. This measure came in the wake of a still more radical vote in the British Parliament which approved by an overwhelming majority the total ban of animals in circuses. Eventually, the German government overturned the Senate legislative move a month later. It is also public knowledge that the British prime minister was promoting an alternative legal framework such as the ones which are in place in several European countries for circuses when members of his own party broke rank and supported the prohibition vote.

As we are advancing into the twenty-first century, the issue of circus animals is raised with increasing intensity worldwide and forces legislators to take side. The prohibitionists have been so far kept at bay in most parts of the world where decisions to allow animal circuses to perform is generally left at the discretion of local authorities. But some countries such as Austria and Bolivia (and now most likely England) have already enforced the total prohibition of wild animals in circuses. In many others, activists who claim to be acting on behalf of sizeable percentages of the population are fuelled by the disposable income of their supporters and organize campaigns to sensitize opinion to the perceived plights of animals in contemporary society. They lobby politicians to encourage them to vote and enact repressive laws concerning the use of animals in laboratories as well as circuses. They are usually more successful regarding the latter which form a more vulnerable social group than the scientific and pharmaceutical establishments. They make great use of disturbing visual documents which are claimed to represent the norm. This phenomenon is a symptom of the general shift of attitude toward animals which we discussed in Chapter 7. This situation cannot be ignored as it puts pressure on the traditional circus to transform itself into a postanimal mode of existence, a process which has been developing for the past 50 years or so.

The ethnographic agenda of this volume has led us to devote a full chapter to the description of cage acts as they can still be observed in many countries where they constitute an important part of the multimodal discourse of the circus. Examples have been deliberately chosen among companies which maintain high standards in the treatment of their animals. However, it is likely that even those who apply humanely acceptable methods of breeding, keeping, and training wild animals will eventually fall victim to the cultural shift which construes animal as necessarily helpless victims and humans as their self-appointed guardians and defenders. A brief discussion of this "cultural revolution" is in order because it significantly impacts the reception of circus performances and heralds the emergence of a new kind of circus, even perhaps a new kind of animal performance.

Animals, though, remain popular in many countries to the extent that some circuses in France, Italy, and Germany, to name only a few for which evidence is available, still advertise the abundant presence of animals in their programs. The animal rights activists' campaigns are countered by testimony from zoologists and veterinarians who consider that by and large circus animals are well taken care of by their owners who have a vested interest in their well-being, and that the training methods are ethically appropriate to the natural behavior of the wild species concerned.

On November 20, 2011, the Chairman of a Circus Working Group appointed by the UK government in 2010, whose mandate was to assess scientific evidence concerning circus animal welfare, reported the unanimous findings of a panel of academic and practicing experts, nominated by both the circus industry and activist organizations. It was concluded that: (1) "Whilst it was accepted that animals kept in circuses were more confined than in the wild the opinion of most of the Panel was that this did not, necessarily, lead to adverse welfare" (para. 5.3.4); (2) "[A]lthough circus animals are transported regularly, there is no evidence that this, of its own nature, causes the animals' welfare to be adversely affected" (para. 5.4.3); (3) "[T]ere is little evidence that the health of circus animals is any better or worse than animals in other captive environments" (para. 5.6.2).

Indeed, commissions of experts in other countries have consistently concluded that, while prosecutions under the law are justified in case of abuses, a total ban of circus animals is a matter of ideology and politics rather than science. But ideology is what drives cultural revolutions and the tide seems irreversible for the time being as the vote of the British Parliament bears witness. Advocates for the circus have pointed out that activists tend to take the law in their own hands and at times produce the evidence which they believe will serve their cause. The video clips with which they flood the internet are few and highly selective, and have never been authenticated. Fortunately, most people concerned with the well-being of animals respect the legal due process, debate with sound arguments, and gather reliable and balanced information. It is this constituency of concerned citizens which has brought about crucial reforms in the management of animals in circuses during the past 50 years and may eventually make culturally irrelevant rather than illegal the presence of wild and domestic animals in the circus ring.

All rituals are destined to become obsolete sooner or later when they become mere empty shells which have lost their transformative powers. They can persist, of course, through a kind of cultural inertia which sustains their dynamic. Their enjoyment then does not proceed from the fresh meanings they produce but from the nostalgic pleasure of reenacting some anachronistic behavior. Once Christian Orthodox icons or statues of Hindu gods are displayed in museums, they may be interpreted historically and admired aesthetically but are not the focus of religious cults, at least in these contexts. In the same manner, the control of large predators which was one of the main vital obsessions of humans and their evolutionary ancestors has ceased to be relevant in most parts of the world. Fear of wolves persisted in Western Europe until the end of the nineteenth century and explains the success of the first traveling wild-animal shows which exhibited trained wolves such as, in France, the Pezon and the Bonnefoux families during the mid-nineteenth century. This kind of act persisted until the beginning of the twentieth century in Western Europe. Rudesindo Roche presented with great success in Paris 14 Russian wolves at the Cirque d'Hiver (1887) and at the Folies Bergere (1888). Note that the animals were featured as exotic, probably cashing on countless references to their deadly attacks in the Slavic literature as well as popular press (Garnier 1979). Wolves were still a part of circus programs in Eastern Europe until the mid-twentieth century. Circus Probst from East Germany carried a wolf act until the 1950s and, as we saw in Chapter 11, the Armenian Circus included wolves in a spectacular wild-animal display in the 1980s. But, at that time, the animals were presented as the trainer's playful partners. We have lost the sense of the haunting presence of wolves not only, of course, as smart, numerous, and deadly rivals, but also as iconic villains in countless folktales and literary texts. Stories of werewolves and uncanny individuals who had control over packs of wolves had the same effects as today's horror movies during storytelling sessions around the fireplace in dark winter nights. As the actual threat from wolves declined with the extinction of this species in most parts of Europe, tales of man-eating tigers and lions took over as they were fostered by the colonial culture principally in England and France. Stories were spread by travelers' memoirs and amplified in popular and literary works. Naturally, the danger of falling victim to a tiger or a lion while toiling in the fields or in the forest was purely an imaginary fear for Europeans who stayed at home but a more realistic risk for those who had been sent to exotic lands in which they were hardly welcomed. Tragic accidents in cage acts and in itinerant wild-animal exhibitions nevertheless kept such fear all the more alive in the population's imagination as entertainers knew how to enhance the apparent ferocity of their animals through tall tales and painted banners, and by provoking resounding roars and growls from their charges during performances. It is in view of such a mostly symbolic background that wild-animal acts were appreciated and their trainers were admired like heroes or martyrs. This was also a time when very little was scientifically known about the natural behavior of these animals and the kind of existence they lead in the wild. In addition, they were then still abundant, assumed to be dispensable, and broadly considered a nuisance. Bengal tigers were slaughtered by the hundreds by British sport hunters as were African lions by French and English colonizers. Reliable knowledge has accrued about these species and about their crucial role in maintaining the ecological balance. They are no longer considered an inexhaustible hunting resource and are theoretically protected by laws which attempt to prevent their total extinction. Their continuing presence in circus shows in the forms in which they were presented in modern times may now legitimately appear in the eyes of many concerned people as culturally obsolete and morally reprehensible. Whether these animals should be prohibited or the modalities of their presence should be changed is an issue we will examine in the last section of this chapter. Let us now turn to the postanimal circus which has become a dominant force in the contemporary landscape of popular entertainment.

The new circus: Human, humane, and humanitarian

The old paternalistic structure of the traditional circus started to change in Europe with the advent of Communist governments and their perception of the circus as a major component of popular culture. Acrobats were no longer allowed to risk their lives for the sake of thrilling their audience and the use of safety nets or lunges was made compulsory during performances. The artistic qualities of the acts were improved by paying greater attention to the staging: costumes, music, and choreography. During the Cold War, as we saw in the previous chapter, the Soviet circus was used as an international tool of propaganda, sometimes through the very ideological and political contents of its multimodal discourse, but more generally as a display of greater humane and humanistic values than the American circus was supposed to foster. Classical music often accompanied acrobatic acts which displayed postures and gestures inspired by the Russian ballet's aesthetic tradition.

At the same time, the training in circus skills was not left to the old circus families and clans which had been preserving from immemorial times the trade secrets of these arts through schooling their children in acrobatics and other disciplines at an early age. Official circus schools with proper medical supervision and concern for the general education of their students were created. Naturally, many knowledgeable circus artists who could not any longer run their traditional family businesses as free enterprises in the new, collectivist system were hired as teachers in these new schools through which they perpetuated their body techniques. When Communist China opened up to the West, circus institutions, such as acrobatic schools, joined the fray and engaged in collaborative ventures, promoting a collectivist style of organization. The People's Republic of China also sponsored official traveling circus spectacles, occasionally featuring a trained panda.

Coincidentally, after the mid-twentieth century, Western European circuses had difficulties adapting to changing technologies, shifts of interest toward other forms of entertainment, and social legislations which impacted negatively on their traditional modes of operation. Many circuses closed or shifted to other activities. But some decided to ride the new wave and created circus schools of their own, which were often subsidized by governments. This proved to be a profitable strategy because, in addition to the financial support they were receiving and the fees they were charging, they produced an oversupply of skilled artists who later accepted to perform in their shows for minimal wages. Only very few, though, could reach stardom, let alone a sustainable professional life in the circus industry, and transferred the basic acrobatic skills they had acquired to the ballet, the theater, or simply the precarious existence of street entertainers, busking on their own time while traveling during the favorable season. Only exceptionally, some founded successful companies which demonstrated artistic creativity and economic sustainability. These entrepreneurs, usually with the backing of their government or less palatable economic powers, earned a place among the cultural institutions of their countries and acquired global status.

The circus schools offered the children of the middle class an alternative to the traumatic "running off to the circus." Some of them developed companies of their own, straddling the circus and theater genres, and proved to be extremely creative in their staging rather than in the intrinsic value of their acrobatics. The New Circus, as it came to be called, had repudiated animals from its programs, making a virtue out of necessity because animal husbandry and training are far more demanding than running small acrobatic troupes which can travel with minimal equipment and can perform in a variety of venues. Keeping circus animals is a lifelong, often multigenerational commitment. Competently breeding, maintaining, and training wild animals cannot be learned quickly and is extraordinarily time-consuming and costly. Even keeping a single horse entails expertise and responsibility.

But the opening of circus schools had a more general impact on society than merely catering to the fantasies of adolescents whose families could afford the registration fees. Social activists who were concerned about the lack of opportunities for underprivileged youths started offering circus training as an attractive alternative to petty criminality. Circus acrobatics was perceived as a way of developing self-discipline and providing proximal guidance. The benefits certainly included better social integration, health monitoring, and virtual professional perspectives for those who would be able to persist and acquire a marketable specialty. This is now a worldwide phenomenon. Even some children of traditional circus families have joined such schools. Another advantage of these new institutions is that they provided employment for older artists who could not earn any longer a living as performers but still could be efficient instructors and offer precious resources concerning the circus tradition to newcomers. There are indications, though, that some of them were reluctant to transmit what they considered to be trade secrets to strangers who did not belong to their family, clan, or ethnic group. They were nevertheless providing sound basic training. The great majority, mainly those who had initially come to the circus as outsiders, were eager to convey to young acrobats the best of their skills and knowledge of the tradition.

However, as a general rule, high-risk acrobatics was not encouraged in the setting of these schools. The emphasis remains nowadays on physical skills involving strength and balance. The goal is to form decent professionals, leaving to their individual decision the development of genuine "death-defying" acts as an attempt to reach celebrity status or simply for the sake of their own drive toward perfection, a kind of intimate mystical urge.

The New Circus has fostered the emergence of a different circus discourse and has proposed both exemplary professional norms and sound ethical grounds. For those who oppose the use of animals in performance, this kind of circus is being touted as virtuous. In spite of occasional scandals relating to the abuse of orphaned children which were enrolled and trained in uncontrolled troupes, the social merits of these New Circus initiatives have on the whole received positive assessments and the theme of "redemption through the circus" as a school of courage, discipline, and artistic beauty has permeated the media.

Let us turn in concluding this section to the exemplary case of the Australian Circus Oz. Its 2012 Circus Class Descriptions (see www.circusoz.com) include programs for adults, children, and young people with disabilities. Adults can undergo training for flying trapeze, aerial, tumbling, acrobatic balance, pole, and contortion. Children 7 to 12 are introduced to tumbling, trapeze, tightwire, pyramids, and juggling among a host of other skills. There is a special program for teenagers. Disabled youths between 8 and 18 can take courses supported by the Australian Department of Human Services. This latter program which includes dance, clowning, acting, and adapted acrobatics is designed to build self-esteem, confidence, social skills, and coordination. This humanitarian work obviously draws from the symbolic capital of the circus to endow physiotherapeutic programs with an added psychological value: becoming a part of the magic dreamworld of the circus.

Circus and subversion: From anticircus to counterculture and activism

All cultures generate counter-cultures. Dropouts from the circus schools and self-taught individuals became proficient practitioners of the circus arts and claimed a stake in the circus realm by building their own performing territories in the margins of the institution, often in violent opposition to its codes. Nothing could be more revealing of this phenomenon than the often quoted statement by Pierre Bidon, the founder of *Cirque Archaos*: "I hated the circus. This is why I became the circus." We already encountered, in the previous chapter, this extraordinary show which shook the circus world with a storm of provocations and, at the same time, laid bare some of the most essential dimensions of its sense-making power. No ring, no sawdust, no animal, no tinsels, no MC, no pomp, no order. The name itself, *Archaos*, pointed to the creative chaos of the origins, the state of the world before order was imposed, a state which was also represented as what was to come after order disappears once institutions have dissolved and returned to nothingness. This circus was always set up in the margins of cities, at the center of desolate suburban areas, preferably among abandoned factories, and was surrounded by wrecked cars and burning heaps of garbage, which evoked the ruins of the civilization of unbridled consumerism of which the classic circus was a part. This provocative multimodal discourse was bent to transgress the expected etiquette and trappings of respectability found in traditional performances. But circus means were used to choreograph and stage this anticircus symbolic explosion.

The absence of animals was compensated by the ever presence of motor vehicles and other machinery which replaced the horse as a means of transportation and work. Cars, trucks, and motorcycles are now more destructive of human lives than predators ever were in earlier times. Bulldozers and chainsaws were profusely used in the shows. These were not look-alike inoffensive models but real, functional ones, as were the lions and tigers of the classic circus. In one of its programs, *Archaos* even featured a vintage steam-locomotive which unexpectedly surged from the back stage and speeded on the rails across the tent roaring and spewing smoke. The virtual fence which, in traditional circuses, separates the performing area from the audience was inexistent, or rather emphatically negated. Videos of the time show disheveled clowns pursuing their victims with chainsaws among the public. The contained violence of the circus was unleashed and taboos were enthusiastically broken. "Good taste" and other signs of class distinction as well as political correctness were the casualties of these iconoclastic rituals which displayed the unthinkable and the unpalatable through the language of a circus of excesses and cruelty.

There have been other examples of systematic transgressions of the classic circus's codes which showed that all language can be used as a metalanguage that takes itself as an object of reflection or derision. The British company Circus Lumiere, which was founded in 1970 by Hilary Westlake in London, was billed as a circus for adults, from which children were barred. It staged systematic inversions of the circus norms, these norms being themselves at odds with those of the contextual culture. For instance, a magician was cutting open a rabbit to extract a top hat from its belly and a group of young men wearing harnesses were directed as liberty horses by an equestrian dominatrix. Clowns were gorging on laundry powder and gobbling containers of toilet bowls cleaning liquids. One of them ate his own brain by apparently scooping it out with a spoon after the top of his skull was sawed off. The discourse of the circus is indeed liable to being used in surrealist or horror registers not only in literature and film but also in the circus medium itself.

The circus as a discourse can articulate a great variety of ideologies and values. *Archaos* and *Lumiere*, each one in its own idiom, transgressed and manipulated the code itself and opened the way to the development of a new genre which inspired others to take to the road and shake up conventions. The twenty-first century witnessed, for instance, the Australian *Caravan of Doom*, a handful of acrobats doubling as cross-dressing clowns who traveled on motorbikes under the leadership of Captain Ruin (Mitch Jones) and cultivated the provocative and the outrageous for the enjoyment of small, young audiences in cramped, smoky venues and on crowded street corners when cash flow was an issue. The counterculture movement generated indeed a proliferation of short-lived underground circuses whose members were frequently the offspring of the first generation of New Circus artists, who had mastered at an early age the handstands, juggling, and somersaulting of their parents, and had inherited their counterculture ethos.

Such libertarian, unconventional, and independent attitudes could also lead to a commitment to social causes and explicit activism. In the previous section, Circus Oz was mentioned for its humanitarian work. This icon of the New Circus movement, which quickly acquired an international profile through being recognized as a genuine Australian culture representative, was founded in Melbourne in 1978 with an activist agenda. Its self-presentation online states: "Circus Oz has a strong belief in tolerance, diversity, and human kindness. For many years the company has engaged in issues associated with social justice and a good time for all, including work each year with many charities and indigenous communities." The company also raises money in support of refugees and asylum seekers. Circus Oz proclaims that it is animal-free, and that it is under collective ownership, promotes gender equity, and operates as a team.

It emphasizes its debt to China's Nanjing Acrobatic Troupe which in the mid-1980s helped its members to develop their skills and reinforced the collectivist ideology of its founders. In contrast with Cirque du Soleil, which had started around the same time with similar premises, Circus Oz has neither corporatized itself, nor spun numerous spectacles under a global brand name. It has gained international status without becoming a part of the huge entertainment industry with all the financial and ideological constraints this entails. It has also preserved its Australian identity and does not shy away from committing itself to sociopolitical causes. It has been successful in recruiting new generations which are determined to pursue its original mission.

The ritual imperative of all human cultures, as we suggested in the first chapter of this book, constantly generates spatial and temporal structures which are embedded with saliency into the loose fabric of everyday social life. Well-defined performative situations are periodically created through which symbols are concentrated and values encapsulated in transformative narratives which involve all the sensorial modalities available to humans. Although a circus show is sometimes referred to as a "representation," as if something were happening by proxy, it definitely makes present actual agents who enact transmutations in the crucible of the ring. The classic circus commonly transforms an apparently old and derelict tramp into a young athlete who triumphs on the trapeze or a fierce lion into an animal to whose jaws a man trusts his head. This circus operates the metamorphosis of raw nature into sophisticated culture. The new circus strives to symbolically transform the harsh society of conflict and exclusion into a civil society of justice and kindness. This can be first achieved in the ring. There is multisensorial contiguity between the performers and the audience to the extent that the transformation is contagious. The distance between the spectacle and the spectators is codified in a way which ensures that they are not mutually alienated because the circular structure creates several degrees of spatial and visual envelopment. The audience can see itself as well as the performers to the point that the performative situation achieves by itself a fusion.

Fusion is indeed the key notion which explains rituals. The activism which drives the artistic agenda of Circus Oz, for instance, is aimed at social integration. It symbolically overcomes exclusions of all kinds not only with respect to the Australian context but also globally as it stands for refuges, asylum seekers, and all ostracized segments of the world population. The exclusion of animals can be construed also as a form of inclusion since it is for the sake of their rights that animals are not exploited as tools of entertainment in its programs. From this point of view, animals are paradoxically present through their very absence. There might be, however, ways of reintegrating them in the circus rituals without adulterating the philosophy and ethics of the New Circus.

The return of the animal?

Although opponents of the presence of trained animals in circuses have been vocal and influential in some countries, they are far from representing an overwhelming majority. Circuses are business enterprises and when they advertise the presence of animals in their programs, it is because there is a popular demand for this. When inquiries are made regarding this issue, everybody seems to agree that violence and abuses are reprehensible, and should be prevented by appropriate legislation as is the case in most civil societies. However, they recognize that wild animals which are kept in circuses, an environment in which most of them were born and raised, are well treated by their keepers and trainers. These kinds of animal-human interactions, which involve safety constraints for the protection of the visitors of traveling zoos and circus audiences, constitute a specific hybrid subculture which has been little studied. Circus folks and their animals construct over their lifetime meaningful networks of signs through which they recognize each other, mutually anticipate their behavior, convey desires, and express emotions. Because of their constant interactions, keepers and their charges progressively construct a cross-specific code according to which trainers commonly produce species-specific vocal sounds which are significant for their animals, and, conversely, these animals adapt to the semiotic systems of the humans with which they interact such as responding to the names they have been given and appropriately reacting to the range of intonations which are typical of human languages. In addition, not only gestures which can be quite arbitrary but also words are used as meaningful cues in everyday interactions as well as in performances. It is this rich semiotic fabric which is constantly woven in the world of the circus, including a whole range of natural signs of which we are not aware, such as pheromones, subliminal sounds and imperceptible movements, olfactory information, and all the body contacts from brushing, scratching, showering the animals which may reciprocate in their own way with a rough lick of the tongue or a playful tussle. Anybody who has witnessed an elephant being washed and brushed can perceive the willingness of the animal to be so tended and the pleasure it experiences in this process.

The public generally enjoys the safe proximity of animals they can admire in action by contrast with the often hardly visible presence of these animals in zoological gardens. Lions, tigers, elephants, and other wild species in the circus have been accustomed since they were born to the proximity of humans with whom they selectively form bonds.

When opponents of the presence of animals in circuses are confronted with scientific evidence that these animals are not suffering from their captive conditions, their second line of argument is that these animals are made to perform demeaning exercises. They mean by this the training of "unnatural" behavior which, in their opinion, causes animals to lose their dignity. There is no doubt that an elephant doing a headstand or a tiger made to ride a specially designed bicycle look silly. These two examples belong to a paradigm of training and staging which includes instances of forced anthropomorphism such as fixing a hat on the top of an animal's head, dressing up bears and primates or monkeys with human garments, and creating the illusion that a horse understands articulate language and can add and subtract as well as mathematicians do. These are cultural fossils, the remnants of a time when the general population as well as the intellectual minority were mostly ignorant of the way of life of animals, their physical and cognitive capacities, the complexity of their social behavior, and the psychological characteristics of each individual. As we saw in Chapter 4, the scientific elite in the late nineteenth century was prone to grant advanced arithmetic skills to some horses. Until the twentieth century, not much progress had been made in this respect since Aristotle. Animals were perceived through the filters of metaphysics and folklore, or reduced to laboratory automata. Modern enlightened audiences who are conversant with the research of Franz de Waal (1989), Cynthia Moss (1988), or Charles McDougal (1977), to mention only a few, cannot possibly enjoy watching a chained baby chimpanzee smoking a cigar, an elephant prodded to sit on a stool with a top hat on its head, or a tiger reluctantly standing straight up on a revolving mirror-studded sphere under the glare of spotlights. Such displays are as mindless and insulting, both to the animals and the spectators, as the countless animation movies which feed children and their willing parents with fairy tale views of animals which, tragically for the animals, spread ignorance among populations which should instead be exposed and sensitized to the natural beauty and behavior of the species which are driven to extinction.

Humans are not complete without their animal complement. In relatively recent evolutionary time, they have evolved in relation to each other as they have always been a defining part of the environments to which both adapted. Domestication worked both ways. Some evolutionary biologists contend that cattle, sheep, and goats first sought protection from their predators by staying in the proximity of humans when the latter's mastery of fire and other weaponry started to keep those predators at bay. Dogs may have first been *Canidae* which were attracted to the benefits of communal hunting with human bands. Nowadays, in the wild life sanctuaries of Indian forests, herds of wild deer gather for the night within the perimeter of the bungalows compounds where tourists are accommodated. These ungulates seek protection from tigers which are wary of getting too close to humans if they can avoid it. Tigers must eat and, in the jungle, not all deer see the dawn of the next day. Patterns of symbiosis and commensalism emerged from such environmental pressures. There are natural affinities between humans and some other animal species which are based on shared sensorial information and form the basis of the very possibility of domestication and training. In many respects, circus animal acts are ways of celebrating ritualistically these immemorial alliances. In accordance with the contemporary state of biological knowledge and standards of welfare, such acts could be more explicitly construed as iconic reenactments of the convergence of some species, including humans, toward common goals of survival. The spectacle of six zebras approaching a trainer in the center of the ring to receive pieces of carrots from her or his hands can be experienced as an immemorial gesture of commensality which preserves the dignity of each.

Human history with the emergence of complex civilizations is inseparable from the domestication of horses and elephants which, for millennia, have mingled with humans in Eurasian and North African urban settlements. Their integration into human cultures originated from a different process initially based on the capture of supplementary sources of energy and strength. However, it evolved into a kind of symbiosis which offered countless examples of psychological bonding. It provides also one of the most cogent examples of genetic and cultural coevolution. The circus rituals also commemorate this crucial founding of human cultures and the interspecific companionship it fostered.

Finally, the inherent violence which regulates the relationship between predators and their prey is transcended in cage acts which demonstrate the possibility of peaceful, even affectionate rapport with large felines. The times when reenacting violence by ritualistically slaughtering lions and tigers in the Roman Empire's amphitheaters have long gone. So is the modern, symbolic version of this violence which was embodied in the fighting confrontations of the nineteenth century when trainers often were wearing gladiators' outfits or colonial army uniforms. The spectacle of an embrace between a human and a full-grown lion or tiger as it is performed by some contemporary trainers implements a mutual triumph over fear and aggression which gives substance to the transformative power of the circus rituals and can be a rich source of reflection, pleasure, and inspiration.

Will animals return to the circus in the long run? It is quite possible that cultural evolution will prompt new modalities in the perception and treatment of animals beyond the current prohibitionist attitude, and that their presence and participation in the rituals of the circus will be reinvented in the context of posthumanism. Ways of displaying the commonality of biological adaptations and behavioral patterns between animals and humans rather than emphatically staging their radical differences could be the source of the new cosmological understanding which some have dubbed "transhumanism." Humanism and its Cartesian legacy have been transcended by the comprehensive vision of Darwinism and the New Synthesis. We can imagine new wild-animal acts in which sequences of natural behavior would be elicited by the construction of relevant situations rather than triggered by Pavlovian reflexes. In a world which is increasingly dominated by virtual experience, the actual, concrete, even brutal presence of animals at close range by means of a ritual would connect humans not only to the continuum of life on earth more efficiently than discourse and statistics but also to themselves. Transhumanism will require its rituals and the affective fusion they achieve through involving all the sensorial modalities which carry information across species in the tumultuous river of life. When we are abstracted from this flow, we become a mere illusion.

Conclusion

Pleasures of the Circus: Attraction, Emotion, and Addiction

Truth and deception

A commonplace which frequently recurs in the critical discourse about the circus is that its spectacles are true and genuine. The acrobat who walks on a high wire cannot cheat. He or she actually does this in front of the spectators' eyes. Such displayed actions are perceived as the opposite of theatrical representations in which actors can only pretend to be capable of performing extraordinary feats of strength and balance. Actors switch from one identity to another and their actions and emotions are mere simulacra. Since the advent of the digital age and the spread of popular technologies such as Photoshop, films and photographs cannot be fully trusted to reflect the real world. By contrast, the circus offers irrefutable evidence of the reality of its performances because consistent information is received through all the sensorial channels available to humans and the time of the perception coincides with the time of the performance to such an extent that the outcome of its actions remains uncertain for the spectators until they are completed. The chronicle of the circus keeps providing reports of a sufficient number of unfortunate accidents to make credible the reality of the risks involved. Unpredictability authenticates the truth of circus performances by making the audience the potential witness of catastrophic outcomes, something which is both feared and desired at the same time. Most humans indeed crave information at any cost. In some respects, watching a circus show is somewhat comparable to attending a theatrical drama in which an actor plays Russian roulette with live bullets. The circus is always essentially a live, open game in spite of the ritualistic formality of its unfolding.

However, another commonplace of the discourse on the circus is that it is a world of lies and deceptions. There has hardly been any chapter in this book in which a delusive trick was not disclosed: acrobats stage a failure in order to construe an action as more difficult than it actually is; horses are supposed to understand articulate language while they merely respond to the hand movements of their trainer; clowns appear to be noisily slapped on the face when the sounds come in fact from the clapping of their own hands. Circus has often been denounced as the realm of illusions. Its history from the time of the medieval fairgrounds to the age of marketing is rife with examples of exaggerated claims designed to capture the attention of the public and attract audiences. The images displayed on banners and posters aggrandize and glamorize the circus icons which at the end may possess more reality in the minds of the spectators than the actual artists they briefly see in the ring. The attractiveness of the circus is indeed supported by powerful iconic waves, constantly renewed through illustrated books, websites, and video clips. Digital photography further contributed to the idealization of the circus by freezing countless instants which offer the possibility of focusing attention on morphological and chromatic details which cannot be consciously perceived and processed during the flow of the performance itself. As a result, many spectators perceive the artists, the animals, and the props of the circus through the filters of their idealized images. As we saw in Chapter 10, literary works, paintings, and films often bias the experience of performances to the extent that they can be considered to be a constitutive part of the multimodal and transartistic discourse of the circus. The pictures in Chapters 2 and 8 offer everlasting glimpses of instants which were abstracted from a fast and continuous flux of multimodal perceptions. It seems that, paradoxically, bluffing and deluding are as much an essential part of the circus as the truth and honesty at the core of the performances which are displayed in the ring. It is through the staging and framing of these feats that the discourse of the circus creates multimodal metaphors and narratives which cause wonderment and embody fantasies.

These two faces of the circus can be considered separately and their cultural evolution can be retraced in historical times. For instance, there is archaeological evidence of acrobatic horsemanship dating from the earliest Chinese kingdoms. Inventions of some spectacular tricks such as the flying trapeze act or the apparent beheading of a person by a magician are well documented. And so are the ways in which these feats have been announced and advertised in successive epochs. For the most part, the circus tradition is indeed a culture-sensitive phenomenon. But it seems to possess universal qualities as well, which relate its body techniques and their modes of public display in live performances to much deeper primal roots. Let us reflect in concluding this volume on the evolution of the social behaviors upon which the circus, under whatever name, is grounded.

The logic of attraction

Luring a prey or a mate is a vital imperative of many social species, at least among mammals. Humans do not escape these constraints of nature. Hunting techniques which succeed in attracting the prey in the vicinity of the predators are highly cost-effective and capturing the attention of a desirable mate is at the heart of courtship behavior. Both imply some forms of staging and performing which target others with semiotic means. The logic of attraction drives the evolution of behavior and may also explain the emergence of some human institutions whose ultimate goal is to serve the survival of their members.

Circuses, as organizations usually belonging to a single family over several generations, as well as individual circus artists compete for attention. The former must secure locations in which they can attract lucrative audiences. The latter must be hired by circuses or other institutions which consider their presence as an asset if they are part of the programs they offer. Both must be attractive at their respective levels in order to survive. Ultimately, their very existence depends on their ability to seduce the population at large and motivate spectators to spend a portion of their disposable income on the purchase of admission tickets. Local businesses in cities usually do not welcome the presence of traveling circuses because they distract significant economic resources from their regular customers. The history of the modern circus records the endless series of successes and failures of circus organizations which competed in very rough market conditions. Those who managed to prosper had demonstrated an outstanding capacity to attract attention and to sustain interest among their constituencies of spectators. This involved an efficient production and manipulation of signs in the literal as well as more general sense of the term. It required balancing bluff and substance. Like natural selection, the selective survival of cultural organizations depends on their adaptive qualities, that is, how well they happen to match the constraints of their evolving environment. A circus clown or a lion trainer must keep attuned to the changing system of values of the society for which they perform. In today's circus the former has better to abstain from making politically incorrect jokes and ethically outrageous gags, and the latter must avoid violent confrontations with the animals. Failing to observe these constraints will cause both to soon disappear by lack of contracts because circus entrepreneurs need to remain sensitive to the community standards of their time if they are to stay in business. Cultural selection is an ever-present process according to which some forms perish and others emerge and prosper. Audiences are indeed consumers who make comparative choices.

Taken abstractly, this dynamic pattern is homologous to a well-documented behavior which is observed in many social species: the display by males of outstanding phenotypic traits in front of females who decide with which they will mate. In these species, males carry extra weight (such as large antlers or long feathery tails) and/or bright colors which expose them to the attention of predators. These are signs of the exceptional adaptive quality of their genes since they have survived to the age of reproduction in spite of these "handicaps" as they have been labeled by some biologists (Zahavi and Zahavi 1997). Male elephants converge toward a female which has been advertising her readiness to mate, and fight with each other in front of her until the victorious animal is allowed to claim its prize. Many male birds, in particular bower birds, build shelters and decorate them with colorful pebbles, flowers, and other bright objects, waiting for female passersby which may be seduced into copulating if they are sufficiently impressed. Some display in addition courtship "dances." But the most striking behavior is what zoologists called *lekking*, a Swedish word which is derived from the verb *leka* (to play). A group of males gather in an open area and display various visual and acoustic feats akin to dance and acrobatics while being watched by the females of their species which assess their respective competencies and eventually choose a mate after having visited several *lekking* areas (Hoglund and Alatalo 1995).

Competitive displays of strength, agility, horsemanship, and vocal, verbal, or instrumental skills are a common feature of folk cultures in which contests among young men were (and still are) traditionally organized at various times of the seasonal cycle. These events can be rightly considered as prototypes of the spectacles which are observed in complex societies. We must not forget that women started to take part in these events only relatively recently after a long struggle for gender equality. The presence of female acrobats who strive to excel in all circus specialties is indeed a modern phenomenon (Tait 2005).

Evoking such social behavior, whose abstract pattern can be observed both in some animal species and in human societies, does not amount to offering a reductionist explanation of circus spectacles (Braithwaite 2008). There are, however, some formal commonalities which point to a primal source, an original structural dynamic which may lead to a deeper understanding of the logic of attraction which is the very basis of the performing arts: capturing the attention of others in order to derive some advantages. But mobilizing a crowd is not without danger because the mobbing instinct can always manifest itself if the performers do not meet the expectations of the crowd. This is why actors as well as circus artists are usually on edge before a show starts. There are many examples of performances turning sour. The notion of attraction implies indeed two complementary roles: the attractor and the attracted. In the following sections, we will consider the kind of gratification which spectators obtain from the experience of watching circus performances.

Information, fear, and empathy

One of the main assets of the circus is its capacity to produce novelties. The rhetoric of the "never seen before" and "attempted for the first time" permeates its marketing on all levels. Objectively, the circus provides an alternative experience through the original spatial organization of its architecture and inner structure; the abnormality of its nomadic existence for sedentary populations; its sudden appearance and disappearance in the midst of cities and villages; the exotic animals it transports and displays; the overload of multimodal information it creates for its audiences; and the extreme behavior its performers exhibit in the ring. In a stable natural and social environment in which the redundancies of everyday life generate boredom, any unexpected event is bound to trigger attention. Even if, as we have seen in the first chapter of this volume, circus acts offer so little variety that they can be considered to be forms of repetitive rituals, the rarity of their occurrence combines with the rhetoric of their staging to endow them with high information value. Their transitory mode of operation allows time to dampen the memory of the spectators from one experience of the circus to another, somewhat like religious celebrations which are revived after a full year's gap and thus can preserve some amount of informational value. The circus is indeed in many respects comparable to these festivals because it arouses strong emotions of attraction, fear, and empathy in a collective setting. Witnessing an audience which showers an artist with thunderous and sustained applause, and which spontaneously stands up to express its enthusiastic appreciation at the end of an act, causes an overwhelming feeling of unanimous passion.

In a previous volume, *Semiotics at the Circus* (2010: 175–84), I have shown that the repertory of aerial acrobatics relates to the survival competencies of the common ancestors of the primates who were tree-dwelling mammals. There is good physiological and behavioral evidence that this past adaptation to arboreal life has left fossil neuromuscular patterns of activation in *Homo sapiens* as well as, probably, some corresponding affects. The discovery of mirror neurons, that is, motor neurons which fire both when we perform a movement and when we see the same movement being performed by someone else, explains to a great extent the dynamic participation which can be observed in spectators whose muscles contract as they witness acrobatic performances. At the same time, they experience emotional uneasiness. The fear of falling is indeed deeply rooted in the evolutionary past of our species. We can jokingly, but pointedly imagined that a fox which notices a squirrel running the risk of losing its balance and dropping to the ground will look forward to this event as a good opportunity for dinner and will not experience any anxiety except perhaps if it is turns out that the squirrel is able to restore its balance on the branch. But for a human, the natural identification with a conspecific in danger of falling from some elevated position usually triggers sympathetic anxiety.

Figure 13.1 For more than two decades, Gérard Edon performed a daring balancing act which consisted of standing on a trapeze both while the trapeze was hanging motionless and while it was swaying. The acrobat was taking various positions, standing laterally or frontally, successively on his feet and on his head. There was neither safety lunge nor net. It was obvious that a fall would have been fatal. The act implemented a progressive increase of the apparent danger as the first part involved the static mode of the trapeze and the second part was performed as it was swaying with maximal amplitude high above the ground. (Rendering by David Blostein of the nerve-racking frontal balancing which concluded the act after a photograph published in Bouissac 1976a.)

The spectators of a high-wire walking act visually assess the risks implied by such actions. As we noticed in Chapter 2 when we analyzed the balancing act of René Sperlich, we are prone to construe the situation which unfolds in front of us as a game with death leading to an uncertain outcome. An important component of this experience is an empathic fear which is amplified by the frustrating knowledge that we are not in a position to help prevent a deadly fall. Furthermore, for many, this feeling is reinforced by a sense of guilt since we have taken an active part in such a potential tragedy by the mere fact of having purchased an admission ticket. We will examine another fundamental consequence of the dynamic of this social structure in the next section of this chapter.

Another range of emotions which are stirred by the circus is our reaction to desirable bodies which are displayed for our visual consumption. We reviewed various aspects of this dimension of circus performances in Chapter 11. This primal arousal combines and blends with our fascination for charismatic smiles which feed our romantic fantasies. Falling in love with the circus may imply both erotic and sentimental drives.

Laughter also enters in this rich, intense cocktail of emotions. Laughing together at a scapegoat is a powerful factor of social integration. It achieves an instant obliteration of differences through the sudden emergence of a unanimous, albeit delusional feeling of communal equality. It is interesting to note that in moments of uncontrollable hilarity, such as those caused by clowns, strangers who happen to seat next to each other suddenly interact through glances and verbal exchanges.

But do the range and intensity of the emotions which are stimulated by the clever marketing and skilled staging of circus acts suffice to explain the force with which large segments of the population are attracted to this form of entertainment like metal chips to a magnet? It seems that there is more to this than the craving for information and the pleasure of experiencing varied and deep emotions. The love of the circus is indeed akin to an infatuation and does not seem to be fully accounted for in terms of the possible motivational factors which have been listed in this section. There is, however, a plausible explanation for such behavior as we will see in the following section. The apparent irrationality of the compulsory attraction to the circus can indeed be understood as a form of addiction which game theory can explain.

Games, rewards, and addiction

For many, the circus is indeed the name of a passion. Let us remember the remarkable case of the Vesque sisters we encountered in Chapter 2. But they are not an isolated phenomenon, even though the form of their dedication was unique. The love for the circus has driven devotees to amass huge collections of items connected to the arts of training, clowning, and acrobatics to include anything from admission tickets and illustrated programs to props and costumes. Some even keep jars full of sawdust they gathered from circus rings. The construction of traveling circuses on miniature scales with all their implements of trucks, wagons, canvas tents, rings, and tiny icons of animals and people gives countless amateurs the illusion of owning a circus through its simulacra. Such fetishistic constructions replicate the iconic and symbolic objects of their fascination rather than the harsh reality of the day-to-day operation of actual circus companies and artists. They are material supports for a kind of cult, the sacred toys with which their imagination plays. Numerous associations of circus fans worldwide bear witness to the role of the circus in the intimate life of sizeable constituencies of individuals who foster a very special relationship to the circus through associations, interest groups, and personal networks. For them, going to the circus is not a trivial event and the pleasure they experience is intense. But what exactly causes this euphoria which is shared to a great extent by all circus audiences even if only a few spectators indulge in some forms of worship?

Pleasure is difficult to define. Being euphoric or high are other ways of referring to a state of satisfaction which is experienced as a point of arrival beyond which there is no desire because there is nothing lacking in the way we feel at that moment. All humans strive to reach such a state and to regain it as soon as it fades away. The neurosciences have uncovered that we experience extreme satisfaction when some parts of the brain which are called "reward centers" are stimulated by neurotransmitters, in particular dopamine, a hormone which is released by some neurons in the dopaminergic systems when we are satiated (food, sex, social recognition, etc.). It is noteworthy that addictive drugs such as cocaine mimic the chemical structure of dopamine and thus create a similar effect. This naturally leads to the question: Could the pleasure felt at the circus be connected with the release of dopamine in the brain of the spectators? Although some food is traditionally consumed during circus shows and, as we saw in Chapter 10, some acts are erotically charged, it does not seem that these aspects are determining factors although they undoubtedly play a role.

An idea which deserves to be further explored is that the euphoria created by circus performances is related to the game structure of the acts which we have pointed out in Chapters 1 and 2. There is indeed some good empirical evidence that the outcome of a game, in the abstract sense propounded by game theory, triggers the release of dopamine in the brains of the players as well as in the brains of those who witness the unfolding of a game. Experimental evidence shows indeed that the activation of dopaminergic neurons is correlated with reward prediction and predictability (Fiorillo et al. 2003; Tobler 2010). Interestingly, about one-third of these neurons "shows a more sustained activation that gradually increases toward the time of risky rewards" (Tobler 2010: 325).

Let us consider again an acrobatic act and discover how it can be structurally equated to a game. In Chapter 2, we showed that the balancing act of René Sperlich was construed by the audience as a game in which the acrobat was challenging death through increasing the odds he had to beat in order to survive. We will now focus on a more complex act which involves two acrobats: the Duo Sorellas to which we alluded in Chapter 11. It is a true challenge to attempt to describe such a complex performance. Moments during which the two acrobats behave symmetrically, in parallel, alternate with moments during which they engage in complementary actions in which the survival of one of them is strictly due to the behavior of the other. They perform on a single trapeze with a bar that is long enough so that they can sit comfortably side by side on it when they pause but short enough that it does not exceed the easy reach of a single man who naturally extends his arms and legs as in the celebrated drawing by Leonardo Da Vinci purporting to exemplify the ideal proportions of the human body. The height at which they perform above the ground makes their actions extremely risky since a fall would cause serious harm if not instant death. They perform without a safety lunge or net.

Video recordings of this act are available on the internet, which show the integral staging and unfolding of this daring performance in two different venues at an interval of several years. They can be found at the following URLs:

www.youtube.com/watch?v=AD2ucEkU3eI&feature=endscreen&NR=1
www.youtube.com/watch?v=6kmFTtgDZdg&feature=related

There are two distinct streams of gestures in this act: first, social gestures which the acrobats direct either to the audience or to one another; second, technical gestures which constitute the substance of their acrobatics. The social gestures frame the technical ones. They are purely semiotic and belong to the staging of the act. The acrobatic construction of the act is constrained by the neuromuscular competence of the two men, their capacity to time their movements in a mutually compatible manner, and the laws of physics.

The two men produce social signs when they are sitting next to one another on the trapeze bar. The public-oriented nonverbal communication combines broad smiles with the hand gestures of greeting. The latter are done by energetically projecting toward the audience the arm which is not used to maintain the grip on the trapeze. The result is that they briefly appear like a single body with two heads looking in opposite directions and two arms, each targeting the audience on its side. For the philosophers who may be attending this performance, this seemingly single body made of two halves may evoke the myth told in Plato's *Symposium*, a dialogue on love according to which contemporary humans are actually only halves of previous beings which, in immemorial times, the gods cut in half to punish their arrogance and weaken them so that they would not be able to mount serious challenges to their divine power. This is why, so the myth claims, we are all looking for our other half and, occasionally, find it. This view purports to explain, among other things, same-sex orientation. The story is in order here because the two acrobats stage their act as a couple and produce signs oriented toward one another which suggest virile intimacy. They alternate synchronous gestures in parallel which suggest harmony and mutual actions which indicate complementarity such as glances, hand contacts, and reciprocal attitudes. The latter cluster of signs symbolizes a deep agreement, a commitment to confront danger and death together. The feats of aerial acrobatics which they perform suppose, indeed, a mutual absolute trust and as such can be construed as a dynamic metaphor of love, all the more so as their performance involves a great deal of intimate body contact.

The act unfolds at a fast pace punctuated by brief pauses for a total duration of slightly over 6 minutes including brief pauses to acknowledge applause while recuperating from muscular fatigue. Each trick is executed in a mere few seconds. Rodrique is the one who catches his partner when Chris is unsupported in the air for a fraction of a second. There are five such instances in the act when Chris lets go his grip on the trapeze or

Rodrique's hands and is caught just in time to prevent a fall. He is successively grabbed by the feet, the armpits, the knee, the calves, and the hands. Rodrique alternately uses his hands, his legs, and his feet to catch Chris. The most daring trick consists of a feet to feet catch when Chris's body slides along his partner's body and hooks his insteps to Rodrique's insteps to stop the fall at the last moment. This is immediately followed by a single foot to foot suspension. These dramatic but extremely short episodes are combined with demonstrations of strength and balance such as when Chris who is hanging by one arm from Rodrique's hand raises himself to a horizontal position and slowly accomplish a full circular movement, or when Rodrique makes an unsupported handstand on Chris's feet which are anchored through his firm pressure at the angles formed by the extremities of the bar and the ropes from which it hangs.

The whole sequence of the act can be formally analyzed as two players making decisions in responses to one another's moves. The successful completion of the act is an equilibrium in which both players win. In theory, one could save pain and energy by not agreeing to play his part. We can consider, for the sake of heuristic speculation, that by letting Chris fall to the ground and likely break his neck, Rodrique would cash the full payment carried by the contract with the circus in which they happen to perform, or even perhaps could cash a life insurance. Chris on his part could fail to provide the firm support of his soles when Rodrique makes an unsupported handstand on them. In fact, either could cause a fatal accident in which the other would perish. The audience may entertain such a fear with respect to the outcome of each segment of this act because countless popular novels and detective movies have set criminal actions in the context of a circus. These fictitious events remain somewhat active in the background memory of the public. It is definitely a part of the imaginary circus we discussed in Chapter 10. Moreover, the chronicle of the circus has recorded fatal accidents which occurred during this type of act. Naturally, the Duo Sorellas' act perceived as a two-player game with an uncertain outcome refers to the point of view of the audience. From the point of view of the acrobats themselves, it must be a different perception. They are sustained by the absolute faith in one another's determination to play fair. The outcome of each trick is as certain as an exercise can be for which they have trained themselves under the guidance of a mentor and which has been rehearsed again and again with all necessary safety measures until they achieved total control on all aspects of the performance.

However, the spectators evaluate the risks from their own point of view which is to a large extent manipulated by the artists. Special announcements informing the audience that a particular trick is going to be attempted for the first time belong to the rhetoric of the circus. It may be sometimes a way to excuse in advance a possible failure on the part of acrobats who have not yet fully mastered their skill. However, most often, such announcements are designed to underline the uncertainty of the outcome and, thus, raise the odds of the game.

Performance, ritual, and meaning

At the end of this itinerary which has explored a variety of circus acts in the context of the programs of which they are a part as well as in relation to the acts which belong to the same specialty, a final reflection on the meaning they produce in the minds of their audiences is in order. In the course of the chapters, we have discovered the resilient dramatic structures according to which these acts are constructed from generation to generation, and the body techniques they implement. In many respects, watching a circus performance consists of participating in a cultural event which, as such, has to be learned by children during the process of development and acculturation. As pure information, that is, as a first, unprepared experience, a circus act does not make sense because it is totally unmotivated: why does this young man build an unstable tower of chairs and climb it not in order to reach something he could not obtain otherwise but simply to climb down once he has kept his balance at the top? Why make a tiger jump through a hoop of fire and a horse dance in rhythm to a tune which is for it mere noise? All this is so absurd in terms of real life's basic survival that the source of the interest it causes has to be located in the symbolic domain which is the realm of rituals.

But there must be something else in this multimodal language of the circus which accounts for both the deep interest it triggers in many and the repulsion it causes in some. The hypothesis which has been proposed in this work is that circus acts can be construed as games in the sense developed by game theory. This is why the circus is experienced as more than a mere succession of repetitive performances such as rituals. But the circus is also endowed with many features characterizing rituals: the construction of a special space and time; the formality of its unfolding; the transcendence of its traditional norms; the emotional involvement it causes; the relevance of its symbols to the natural and cultural environment of its participants; and the transformative power of its representations. All these components have been addressed as we moved along the chapters in this book, alternating personal experiences, ethnographic accounts, and theoretical reflections.

Meaning is a complex phenomenon, both emotional and cognitive. Pure information generates anxiety until we can relate such happenings to something with which we are familiar. Meaning is the emotion we feel when we discover connecting patterns to which we are in some ways related. Meaning emerges from the echoes we discern between patterns within a comprehensive whole, whether such insights are real or delusional. The circus encapsulates all the challenges of human existence. The fundamentally same game is refracted from act to act. The odds follow a crescendo which eventually leads to a soft landing in the cradle of unanimity. The circus provides us with a sense of fusion, risk, and triumph.

Bibliography

Alain-Fournier, H., 1913. *Le grand Meaulnes*. Paris: Emile-Paul Frères.
Assael, B., 2005. *The Circus and Victorian Society*. Charlottesville, VA: University of Virginia Press.
Banville, T. de, 1853. *Les pauvres saltimbanques*. Paris: Michel Levy Frères.
Bekoff, M., 2007. *The Emotional Lives of Animals*. New York: New World Library.
— 2010. *The Animal Manifesto. Six Reasons for Expanding Our Compassion Footprint*. Novato: New World Library.
Bell, C., 1997. *Ritual: Perspectives and Dimensions*. New York: Oxford University Press.
Berland, J. C., 1982. *No Five Fingers Are Alike*. Cambridge, MA: Harvard University Press.
Blake, H., 1975. *Talking with Horses: A Study of Communication between Man and Horse*. London: Souvenir Press.
Bordez, C. and G. Iuliani, 2002. *Dernier tour de piste*. Chicoutimi, QC: JCL.
Bouissac, P., 1973. *La mesure des gestes*. Berlin: De Gruyter Mouton.
— 1976a. *Circus and Culture*. Bloomington, IN: Indiana University Press.
— (ed.), 1976b. *L'oeuvre de Marthe et Juliette Vesque: Le cirque en France de la Belle Epoque a la fin de la fin de la deuxieme guerre mondiale*. Volume I. Microfiches. Paris: L'Institut d'Ethnologie, Archives, Musee de l'Homme.
— 1977. "Semiotics and spectacles: the circus institution and representations." In T. A. Sebeok (ed.), *A Perfusion of Signs*. Bloomington: Indiana University Press, pp. 143–52.
— (ed.), 1991. "Semiotics of the circus." *Semiotica*, 85 (3/4) [special issue].
— 2010. *Semiotics at the Circus*. Berlin: De Gruyter Mouton.
Boustany, B. (ed.), 1992. *En piste: le cirque en images des soeurs Vesque*. Paris: Gallimard.
Braithwaite, J., 2008. "Lekking displays in contemporary organizations." *Journal of Health, Organization, and Management*, 22 (5), 529–59.
Carmeli, Y., 1987. "Why does 'Jimmy Brown Circus' travel? A semiotic approach to the analysis of circus ecology." *Poetics Today*, 8 (2), 219–44.
— 1991. "Performance and family in the world of British circus." *Semiotica*, 85 (3/4), 257–89.
— 2003. "Lion on display: culture, nature, and totality in a circus performance." *Poetics Today*, 24 (1), 65–90.
— 2007. "Travelling and family in the 1970s British circus." *Semiotica*, 167 (1/4), 369–85.
Clifford, J. and G. E. Marcus, 1986. *Writing Culture*. Berkeley, CA: University of California Press.
Coppa, F., L. Hass, and J. Peck (eds), 2008. *Performing Magic on the Western Stage from the Eighteenth Century to the Present*. New York: Palgrave MacMillan.
Coxe, A. D. H., 1951. *A Seat at the Circus*. London: Evans.
Croft-Cooke, R., 1941. *The Circus Has No Home*. London: Methuen.
De Coppet, D. (ed.), 1992. *Understanding Rituals*. London: Routledge.
De Goncourt, E., 1879. *Les frères Zemganno*. Paris: G. Charpentier.

De L'Estoile, P., 1978 [1601]. "Moraco, le cheval de l'écossais." Ed. M. C. Dumez. *Le Cirque dans l'Univers*, 110 (1978), 11–12.
De Waal, F., 1989. *Peace Making among Primates*. Cambridge, MA: Harvard University Press.
Douglas, M., 1966. *Purity and Danger*. London: Routledge.
Driver, T. F., 1991. *Magic Ritual: Our Need for Liberating Rites That Transform Our Lives & Our Communities*. San Francisco, CA: Harper.
During, S., 2002. *Modern Enchantments: The Cultural Power of Secular Magic*. Cambridge: Harvard University Press.
Durkheim, J., 1955. *Le cirque*. Paris: Nathan.
Eco, U., 1976. *A Theory of Semiotics*. Bloomington: Indiana University Press.
Eibl-Ebesfeldt, I., 1975. *Ethology: The Biology of Behavior*. Trans. E. Klinghammer. New York: Holt, Rhinehart, and Winston.
Fensham, F. C., 1988. "Liability of animals in biblical and ancient Near Eastern law." *Journal of Northwest Semitic Languages*, 14, 85–90.
Finkelstein, J. J., 1973. "The goring ox: some historical perspectives on deodands, forfeitures, wrongful death and the Western notion of sovereignty." *Temple Law Quarterly*, 46, 169–290.
— 1981. "The ox that gored." *Transactions of the American Philosophical Society*, Vol. 72, Part 2. Philadelphia: American Philosophical Society.
Frega, D., 2001. *Women of Illusion: A Circus Family Story*. London: Palgrave.
Gaignebet, C., 1986. *A plus hault sens: l'ésotérisme spirituel et charnel de Rabelais*, 2 vols. Paris: Maisonneuve.
Garnier, J., 1979. "Le dressage des loups [the training of wolves]." *Le Cirque dans l'Univers*, 114, 3–5.
Genet, J., 1958. *Le funambule*. Decines (Rhone): L'Arbalete.
Girgen, J., 2003. "The historical and contemporary prosecution and punishment of animals." *Animal Law*, 9, 97–133 (www.animallaw.info/journals/jo_pdf/lralvol9_p97.pdf).
Glen, J., 1983. Director of *Octopussy*, a James Bond 007 film.
Goodall, J., 1990. *Through a Window*. New York: Houghton Mifflin.
Goodall, J. and L. Pintea, 2010. "Securing a future for chimpanzees." *Nature*, 466 (July 8), 180–1.
Grandin, T. and C. Johnson, 2005. *Animals in Translation: Using the Mysteries of Autism to Decode Animal Behavior*. New York: Scribner.
Grathoff, R. H., 1970. *The Structure of Social Inconsistencies: A Contribution to a Unified Theory of Play, Game, and Social Action*. The Hague: Martinus Nijhoff.
Grimm, D., 2010. "Is a dolphin a person?" *Science*, 327 (February 26), 1070–1.
Hachet-Souplet, P., 1905. *Le dressage des animaux*. Paris: Didot.
Hammersley, M., 1992. *What Is Wrong with Ethnography?* London: Routledge.
Handelman, D., 1991. "Symbolic types, the body, and circus." *Semiotica*, 85 (3/4), 205–25.
Hass, L., 2008. "Life magic and staged magic: a hidden intertwining." In F. Coppa, L. Hass, and J. Peck (eds), *Performing Magic on the Western Stage*. New York: Palgrave MacMillan, pp. 13–31.
Hearne, V., 1983. *In the Absence of Horses*. Princeton: Princeton University Press.
— 1986. *Adam's Task: Calling Animals by Name*. New York: Alfred A. Knopf.
Heine, H., 1913. *Atta Troll*. London: Sidgwick & Jackson.
Hoeglund, J. and R. V. Alatalo, 1995. *Leks*. Princeton, NJ: Princeton University Press.
Ingold, T. (ed.), 1988. *What Is an Animal?* London: Unwin Hyman.
Inomata, T. and L. S. Coben (eds), 2006. "Archaeology of performance: theater of power," *Community, and Politics*. New York: Altamira.

Jackson, B.S., 1975. *Essays in Jewish and Comparative Legal History*. Leiden: E.J. Brill.
— 2011. "Liability of animals: an historico-structural comparison." *International Journal for the Semiotics of Law*, 24 (3), 259–89.
Jackson, P., 2012. "Apparition and apparatuses: on the framing and staging of religious events." *Method and Theory in the Study of Religion*, 24, 1–10.
Jakobson, R., 1968. "Poetry of grammar and grammar of poetry." *Lingua*, 21, 597–609.
— 1970. "On the verbal art of William Blake and other poets painters." *Linguistic Inquiry*, I.1, 1–68.
Kahn, G., 1898. *Le cirque solaire*. Paris: La Revue Blanche.
Klingel, H., 1977. "Communication in perissodactyla." In T. A. Sebeok (ed.), *How Animals Communicate*. Bloomington: Indiana University Press, pp. 715–27.
Kristeva, J., 1974. *La révolution du langage poétique*. Paris: Seuil.
Kyriakidis, E. (ed.), 2007. *The Archaeology of Ritual*. Los Angeles, CA: Cotsen Institute of Archaeology, University of California at Los Angeles.
Lawrence, E. A., 1982. *Rodeo: An Anthropologist Looks at the Wild and the Tame*. Knoxville: University of Tennessee Press.
— 1985. *Hoofbeats and Society: Studies in Human-Horse Interactions*. Bloomington, IN: Indiana University Press.
— 1989. *His Very Silence Speaks: Comanche—The Horse Who Survived Custer's Last Stand*. Detroit: Wayne State University.
Leach, E., 1964. "Anthropological aspects of language: animal categories and verbal abuse." In E. H. Lenneberg (ed.), *New Directions in the Study of Language*. Cambridge: MIT Press, pp. 23–63.
Lévi-Strauss, C., 1962. *La pensée sauvage*. Paris: Plon.
— 1966. *The Savage Mind*. London: Weidenfeld and Nicolson.
Lotman, J., 1977. *The Structure of the Artistic Text*. Trans. R. Vroom. Ann Arbor, MI: University of Michigan Press.
Mallarmé, S., 1945. *Oeuvres complètes*. Paris: Gallimard.
Malot, H., 1878. *Sans famille*. Paris: Dentu.
Mangan, M., 2007. *Performing Dark Arts: A Cultural History of Conjuring*. Bristol: Intellect Books.
Markham, G., 1607. *Cavelarice, or the English Horseman*. London: E. White.
Mauriange, E. and P. Bouissac (eds), 1977. *Marthe et Juliette Vesque. Le cirque en images. Archives d' ethnologie française, 5*. Paris: Maisonneuve & Larose.
McDougal, C., 1977. *The Face of the Tiger*. London: Rivington Books.
McGreavy, P. D. and A. N. McLean, 2007. "Roles of learning theory and ethology in equitation." *Journal of Veterinary Behavior*, 2 (4), 108–18.
McManus, D., 2003. *No Kidding! Clown as Protagonist in Twentieth-Century Theater*. Newark, DE: University of Delaware Press.
Miller, H., 1953. *The Smile at the Foot of the Ladder / Le sourire au pied de l'échelle*. Paris: Correa.
Moss, C., 1988. *Elephant Memories*. New York: Morrow.
Muir, E., 1976. "The Horses." In Edwin Muir, *Collected Poems*. London: Faber and Faber, pp. 246–8.
Murphy, J., C. Hall, and S. Arkins, 2009. "What horses and humans see: a comparative review." *International Journal of Zoology*, 2009, 1–15.
Nietzsche, F., 1872. *Die Geburt der Tragödie aus der Geiste der Musik*. Leipzig: Verlag von F. W. Fritzsch.
— 1954. *Also Sprach Zarathustra / Ainsi parlait Zarathoustra*. Paris: Aubier.

Olsen, S. L., S. Grant, A. M. Choyke, and L. Bartosiewicz (eds), 2006. *Horses and Humans: The Evolution of Human-Equine Relationships*. Oxford: British Archaeology Reports, International Series 1560.

Otte, M., 2006. *Jewish Identities in German Popular Entertainment, 1890–1933*. Cambridge: Cambridge University Press.

Peterson, M., 2007. "The animal apparatus: from a theory of animal acting to an ethics of animal acts." *TDR The Drama Review*, 51 (1), 33–48.

Petit, P., 1985. *The High Wire*. New York: Random House.

— 1997. *Traité du funambulisme*. Arles: Actes Sud.

Pfungst, O., 1911 [1907]. *Clever Hans (The Horse of Mr. von Osten): A Contribution to Experimental Animal and Human Psychology*. Trans. C. L. Rahn. New York: Henry Holt.

Prieto, L., 1966. *Messages et signaux*. Paris: Presses Universitaires de France.

Propp, V., 1968 [1928]. *Morphology of the Folktale*. Trans. L. Scott. Austin: University of Texas Press.

Ramirez, F. and C. Rolot, 1977. *Joies du cirque*. Paris: Hachette.

Rémy, T., 1962. *Entrées clownesques*. Paris: L'Arche.

— 1979. "Le cirque Fernando: vingt-cinq ans de cirque (1873–1897)." *Le Cirque dans l'Univers*, 115. Numéro spécial, 7–72.

Riggins, S. H., 2003. *The Pleasures of Time*. Toronto: Insomniac Press.

Rilke, R. M., 1943. *Les élégies de Duino. Edition bilingue*. Paris: Aubier.

Ritter, N., 1989. *Art as Spectacle: Images of the Entertainer since Romanticism*. Columbus, MO: University of Missouri Press.

Rubenstein, D. I., 1986. "Ecology and sociality in horses and zebras." In D. I. Rubenstein and R. W. Wrangham (eds.). *Ecological Aspects of Social Evolution: Birds and Mammals*. Princeton: Princeton University Press.

Schäfer, M., 1975. *The Language of the Horse*. Trans. D. Machin Goodall. London: Kaye and Ward.

Schaller, G. B., 1969. *The Deer and the Tiger: A Study of Wildlife in India*. Chicago, IL: University of Chicago Press.

— 1972. *The Serengeti Lion: A Study of Predator-Prey Relation*. Chicago, IL: University of Chicago Press.

Shanklin, E., 1985. "Sustenance and symbols: anthropological studies of domesticated animals." *Annual Review of Anthropology*, 14, 375–403.

Siegel, L., 1991. *Net of Magic: Wonders and Deceptions in India*. Chicago, IL: University of Chicago Press.

Sorenson, J., 2010. *About Canada: Animal Right*. Black Point: Fernwood Publishing.

Starobinski, J., 1970. *Portrait de l'artiste en saltimbanque*. Geneve: Skira.

Stoddart, H., 2000. *Rings of Desire*. Manchester: Manchester University Press.

Stroud, N., 2000. *Josser: The Secret Life of a Circus Girl*. London: Virago Press.

Tait, P., 2005. *Circus Bodies*. London: Taylor & Francis.

Tambiah, S., 1969. "Animals are good to think and good to prohibit." *Ethnology*, 8 (4), 423–59.

Thétard, H., 1978 [1947]. *La merveilleuse histoire du cirque*. Paris: Prisma.

Tobler, P. N., 2010. "Behavioral functions of dopamine neurons." In L. L. Iversen, S. D. Iversen, S. B. Dunnett, and A. Bjoerklund (eds), *Dopamine Handbook*. Oxford: Oxford University Press, pp. 316–30.

Toole-Stott, R., 1958. *Circus and Allied Arts: A World Bibliography*. Derby: Harpur and Sons.

Turner, V., 1969. *The Ritual Process: Structure and Anti-Structure*. Harmondsworth: Penguin.
— 1974. *Dramas, Fields, and Metaphors*. Ithaca: Cornell University Press.
Van Hooff, J. A. R. A. M., 1972. "A comparative approach to the phylogeny of laughter and smiling." In R. A. Hinde (ed.), *Nonverbal Communication*. Cambridge: Cambridge University Press, pp. 209–38.
Van Maanen, J., 1988. *Tales of the Field: On Writing Ethnography*. Chicago, IL: University of Chicago Press.
White, D. G., 1991. *Myths of the Dog-Man*. Chicago: University of Chicago Press.
Willis, R. (ed.), 1974. *Signifying Animals: Human Meaning in the Natural World*. London: Routledge.
Zahavi, A. and A. Zahavi, 1997. *The Handicap Principle: A Missing Piece of Darwin's Puzzle*. New York: Oxford University Press.
Zeeb, K., 1976. *Les chevaux de Frédy Knie*. Lausanne: Payot.

Index

accidents 27, 31–4
acrobats,
    equilibrists 39–47
    funambulists 168–9, 175–6
    trapezists 170–8, 203
actions 92–7
activism 193–5
animal trainers,
    Alexander Lacey 9, 110, 118–29, 133–43
    Brenda Hani 67–9
    Clyde Beatty 130–1
    Damoo Dothre 107
    David Rosaire 100–3
    Derrick Rosaire 62–7, 71–3
    Douglas Kossmayer (Eddie Windsor) 98–103
    Eloize Berchtold 31–3
    Freddy Knie Jr 78–84, 88–90
    Henri Dantès 131–3
    James Puydebois 37
    Jana Mandana 37
    John Banks 60–2, 109
    Julio Hani 67–9
    Kara Kawak 108
    Marek Jama 40
    Marfa the Corsican 107
    Trude Stosch-Sarrasani 82
animals 104–14, 195–8
artists,
    Agathe 175
    Amélie 176
    André Kole 53
    Andrews, The 177
    Antoine 175
    Charlie Cairoli 147–58
    Chris Christiansen 167–8
    Duo à Deux 172
    Duo Lapsus 145–6
    Duo Sorellas 173, 205–7
    Erik 176
    Gérard Edon 203
    Philippe Petit 168–9
    René Sperlich 39–47, 205

Bekoff, M. 113
Berland, J. 52
Blostein, D. 9

Canestrini, D. 184
Carmeli, Y. 128, 163, 174
circus,
    Alexis Gruss 25–6
    Apollo 24–5
    Archaos 178–9, 193–4
    Arizona 66–7
    Arlette Gruss 104–5
    Armenian 180–1
    Barbarie 174
    Blackpool Tower Circus 49, 147–58
    Bouglione 131–3
    Bureau 11–12, 105
    Charles Knie 10–13, 16–20, 39–46, 118–27, 133–9, 179–80
    Chinese 191
    Constanze Busch 13–14
    Gatini 31
    Knie 78–90, 145–7
    Krone 34–9
    Lumiere 194–5
    Moscow 181–4
    Oz 192–3, 195
    Robert Fossett 67–9
    Romanès 163
    Roncalli 97, 174
    Soleil 178, 195
    Vargas 39
    Venus 184–7
    William 13–14
Clever Hans 58, 70–2

Index

clowns 2–3, 17, 144–58, 165–6, 184–7
Croft-Cooke, R. 164

De Banville, T. 161, 163
De L'Estoile, P. 59
De Wilde, J. 171
dogs 97–103, 109

elephants 24–6, 34–9
emotions 199–208
ethnography 20–3, 28–47

fire 1–6
funambulist 168–9

game theory 41–7, 205–7
gay body politics 174
Gay Circus Night 179–80
Genet, J. 161–2
Goodall, J. 113–14
Greimas, A. J. 92–4
Grodotzki, S. 9

Hachiko 109
Handelman, D. 164
horses,
  breeds 77–8
  educated 58–73
  liberty 74–91

ideology 170–87

Jackson, B. S. 108
juggler 166–8

Kahn, G. 161

Lawrence, E. A. 89–90
lions 129–37

McDougal, C. 115–16, 197
magic 48–57
Mallarmé, S. 160–1
malleability 30, 34, 39–47
Mangalat, M. 184–7
Marcuse, H. 150–3
Mattu, G. 8
metaphors 74–91
Miller, H. 165–6
Muir, E. 91

Nietzsche, F. 166–7

Peperberg, I. 112–13
pickpocket 55–6
politics 170–87

Relleke, C. 171
Riggins S. H. 9
ritual 1, 4–6, 23–7, 207–8
Roguszka, Z. 9, 120

seals 19
Siegel, L. 51–2
Skidmore, J. 187
snake charmers 50–3

text 28
textility 28–31, 39–47
tigers 5, 115–43
Toole-Stott, R. 60–2

ventriloquist 56–7
Vesque, J. 22, 29–30
Vesque, M. 22, 29–30

wolves 190

zebras 4, 77, 197